PostgreSQL for Data Architects

Discover how to design, develop, and maintain your database application effectively with PostgreSQL

Jayadevan Maymala

[PACKT] open source*
community experience distilled
PUBLISHING

BIRMINGHAM - MUMBAI

PostgreSQL for Data Architects

Copyright © 2015 Packt Publishing

All rights reserved. No part of this book may be reproduced, stored in a retrieval system, or transmitted in any form or by any means, without the prior written permission of the publisher, except in the case of brief quotations embedded in critical articles or reviews.

Every effort has been made in the preparation of this book to ensure the accuracy of the information presented. However, the information contained in this book is sold without warranty, either express or implied. Neither the author, nor Packt Publishing, and its dealers and distributors will be held liable for any damages caused or alleged to be caused directly or indirectly by this book.

Packt Publishing has endeavored to provide trademark information about all of the companies and products mentioned in this book by the appropriate use of capitals. However, Packt Publishing cannot guarantee the accuracy of this information.

First published: March 2015

Production reference: 1240315

Published by Packt Publishing Ltd.
Livery Place
35 Livery Street
Birmingham B3 2PB, UK.

ISBN 978-1-78328-860-1

www.packtpub.com

Cover image by Kai Stachowiak (kalhh@web.de)

Credits

Author
Jayadevan Maymala

Reviewers
Pascal Charest
Bahman Movaqar
Ângelo Marcos Rigo
Hans-Jürgen Schönig
Stéphane Wirtel

Commissioning Editor
Anthony Albuquerque

Acquisition Editor
Sonali Vernekar

Content Development Editors
Rahul Nair
Sharvari Tawde

Technical Editor
Shashank Desai

Copy Editor
Relin Hedly

Project Coordinator
Judie Jose

Proofreaders
Maria Gould
Clyde Jenkins
Chris Smith
Jonathan Todd

Indexer
Hemangini Bari

Graphics
Sheetal Aute
Abhinash Sahu

Production Coordinator
Aparna Bhagat

Cover Work
Aparna Bhagat

About the Author

Jayadevan Maymala is a database developer, designer, and architect. He started working with the Oracle database in 1999. Over the years, he has worked with DB2, Sybase, and SQL Server. Of late, he has been working with open source technologies. His database of choice is PostgreSQL. In his career, he has worked in different domains spanning supply chain management, finance, and travel. He has spent an equal amount of time working with databases supporting critical transaction processing systems as well as data warehouses supporting analytical systems.

When he is not working on open source technologies, he spends time reading and updating himself on economic and political issues.

> I would like to thank my wife, Uma, for putting up with my marathon writing sessions over weekends. I am also deeply indebted to the PostgreSQL community, which has individuals who are always promptly replying to my basic and not-so-basic queries. It's an amazing team that has been working tirelessly to build such a great database and then give it away for free with such liberal licensing terms. Thank you.

About the Reviewers

Pascal Charest is a cutting-edge technology professional working with a very wide array of open source technologies.

He is currently leading system administrators in strategic planning of networked infrastructures and is often consulted for system architecture design. He can be reached via his LinkedIn profile at `http://www.linkedin.com/in/pascalcharest`.

> I'd like to thank Anthony and Zachary for keeping me awake, day and night.

Bahman Movaqar has been developing, deploying, and delivering software for the past 14 years, ranging from embedded operating systems to ERP implementations. He's an open source believer and a passionate amateur chess player. He blogs at `http://bahmanm.com/`.

> I'd like to thank my lovely wife, Nahid, who has taught me how to be strong.

Ângelo Marcos Rigo has a strong background in web development since 1998, focusing on content management systems. For the past 7 years, he has been managing, customizing, and developing extensions for Moodle LMS. He can be reached at his website http://www.u4w.com.br/novosite/index.php for CMS or Moodle LMS consulting. He has reviewed *Moodle Security*, *Packt Publishing*.

> I would like to thank my wife, Janaina de Souza, and my daughter, Lorena Rigo, for their support when I was away reviewing this book.

Hans-Jürgen Schönig has been involved in professional PostgreSQL training, consulting, and support for more than 15 years now. He and his company Cybertec Schönig & Schönig GmbH (http://www.cybertec.at/) are serving clients around the globe and have worked on some of the world's largest PostgreSQL deployments.

Stéphane Wirtel is an enthusiast software craftsman who is interested in high availability, replication, and distributed systems. Since 2000, he has been using PostgreSQL with the Python programming language. Stephane gives talks on Python and PostgreSQL in several conferences in Europe. The last one was called Python & PostgreSQL, a Wonderful Wedding. He is also a former core developer of the Odoo project, having worked on it for 6 years.

Stéphane is also a member of the Python Software Foundation and the EuroPython Society. He promotes the Python programming language via the PythonFOSDEM event at Brussels. You can reach him at http://wirtel.be/ or via Twitter @matrixise.

He works for Mgx.IO, a company that specializes in Python and Erlang developments. You can reach this company at http://mgx.io/ or via Twitter @mgxio. He has also reviewed the books *Getting Started with PhantomJS* and *PhantomJS Cookbook*, both by Packt Publishing.

> I would like to thank my wife, Anne, my daughter, Margaux, my family and friends for their support, and the PostgreSQL and Python communities for the awesome tools.

www.PacktPub.com

Support files, eBooks, discount offers, and more

For support files and downloads related to your book, please visit www.PacktPub.com.

Did you know that Packt offers eBook versions of every book published, with PDF and ePub files available? You can upgrade to the eBook version at www.PacktPub.com and as a print book customer, you are entitled to a discount on the eBook copy. Get in touch with us at service@packtpub.com for more details.

At www.PacktPub.com, you can also read a collection of free technical articles, sign up for a range of free newsletters and receive exclusive discounts and offers on Packt books and eBooks.

PACKTLib

https://www2.packtpub.com/books/subscription/packtlib

Do you need instant solutions to your IT questions? PacktLib is Packt's online digital book library. Here, you can search, access, and read Packt's entire library of books.

Why subscribe?

- Fully searchable across every book published by Packt
- Copy and paste, print, and bookmark content
- On demand and accessible via a web browser

Free access for Packt account holders

If you have an account with Packt at www.PacktPub.com, you can use this to access PacktLib today and view 9 entirely free books. Simply use your login credentials for immediate access.

Table of Contents

Preface	**vii**
Chapter 1: Installing PostgreSQL	**1**
Installation options	**1**
Downloading and extracting the source	2
Inspecting the contents	3
Dependencies to compile the source	**4**
Configuring and creating the makefile	**5**
Building and creating the executables	**8**
Installing and moving the files to where they belong	**9**
Inspecting the changes	10
Initializing a cluster	**11**
A quick walk through the directories	14
Processes created	17
Important files created	17
Working with extensions	**18**
Summary	**19**
Chapter 2: Server Architecture	**21**
Starting with the daemon process	**21**
Understanding the shared buffer	**23**
Inspecting the buffer cache	25
Checkpoint	**29**
WAL and the WAL writer process	**32**
Recovery	34
Incremental backup and point-in-time recovery	34
Replication	34
The background writer	**36**
The autovacuum launcher process	**37**

[i]

Table of Contents

The logging process	41
The stats collector process	46
The WAL sender and WAL receiver	49
Sorting in memory with work_mem	49
Maintenance with maintenance_work_mem	51
Understanding effective_cache_size	53
Summary	**54**
Chapter 3: PostgreSQL – Object Hierarchy and Roles	**55**
The PostgreSQL cluster	55
Understanding tablespaces	56
Managing temporary objects with temporary tablespaces	59
Views	61
Databases, schemas, and search_path	61
Schemas – use cases	67
Roles and privileges	67
Summary	**72**
Chapter 4: Working with Transactions	**73**
Understanding transactions	73
ACID properties of transactions	76
A for atomicity	76
C for consistency	76
I for isolation	76
D for durability	85
PostgreSQL and MVCC	86
Summary	**90**
Chapter 5: Data Modeling with SQL Power Architect	**91**
Tools for databases and their uses	91
Database design tools	93
SQL Power Architect – downloading and installing	93
Creating tables	95
Generating SQL	97
Reverse engineering and making changes	100
Exporting the data model	101
Profiling	102
Summary	**103**
Chapter 6: Client Tools	**105**
GUI tools and command-line tools	105
pgAdmin – downloading and installation	105
Adding a server	106

The pgAdmin main window	108
The Query tool	111
psql – working from the command line	**114**
psql – connection options	114
The power of \d	115
More meta-commands	117
Setting up the environment	120
History of commands	121
Summary	**122**
Chapter 7: SQL Tuning	**123**
Understanding basic facts about databases	**123**
Fact 1 – databases are more frequently read from than written to	123
Fact 2 – data is always read in blocks or pages, not as individual records or columns	124
Approaches to reducing the number of blocks read/written	125
Query execution components	**125**
Planner	126
Access methods	126
Join strategies	127
Finding the execution plan	**128**
Optimization guidelines and catches	**130**
Indexing foreign keys	130
Using SELECT *	132
Using ORDER BY	133
Using DISTINCT	134
Using UNION ALL instead of UNION	134
Using functions in the FILTER clause	134
Reducing the number of SQL statements	137
Reducing function executions	138
Not using indexes	140
Partial indexes	142
Optimizing functions	143
Summary	**145**
Chapter 8: Server Tuning	**147**
Server-wide memory settings	**147**
shared_buffers	147
effective_cache_size	148
Managing writes, connections, and maintenance	**149**

Table of Contents

Seek/scan cost and statistics parameters	**151**
CPU costs	155
Materialized views	**157**
Partitioned tables	**160**
Summary	**165**
Chapter 9: Tools to Move Data in and out of PostgreSQL	**167**
Setting up the production database – considerations	**167**
COPY	**168**
Fast loading with pg_bulkload	**171**
pg_dump	**173**
Filtering options	**175**
pg_dumpall	176
pg_restore	176
Summary	**178**
Chapter 10: Scaling, Replication, and Backup and Recovery	**179**
Scalability	**179**
Vertical scaling	181
Horizontal scaling	182
Master-slave(s) with read/write separation	182
Streaming replication	184
Connection pooling, load balancing, and failover with pgpool-II	189
Sharding	199
Multi-master full replication	201
Point-in-time recovery	**202**
Summary	**206**
Chapter 11: PostgreSQL – Troubleshooting	**207**
Connection issues	**207**
Authentication and permission issues	**208**
Parameter changes not effective	**210**
Query not responding	**212**
Summary	**216**
Chapter 12: PostgreSQL – Extras	**217**
Interesting data types	**217**
RANGE	218
Using network address types	220
hstore for key-value pairs	222
json/jsonb	224
XML	227
Inserting and verifying XML data	228
Generating XML files for table definitions and data	228

Geometry and geography	229
Foreign Data Wrappers	229
FDW for files	230
PostgreSQL FDW	231
Data wrappers – other aspects	232
pgbadger	233
Features over time	**236**
Interesting features in 9.4	236
Keeping the buffer ready	236
Better recoverability	238
Easy-to-change parameters	238
Logical decoding and consumption of changes	239
Summary	**240**
Index	**241**

Preface

PostgreSQL is an incredibly flexible and dependable open source relational database. Harnessing its power will make your applications more reliable and extensible without increasing costs. Using PostgreSQL's advanced features will save you work and increase performance, once you've discovered how to set it up.

PostgreSQL for Data Architects will teach you everything you need to learn in order to get a scalable and optimized PostgreSQL server up and running.

The book starts with basic concepts (such as installing PostgreSQL from source) and covers theoretical aspects (such as concurrency and transaction management). After this, you'll learn how to set up replication, use load balancing to scale horizontally, and troubleshoot errors.

As you continue through this book, you will see the significant impact of configuration parameters on performance, scalability, and transaction management. Finally, you will get acquainted with useful tools available in the PostgreSQL ecosystem used to analyze PostgreSQL logs, set up load balancing, and recovery.

What this book covers

Chapter 1, *Installing PostgreSQL*, provides an overview of the process to install PostgreSQL from source. The chapter covers the prerequisites to compile from source, and the process to initialize a cluster in Unix/Linux environment. It also covers the directory structure.

Chapter 2, *Server Architecture*, covers the important processes started when we start a PostgreSQL cluster and how they work along with the memory structures to provide the functionality expected from a database management system.

Chapter 3, *PostgreSQL – Object Hierarchy and Roles*, explains various object types and objects provided by PostgreSQL. Important concepts such as databases, clusters, tablespaces, and schemas are covered in this chapter.

Chapter 4, *Working with Transactions*, covers ACID properties of transactions, isolation levels, and how PostgreSQL provides them. Multiversion concurrency control is another topic dealt with in this chapter.

Chapter 5, *Data Modeling with SQL Power Architect*, talks about how we can model tables and relationships with SQL Power Architect. Some of the aspects that should be considered when we choose a design tool are also covered in this chapter.

Chapter 6, *Client Tools*, covers two clients tools (pgAdmin: a UI tool and psql: a command-line tool). Browsing database objects, generating queries, and generating the execution plan for queries using pgAdmin are covered. Setting up the environment variables for connecting from psql, viewing history of SQL commands executed, and meta-commands are also covered in this chapter.

Chapter 7, *SQL Tuning*, explains query optimization techniques. To set the context, some patterns about database use and theory on how the PostgreSQL optimizer works are covered.

Chapter 8, *Server Tuning*, covers PostgreSQL server settings that have significant impact on query performance. These include memory settings, cost settings, and so on. Two object types: partitions and materialized views are also covered in this chapter.

Chapter 9, *Tools to Move Data in and out of PostgreSQL*, covers common tools/utilities, such as pg_dump, pg_bulkload, and copy used to move data in and out of PostgreSQL.

Chapter 10, *Scaling, Replication, and Backup and Recovery*, covers methods that are usually used for achievability. A step-by-step method to achieve horizontal scalability using PostgreSQL's streaming replication and pgpool-II is also presented. Point-in-time recovery for PostgreSQL is also covered in this chapter.

Chapter 11, *PostgreSQL – Troubleshooting*, explains a few of the most common problems developers run into when they start off with PostgreSQL and how to troubleshoot them. Connection issues, privilege issues, and parameter setting issues are also covered.

Chapter 12, *PostgreSQL – Extras*, covers quite a few topics. Some interesting data types that every data architect should be aware of, a couple of really useful extensions, and a tool to analyze PostgreSQL log files are covered. It also covers a few interesting features available in PostgreSQL 9.4.

What you need for this book

A computer with access to the Internet is mandatory. It will definitely help if the computer is running on a Unix/Linux operating system.

Who this book is for

You are expected to have some exposure to databases. Basic familiarity with database objects such as tables and views is expected. You will find this book really useful if you have no or a little exposure to PostgreSQL. If you have been working with PostgreSQL for a few years, you should still find a few useful commands that you were not aware of or a couple of optimization approaches you have not tried. You will also gain more insight into how the database works.

Conventions

In this book, you will find a number of text styles that distinguish among different kinds of information. Here are some examples of these styles and an explanation of their meaning.

Code words in text, database table names, folder names, filenames, file extensions, pathnames, dummy URLs, user input, and Twitter handles are shown as follows: "We will use the following `wget` command to download the source."

A block of code/SQL at psql prompt as well as the output from the server at psql is set as follows:

```
CREATE TABLE emp(id serial, first_name varchar(50));
```

Commands executed at shell/command prompt, the output, and parameters and settings are formatted as follows:

```
[root@MyCentOS ~]# ps f -U postgres
  PID TTY      STAT   TIME COMMAND
 1918 tty1     S      0:00 /usr/local/pgsql/bin/postgres
```

New terms and **important words** are shown in bold.

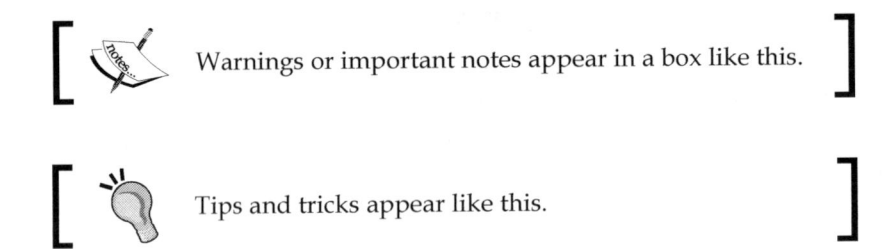

Preface

> Warnings or important notes appear in a box like this.

> Tips and tricks appear like this.

Reader feedback

Feedback from our readers is always welcome. Let us know what you think about this book—what you liked or disliked. Reader feedback is important for us as it helps us develop titles that you will really get the most out of.

To send us general feedback, simply e-mail feedback@packtpub.com, and mention the book's title in the subject of your message.

If there is a topic that you have expertise in and you are interested in either writing or contributing to a book, see our author guide at www.packtpub.com/authors.

Customer support

Now that you are the proud owner of a Packt book, we have a number of things to help you to get the most from your purchase.

Downloading the example code

You can download the example code files from your account at http://www.packtpub.com for all the Packt Publishing books you have purchased. If you purchased this book elsewhere, you can visit http://www.packtpub.com/support and register to have the files e-mailed directly to you.

Errata

Although we have taken every care to ensure the accuracy of our content, mistakes do happen. If you find a mistake in one of our books—maybe a mistake in the text or the code—we would be grateful if you could report this to us. By doing so, you can save other readers from frustration and help us improve subsequent versions of this book. If you find any errata, please report them by visiting http://www.packtpub.com/submit-errata, selecting your book, clicking on the **Errata Submission Form** link, and entering the details of your errata. Once your errata are verified, your submission will be accepted and the errata will be uploaded to our website or added to any list of existing errata under the Errata section of that title.

To view the previously submitted errata, go to https://www.packtpub.com/books/content/support and enter the name of the book in the search field. The required information will appear under the **Errata** section.

Piracy

Piracy of copyrighted material on the Internet is an ongoing problem across all media. At Packt, we take the protection of our copyright and licenses very seriously. If you come across any illegal copies of our works in any form on the Internet, please provide us with the location address or website name immediately so that we can pursue a remedy.

Please contact us at copyright@packtpub.com with a link to the suspected pirated material.

We appreciate your help in protecting our authors and our ability to bring you valuable content.

Questions

If you have a problem with any aspect of this book, you can contact us at questions@packtpub.com, and we will do our best to address the problem.

Installing PostgreSQL

This chapter gives you an overview of the process to install PostgreSQL from the source. The system used for installation and providing examples in the following sections is a 64-bit CentOS (6.4) machine. Other Unix/Linux systems typically have similar commands. For those using Windows systems, there is a set of utilities available at http://sourceforge.net/projects/unxutils/, which makes it possible to execute most of the Unix commands (`find`, `grep`, `cut`, and so on) in the Windows environment. The steps to be followed to install PostgreSQL on Windows are very different compared to those for Unix/Linux systems and are not covered in this chapter.

Installation options

There are many possible ways to install PostgreSQL on a system. For Windows, downloading the Graphical Installer and using this is the easy way. For Linux systems such as Red Hat Enterprise Linux or CentOS, we could either use **Yellow dog Updater Modified** (**yum**) or **Red Hat Package Manager** or **RPM Package Manager** (**rpm**) commands to install PostgreSQL. For Ubuntu, PostgreSQL can be installed using the `apt-get` command, which in turn works with Ubuntu's **Advanced Packaging Tool** (**APT**). While these options work, we do not get to see what is happening when we execute these commands, except, of course, that the database gets installed.

Then there are situations where we might want to build from the source. Assume that all we have is one production server and one development or staging server. We are on version 9.3. Version 9.4 is about to be released and there are quite a few interesting features in 9.4 that we want to try out. If we want to install 9.4 in the test server and use it alongside 9.3, without the installations stepping on each other's toes, compiling from the source with the `--prefix=` option and specifying different installation directories is the right approach. We could also set different default ports. It's also possible that the new version (source) is ready, but the package for our Linux distribution is not ready yet.

We might use a flavor of Linux for which an installation package is not available at all. Installation from source is the way forward in these situations. One advantage with installing from the source is that we don't have to worry too much about which package to download, the version of operating system (CentOS 6.3 or 6.4?), architecture (32 bit or 64 bit), and so on. These are more or less irrelevant. Of course, we should be using an operating system/architecture that is supported by the database, but that's about it! We also need to download and install all the tools and utilities necessary to compile and make the software, in this case, PostgreSQL.

So let's get down to it.

Downloading and extracting the source

The source for PostgreSQL is available at http://www.postgresql.org/ftp/source/.

We can see a number of versions all the way down to version 1 when it was called Postgres95 and up to the latest production and beta versions. If you belong to the group who believe that one shouldn't try software that is not at least a few months old, so that its teething issues are resolved, you should opt for the last-but-one version. It's a good idea to opt for the latest stable version. The latest versions have added quite a few very useful features, such as materialized views and an improved set of JSON functions and operators.

We will use the following wget command to download the source:

```
wget http://ftp.postgresql.org/pub/source/v9.3.0/postgresql-9.3.0.tar.gz
```

> It's a good idea to opt for the latest stable version.

Executing this command will give us a window that looks like this:

```
[jay@MyCentOS sw]$ wget http://ftp.postgresql.org/pub/source/v9.3.0/postgresql-9.3.0.tar.gz
--2013-10-07 14:37:55--  http://ftp.postgresql.org/pub/source/v9.3.0/postgresql-9.3.0.tar.gz
Resolving ftp.postgresql.org... 67.192.136.133, 213.189.17.228, 87.238.57.227, ...
Connecting to ftp.postgresql.org|67.192.136.133|:80... connected.
HTTP request sent, awaiting response... 200 OK
Length: 22140691 (21M) [application/x-tgz]
Saving to: `postgresql-9.3.0.tar.gz"

 3% [===>                                                           ] 874,117     195K/s  eta 2m 6s
```

As we can see, the tarred and gzipped source code comes to about 21 MB. As an aside, the installation files of Oracle—the big RDBMS out here—weighs over 2.2 GB.

The files can be extracted using the following command:

```
tar -xvf postgresql-9.3.0.tar.gz
```

The `tar` command is used to create or extract `TapeARchive` files. In the preceding command, the `x` option is used to extract, `v` for verbose is used so that we can see the list of files and folders getting extracted, and the `f` option is for, well, passing the name of the file, which will undergo the extraction process. We might need to provide the `z` option, so the command will be `tar -xzvf` if the preceding code in the `tar` command does not work. Some versions of `tar` are intelligent enough to figure out whether it is a gzipped file or not and will unzip it automatically. The untarred unzipped files come to around 115 MB.

Inspecting the contents

Let's inspect the contents:

```
cd postgresql-9.3.0

find ./ -maxdepth 1 -type d
```

The `find` command searches for files meeting specific criteria. Here, we instructed `find` to limit itself to scanning just one level of subdirectories using `maxdepth 1`. We used the `type` option along with `d` to tell `find` that we need files of type directory, as shown in the following screenshot:

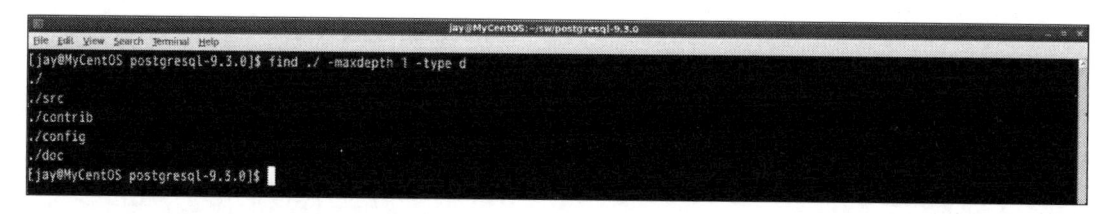

```
[jay@MyCentOS postgresql-9.3.0]$ find ./ -maxdepth 1 -type d
./
./src
./contrib
./config
./doc
[jay@MyCentOS postgresql-9.3.0]$
```

There are four directories:

- `src`: This directory has most of the core code, namely, code for the backend processes, optimizer, storage, client utilities (such as `psql`) and code to take care of replication, and so on. It also contains the makefiles for various distributions. For example, we have the files `Makefile.hpux`, `Makefile.linux`, `Makefile.openbsd`, and `Makefile.sco` under `src/makefile`.

Installing PostgreSQL

- `doc`: This directory has the source for documentation written in DocBook, DocBook being an application of **Standard Generalized Markup Language (SGML)**. It's possible to generate documentation in an HTML format, PDF format, and a few other formats.
- `contrib`: This directory is where many extensions are available. These are add-on modules that do not form part of the core installation, but can be installed as needed. For example, those who have to connect to other PostgreSQL databases can install the Foreign Data Wrapper extension: `postgres_fdw`. For those who want to access the contents of a file on the server from a table, there is the `file_fdw` extension.
- `config`: This directory contains a few macros that help you configure and compile the package.

Now let's move on to the dependencies, configuration options, and the actual installation itself.

Dependencies to compile the source

To compile and build PostgreSQL from source, we need GNU Make Version 3.8 or higher. The `gmake -v` command will tell us whether we have `gmake` and its version.

A compiler is also necessary. **GNU Compiler Collection (GCC)** is one such toolset that is included in almost all the Unix systems. The `gcc -v` command will provide you with the version of `gcc` as well as options with which it was configured on the system, as shown in the following screenshot:

```
[jay@MyCentOS postgresql-9.3.0]$ gcc -v
Using built-in specs.
Target: x86_64-redhat-linux
Configured with: ../configure --prefix=/usr --mandir=/usr/share/man --infodir=/usr/share/info --with-bugurl=http://bugzilla.redhat.com/bugzilla --enable-bootstrap --enable-shared --enable-threads=posix --enable-checking=release --with-system-zlib --enable-__cxa_atexit --disable-libunwind-exceptions --enable-gnu-unique-object --enable-languages=c,c++,objc,obj-c++,java,fortran,ada --enable-java-awt=gtk --disable-dssi --with-java-home=/usr/lib/jvm/java-1.5.0-gcj-1.5.0.0/jre --enable-libgcj-multifile --enable-java-maintainer-mode --with-ecj-jar=/usr/share/java/eclipse-ecj.jar --disable-libjava-multilib --with-ppl --with-cloog --with-tune=generic --with-arch_32=i686 --build=x86_64-redhat-linux
Thread model: posix
gcc version 4.4.7 20120313 (Red Hat 4.4.7-3) (GCC)
[jay@MyCentOS postgresql-9.3.0]$
```

> We can use the following commands to install the necessary packages if they are missing:
> - On Ubuntu: `sudo apt-get install build-essential`
> - On RHEL/CentOS: `sudo yum groupinstall 'Development Tools'`

[4]

The process of building a package from source involves preprocessing the source (including the header files, expanding macros, and so on), compiling, assembly, and linking (linking the libraries). The make utility automates the process of building the executable from source code. The make command uses a makefile, which contains rules on how to build the executables.

Other than GNU Make and a compiler, there is nothing else that is really necessary to continue. However, it is better to have at least the following two components:

- readline: The GNU readline library is very useful once we start using psql, the PostgreSQL command-line client, which is covered later. Having readline helps us work in a very "bash-like" environment, using *Tab* to autocomplete/suggest table names and up and down keys to browse command history, and so on and so forth. It also helps to have zlib in place before we proceed with the installation.
- zlib: This compression library can be handy when we are taking backups (a process definitely to be followed when we have a database).

Adding SQL/XML support will also be useful as sooner or later we will want to extract data from tables in an XML format or load data from the XML files to tables. Still, this might not be as useful as the other two, namely, readline and zlib.

Configuring and creating the makefile

The next step is to execute configure. This is a shell script which will run, to quote documentation, a number of tests to determine several system dependent variables. It will also create many files that will be used during compilation. We can get an idea about the options by executing the following command:

```
./configure --help > /tmp/config.txt
```

We can vi /tmp/config.txt and verify that there are over 80 options that can be used. These options can be broadly grouped into the following categories:

- Related to choosing directories. If architecture-independent files go to /usr/local/pgsql or elsewhere, where should the binaries go, where should the documentation files go, and so on.
- Related to debugging, profiling, tracing, and so on to be used with care in production.

Installing PostgreSQL

- Related to choosing nondefault settings for parameters such as blocksize, port, and segment size. Changing default setting for parameters such as blocksize can have significant impact on performance. So, we need to be cautious here. Changing the default port is a good idea from a security perspective. It can be changed later in the configuration file also.
- Related to enabling options, such as OpenSSL support, SELinux support, and LDAP support.
- Related to building modules for several languages (Perl, Python, and PL/TcL).
- Related to disabling a few features (such as `zlib` and `readline`).

> Pay attention to the `--prefix` option. If you would like to do a clean upgrade without causing disruption to the existing environment, provide a directory in which the installation files should be written to. This way, each version will be in a different directory. For example:
>
> `./configure    --prefix=/opt/pg/9.3`

When we run `./configure`, it's likely that we get an output like this:

```
checking for perl... /usr/bin/perl
configure: using perl 5.10.1
checking for main in -lm... yes
checking for library containing setproctitle... no
checking for library containing dlopen... -ldl
checking for library containing socket... none required
checking for library containing shl_load... no
checking for library containing getopt_long... none required
checking for library containing crypt... -lcrypt
checking for library containing fdatasync... none required
checking for library containing gethostbyname_r... none required
checking for library containing shmget... none required
checking for library containing readline... no
configure: error: readline library not found
If you have readline already installed, see config.log for details on the
failure.  It is possible the compiler isn't looking in the proper directory.
Use --without-readline to disable readline support.
[jay@MyCentOS postgresql-9.3.0]$ yum list installed | grep readline
readline.x86_64              6.0-4.el6             @anaconda-CentOS-201303020151.x86_64/6.4
[jay@MyCentOS postgresql-9.3.0]$
```

The output tells us that `readline` is not available. However, if we list installation packages, it is very much there. The reason is that `readline-devel` is missing. It contains files needed by programs (such as `psql`) that use the `readline` library. This can be installed using the following command:

```
yum install readline-devel.x86_64
```

It also installs `ncurses-devel`. You will have to execute the command using `sudo` or `root`. You might also get a similar error for `zlib`, although `zlib` itself is already installed. Again, the corrective action is to install `devel`, in this case, `zlib-devel`.

Once this is done, we can run `configure` again and it should go through without any issues, as shown in the following screenshot:

```
checking for uint64... no
checking for sig_atomic_t... yes
checking for POSIX signal interface... yes
checking for working memcmp... yes
checking for onsgmls... no
checking for nsgmls... no
checking for openjade... no
checking for jade... no
checking for DocBook V4.2... no
checking for DocBook stylesheets... no
checking for collateindex.pl... no
checking for xsltproc... xsltproc
checking for osx... no
checking for sgml2xml... no
checking for sx... no
checking thread safety of required library functions... yes
checking whether gcc supports -Wl,--as-needed... yes
configure: using compiler=gcc (GCC) 4.4.7 20120313 (Red Hat 4.4.7-3)
configure: using CFLAGS=-O2 -Wall -Wmissing-prototypes -Wpointer-arith -Wdeclaration-after-statement -Wendif-labels -Wmissing-format-attribute -Wformat-security -fno-strict-aliasing -fwrapv
configure: using CPPFLAGS= -D_GNU_SOURCE
configure: using LDFLAGS=  -Wl,--as-needed
configure: creating ./config.status
config.status: creating GNUmakefile
config.status: creating src/Makefile.global
config.status: creating src/include/pg_config.h
config.status: creating src/include/pg_config_ext.h
config.status: creating src/interfaces/ecpg/include/ecpg_config.h
config.status: linking src/backend/port/tas/dummy.s to src/backend/port/tas.s
config.status: linking src/backend/port/dynloader/linux.c to src/backend/port/dynloader.c
config.status: linking src/backend/port/sysv_sema.c to src/backend/port/pg_sema.c
config.status: linking src/backend/port/sysv_shmem.c to src/backend/port/pg_shmem.c
config.status: linking src/backend/port/unix_latch.c to src/backend/port/pg_latch.c
config.status: linking src/backend/port/dynloader/linux.h to src/include/dynloader.h
config.status: linking src/include/port/linux.h to src/include/pg_config_os.h
config.status: linking src/makefiles/Makefile.linux to src/Makefile.port
[jay@MyCentOS postgresql-9.3.0]$
```

The two files are now created in the current directory in addition to a few more files in subdirectories. One is `config.status` and the other (`config.log. config.status`) is a bash script that can be executed to recreate the configuration. The `config.log` file can be reviewed to understand the various options used, variables, and errors, if any. It's possible that the `config.log` file has a few errors that are marked fatal, and the compilation process can still be completed without any issue.

Installing PostgreSQL

Building and creating the executables

This step compiles all the source files and generates the executables. The makefile created in the configure step is used by the `gmake` utility. These files are not copied to standard directories, such as `bin`, `/usr/bin`, `/usr/local/bin`, and so on. We have the option to make all the options available (the `contrib` modules, source, and so on), or just the core. It's also possible to build just the core now and add the necessary `contrib` modules later on. We will build everything now, rather than adding the necessary modules later. Hence, the command is:

`gmake world`

The process takes a few minutes to complete, and in the end says `PostgreSQL, contrib, and documentation successfully made. Ready to install,` as shown in the following screenshot:

Installing and moving the files to where they belong

This is the step where the files are copied to the correct directories. As the installation process involves writing files to directories, which an ordinary user cannot write to, we need to use `su` for this step:

`su`

If you are interested in seeing what happens during the installation step, redirect the output to a file, for example, `gmake install-world > /tmp/install.out`.

We used the keyword `world` for make. We will use a similar option for installation too:

`gmake install-world`

If all goes well, we will see a message that says `PostgreSQL, contrib, and documentation successfully made. Ready to install`. If the output was directed to a file as mentioned, we can open it and see that the installation process created a `/usr/local/pgsql` directory with a few subdirectories for various components. Then, the `install` command copied the directories and files to target directories and set attributes such as permissions. Refer to the highlighted portion in the following screenshot:

```
/bin/mkdir -p '/usr/local/pgsql/bin' '/usr/local/pgsql/share'
/usr/bin/install -c  postgres '/usr/local/pgsql/bin/postgres'
ln -s postgres '/usr/local/pgsql/bin/postmaster'
gmake -C catalog install-data
gmake[3]: Entering directory `/home/jay/sw/postgresql-9.3.0/src/backend/catalog'
/bin/mkdir -p '/usr/local/pgsql/share'
/usr/bin/install -c -m 644 `for f in ./postgres.bki; do test -r $f && echo $f && break; done` '/usr/local/pgsql/share/postgres.bki'
/usr/bin/install -c -m 644 `for f in ./postgres.description; do test -r $f && echo $f && break; done` '/usr/local/pgsql/share/postgres.descript
ion'
/usr/bin/install -c -m 644 `for f in ./postgres.shdescription; do test -r $f && echo $f && break; done` '/usr/local/pgsql/share/postgres.shdesc
ription'
/usr/bin/install -c -m 644 ./system_views.sql '/usr/local/pgsql/share/system_views.sql'
/usr/bin/install -c -m 644 ./information_schema.sql '/usr/local/pgsql/share/information_schema.sql'
/usr/bin/install -c -m 644 ./sql_features.txt '/usr/local/pgsql/share/sql_features.txt'
gmake[3]: Leaving directory `/home/jay/sw/postgresql-9.3.0/src/backend/catalog'
gmake -C tsearch install-data
gmake[3]: Entering directory `/home/jay/sw/postgresql-9.3.0/src/backend/tsearch'
/bin/mkdir -p '/usr/local/pgsql/share' '/usr/local/pgsql/share/tsearch_data'
/usr/bin/install -c -m 644 ./synonym_sample.syn ./thesaurus_sample.ths ./hunspell_sample.affix ./ispell_sample.affix ./ispell_sample.dict '/usr
/local/pgsql/share/tsearch_data/'
gmake[3]: Leaving directory `/home/jay/sw/postgresql-9.3.0/src/backend/tsearch'
```

Inspecting the changes

As we did not make any changes to the default options, the installation files will be at `/usr/local/pgsql`. In this, we have four directories, namely `include`, `lib`, `share`, and `bin`. The `include` directory contains header files (`.h`) extension, and the `lib` directory contains all the libraries to be linked dynamically (`.so` in the case of Linux/Unix systems and `.dll` in the case of Windows systems). The `bin` directory, of course, contains executables.

It is the `share` directory that is a bit more interesting. Here, we have a number of sample files, namely, `pg_hba.conf.sample`, `pg_ident.conf.sample`, `pg_service.conf.sample`, `postgresql.conf.sample`, `psqlrc.sample`, and `recovery.conf.sample`. Once we initialize a cluster and make changes to various configuration files and then lose track of the changes, we can compare with these files and understand what changes have been made or roll back the changes if necessary.

This directory also has a few SQL files such as `information_schema.sql` and `system_view.sql`, which go into creating metadata views when a database cluster is initialized.

At the next level of directories under `share`, we have the `doc` directory that holds the documentation, and the `man` directory that holds the manual pages, and so on. The directory of interest under `share` is the one named `extension`. Here, we can see all the extensions, which we can install as per our need. Most extensions have a `.control` file that provides basic information, as shown here:

```
[jay@MyCentOS extension]$ more dblink.control
# dblink extension
comment = 'connect to other PostgreSQL databases from within a database'
default_version = '1.1'
module_pathname = '$libdir/dblink'
relocatable = true
```

There will be SQL files that correspond to each extension, and these will be used when we install the extension in a database we choose.

The documentation to install PostgreSQL from source is at `http://www.postgresql.org/docs/current/static/installation.html`.

Note that we have just installed the database software. There is no database available to connect to yet. Adding a user for the database administration tasks and initializing a database cluster are the next steps.

Initializing a cluster

First we add an OS user. This user will be used to start/stop/restart the database. This user will also be the superuser for the cluster. The following command has to be executed as root or with sudo:

```
adduser postgres
```

> The new user need not be named postgres. It can be mydbadmin, mydba, or anything we fancy.

Next, we create a directory that will be the base directory for the new cluster. This could be anywhere. A standard location can be /usr/local/pgsql/data. However, you might want to have the database cluster on a separate partition. In the event of an OS and associated file system crash, your database data remains intact. It can also be that you want to use faster spinning disks or Solid State Disks for the database cluster to improve performance. In short, performance and/or reliability concerns can make you choose a location other than the default location to initialize the database cluster. As root, we execute the commands:

```
[root@MyCentOS extension]# mkdir -p /pgdata/9.3
```

The -p option ensures that the parent directory is also created if it is nonexistent:

```
[root@MyCentOS extension]# chown postgres /pgdata/9.3
```

Then, we switch user to postgres. This is necessary because when we initialize the cluster, the user under which the command was executed becomes the owner of the cluster. The server process will also be owned by this user. We will go with the standard user -postgres, which we created:

```
su - postgres
```

The next step is to run the initdb script. Well! Not exactly. If we run initdb now, we will get an error:

```
[postgres@MyCentOS ~]$ initdb
-bash: initdb: command not found
```

This is because we haven't added the directory containing the PostgreSQL executables to the environment variable PATH yet. We could provide the absolute path and make it work. However, it is better to set the variables.

Installing PostgreSQL

In `.bash_profile` of `postgres`, we have the following lines:

```
PATH=$PATH:$HOME/bin
export PATH
```

Just before the export PATH line, add:

```
PATH=$PATH:/usr/local/pgsql/bin
```

Then, try this:

```
[postgres@MyCentOS ~]$ which initdb
/usr/bin/which: no initdb in
(/usr/local/bin:/bin:/usr/bin:/usr/local/sbin:/usr/sbin:/sbin:/home/p
ostgres/bin)
```

Not surprisingly, as `.bash_profile` doesn't get executed unless we source it or log out and log in. Log out, log in, and try again:

```
[postgres@MyCentOS ~]$ exit
logout
[root@MyCentOS ~]# su - postgres
[postgres@MyCentOS ~]$ which initdb
/usr/local/pgsql/bin/initdb
```

Now we are good to go! It's a good idea to execute the following:

```
initdb --help | more
```

Among the many parameters available, the important ones, in most cases, will be `-D` or `--pgdata`. This parameter is used to define the directory where the cluster will be initialized (where the database cluster should be stored). This is the only mandatory parameter. Another parameter that can be useful is `--pwprompt`. Using this, we can set the password for the database superuser. So, we execute the following command:

```
initdb --pgdata=/pgdata/9.3 --pwprompt
```

[12]

Chapter 1

If this is not set now and password authentication is to be used, we have to set the password later, as shown here:

```
[postgres@MyCentOS ~]$ initdb --pgdata=/pgdata/9.3 --pwprompt
The files belonging to this database system will be owned by user "postgres".
This user must also own the server process.

The database cluster will be initialized with locale "en_US.UTF-8".
The default database encoding has accordingly been set to "UTF8".
The default text search configuration will be set to "english".

Data page checksums are disabled.

fixing permissions on existing directory /pgdata/9.3 ... ok
creating subdirectories ... ok
selecting default max_connections ... 100
selecting default shared_buffers ... 128MB
creating configuration files ... ok
creating template1 database in /pgdata/9.3/base/1 ... ok
initializing pg_authid ... ok
Enter new superuser password:
Enter it again:
setting password ... ok
initializing dependencies ... ok
creating system views ... ok
loading system objects' descriptions ... ok
creating collations ... ok
creating conversions ... ok
creating dictionaries ... ok
setting privileges on built-in objects ... ok
creating information schema ... ok
loading PL/pgSQL server-side language ... ok
vacuuming database template1 ... ok
copying template1 to template0 ... ok
copying template1 to postgres ... ok
syncing data to disk ... ok

WARNING: enabling "trust" authentication for local connections
You can change this by editing pg_hba.conf or using the option -A, or
--auth-local and --auth-host, the next time you run initdb.
```

As seen in the preceding screenshot, the process asks for the superuser password. Towards the end, it gives a warning that the trust authentication is enabled for local connections. This means that it will be possible to make connections from the localhost without being prompted for a password. It's a good idea to change this setting. We will come to this later. For more options available for `initdb`, please refer to http://www.postgresql.org/docs/current/static/app-initdb.html.

Installing PostgreSQL

As always, let's see what happened; which directories got created when we initialized the cluster:

```
cd /pgdata/9.3
[postgres@MyCentOS 9.3]$ find ./ -maxdepth 1 -type d
./
./base
./pg_stat
./pg_clog
./pg_xlog
./pg_tblspc
./pg_twophase
./pg_subtrans
./global
./pg_notify
./pg_stat_tmp
./pg_snapshots
./pg_multixact
./pg_serial
```

A quick walk through the directories

We will start the cluster as it will help us to relate the files system with the databases:

```
[postgres@MyCentOS base]$ export PGDATA=/pgdata/9.3/
```

PGDATA is the default data directory location.

```
[postgres@MyCentOS base]$ pg_ctl start
server starting
[postgres@MyCentOS base]$ LOG:   database system was shut down at 2013-10-13 13:48:07 IST
LOG:   database system is ready to accept connections
LOG:   autovacuum launcher started
```

The `pg_ctl` is a utility to start, stop, check the status, or restart the database cluster. Passing `init` or `initdb` as a parameter results in the initialization of a cluster. More options can be explored at http://www.postgresql.org/docs/current/static/app-pg-ctl.html.

Now, we will go through the directories:

- `base`: This directory holds the databases that will be created by database users. This also holds the `pg_defaulttablespace` with the databases: `postgres`, `template0`, and `template1`:

    ```
    [postgres@MyCentOS base]$ pwd
    /pgdata/9.3/base
    [postgres@MyCentOS base]$ find ./ -type d
    ./
    ./1
    ./12891
    ./12896
    [postgres@MyCentOS base]$ oid2name
    All databases:
    Oid   Database Name   Tablespace
    ----------------------------------
    12896        postgres   pg_default
    12891        template0  pg_default
        1        template1  pg_default
    ```

    - We can see here that `Oid` points to the directory names. We can try creating and dropping a database, as shown in the following code:

        ```
        [postgres@MyCentOS base]$ pwd
        /pgdata/9.3/base
        [postgres@MyCentOS base]$ psql
        psql (9.3.0)
        Type "help" for help.

        postgres=# \! ls
        1   12891   12896
        postgres=# CREATE DATABASE test;
        CREATE DATABASE
        postgres=# \! ls
        1   12891   12896   16385
        postgres=# DROP DATABASE test;
        DROP DATABASE
        postgres=# \! ls
        1   12891   12896
        ```

[15]

Installing PostgreSQL

> OID stands for Object Identifier. They are used internally by PostgreSQL as primary keys for various system tables. Objects created in the cluster (tables, databases, and so on) will have OIDs associated with them. The `oid2name` utility is available as a `contrib` module and helps us examine the databases, tables, and related file nodes.

  - We note a few things here. First, we were not prompted for a password (remember the warning about trust authentication?). Next, we can execute host commands from `psql` (more on this in a later chapter). Third, creating/dropping databases are actually similar to creating/deleting directories. PostgreSQL does do quite a bit of internal book-keeping when we create or drop objects in addition to manipulating directories.

- `global`: This directory contains cluster-wide tables. There are many tables and associated views that keep track of the entire cluster, namely, database roles, system catalog data, and so on.
- `pg_clog`: This directory contains the transaction commit status data.
- `pg_multixact`: This directory contains multitransaction status data (concurrent transactions waiting for a lock).
- `pg_notify`: This directory contains the LISTEN/NOTIFY status data.
- `pg_serial`: This directory contains information about committed serializable transactions.
- `pg_snapshots`: This directory contains exported snapshots.
- `pg_stat_tmp`: This directory contains temporary files for the statistics subsystem.
- `pg_subtrans`: This directory contains subtransaction status data.
- `pg_tblspc`: This directory contains symbolic links to tablespaces.
- `pg_twophase`: This directory contains state files for prepared transactions.
- `pg_xlog`: This directory contains **Write Ahead Log (WAL)** files.

In short, we have directories to hold containers of real user created data (tables and tablespaces), directories to hold data about all the data and data structures (metadata), and then directories to hold data about the state of transactions.

Processes created

Let's take a look at the processes spawned when we started PostgreSQL:

```
[root@MyCentOS ~]# ps    -fupostgres
```

The following screenshot illustrates the processes spawned:

```
UID        PID   PPID  C STIME TTY          TIME CMD
postgres  1566      1  0 10:03 ?        00:00:00 /usr/local/pgsql/bin/postmaster -D /pgdata/9.3
postgres  1624   1566  0 10:03 ?        00:00:00 postgres: logger process
postgres  1654   1566  0 10:03 ?        00:00:00 postgres: checkpointer process
postgres  1655   1566  0 10:03 ?        00:00:00 postgres: writer process
postgres  1656   1566  0 10:03 ?        00:00:00 postgres: wal writer process
postgres  1657   1566  0 10:03 ?        00:00:00 postgres: autovacuum launcher process
postgres  1658   1566  0 10:03 ?        00:00:00 postgres: stats collector process
```

We can see that there is one parent process (`pid1566`), which spawned a few child processes.

Important files created

One important file that gets created when we initialize a database cluster is `postgresql.conf`. This file contains a number of critical parameters related to the server processes and resource allocation, memory management, logging, file locations, and so on. Another file is `pg_hba.conf`. "hba" (which stands for host-based authentication). Changes to these files are necessary to enable client connection to the database from a different machine. Both of these are in the PGDATA folder.

The `postmaster.pid` file in the same directory is used by `pg_ctl` to determine whether the database is running:

```
[postgres@MyCentOS 9.3]$ pg_ctl status
pg_ctl: server is running (PID: 1566)
```

The contents of the file are as follows:

```
[postgres@MyCentOS 9.3]$ head -1 postmaster.pid
1566
```

The `1566` number in the `pid` file is the same as what we got for the parent process when we did a process listing earlier.

Working with extensions

We have so far initialized the database cluster. However, we made quite a few extensions available using the `world` option. What about them? We can list the installed extensions using the `dx` (describe extension) command at the `psql` prompt:

```
postgres=# \dx
                List of installed extensions
   Name   | Version |   Schema   |         Description
---------+---------+------------+------------------------------
 plpgsql |   1.0   | pg_catalog | PL/pgSQL procedural language
(1 row)
```

To get a list of available extensions, we can query the `pg_available_extensions` view, as shown here:

```
postgres=# SELECT name,comment  FROM pg_available_extensions limit 5;
    name    |                          comment

------------+--------------------------------------------------------------
 dblink     | connect to other PostgreSQL databases from within a database
 isn        | data types for international product numbering standards
 file_fdw   | foreign-data wrapper for flat file access
 tsearch2   | compatibility package for pre-8.3 text search functions
 unaccent   | text search dictionary that removes accents
(5 rows)
```

Let's try installing one extension and then see the list of installed extensions again:

```
postgres=# CREATE EXTENSION dblink ;
CREATE EXTENSION
postgres=# \dx
                List of installed extensions
   Name   | Version |   Schema   |              Description
---------+---------+------------+---------------------------------------
 dblink  |   1.1   | public     | connect to other PostgreSQL databases from within a database
 plpgsql |   1.0   | pg_catalog | PL/pgSQL procedural language
(2 rows)
```

The `dblink` extension has been added to the list of installed extensions. To remove it, just drop it:

```
postgres=# DROP EXTENSION dblink ;
DROP EXTENSION
postgres=# \dx
              List of installed extensions
  Name   | Version |   Schema   |         Description
---------+---------+------------+------------------------------
 plpgsql | 1.0     | pg_catalog | PL/pgSQL procedural language
(1 row)
```

> **Downloading the example code**
>
> You can download the example code files from your account at http://www.packtpub.com for all the Packt Publishing books you have purchased. If you purchased this book elsewhere, you can visit http://www.packtpub.com/support and register to have the files e-mailed directly to you.

Summary

In this chapter, we covered the steps to install PostgreSQL from the source: downloading, configuring, building and installing. We went through the directory structure of the source tree, the cluster initialization process, the resultant directories and files, as well as the process to install and remove extensions.

In the next chapter, we will cover PostgreSQL Server Architecture. We will cover the various background processes, their functions, memory structures and how they all work with each other to provide the many features available in PostgreSQL.

2
Server Architecture

In the previous chapter, we saw that starting a PostgreSQL cluster kicks off a few processes. The processes manage quite a bit of file I/O, manage other processes, and deal with memory allocation and a lot of other work. In this chapter, we will focus on the processes and their roles, memory management, and how they work together.

We will start by listing the processes once again. No client is connected to any of the databases yet:

```
[root@MyCentOS ~]# ps f -U postgres
   PID TTY      STAT   TIME COMMAND
  1918 tty1     S      0:00 /usr/local/pgsql/bin/postgres
  1920 ?        Ss     0:00  \_ postgres: checkpointer process
  1921 ?        Ss     0:00  \_ postgres: writer process
  1922 ?        Ss     0:00  \_ postgres: wal writer process
  1923 ?        Ss     0:00  \_ postgres: autovacuum launcher process
  1924 ?        Ss     0:00  \_ postgres: stats collector process
```

Starting with the daemon process

The first process that is started when we start PostgreSQL is `/usr/local/pgsql/bin/postgres`. This process has quite a few responsibilities such as performing recovery, initializing shared data structures/memory space, and kicking off the mandatory and optional processes. These processes are also referred to as utility processes and include `bgwriter`, `checkpointer`, `autovacuum launcher`, `log writer`, `stats collector process`, and so on. The daemon process also listens for connection requests, receives requests for connections from clients, and spawns server processes for the client. It's obvious that the daemon itself is a mandatory process that should be running for a user to connect to the database.

Server Architecture

Let's focus on the user connecting-issuing-commands scenario and other pieces should fall in place. The following diagram walks you through the process of how the daemon process receives a connection request and starts (forks) a backend process. The backend process will, on successful authentication, start handling requests from that client:

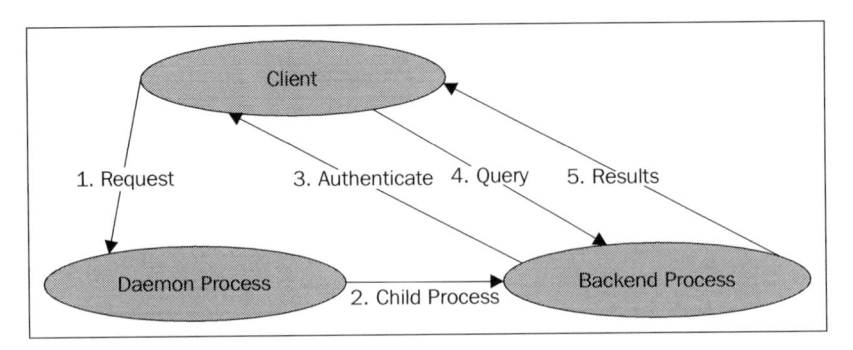

The process is repeated for all connection requests (unless we hit the `max_connections` settings, in which case we get an error).

So, an active server, after a period of time, will have the processes that were there when the server started, plus quite a few processes to serve client connections, as shown in the following diagram:

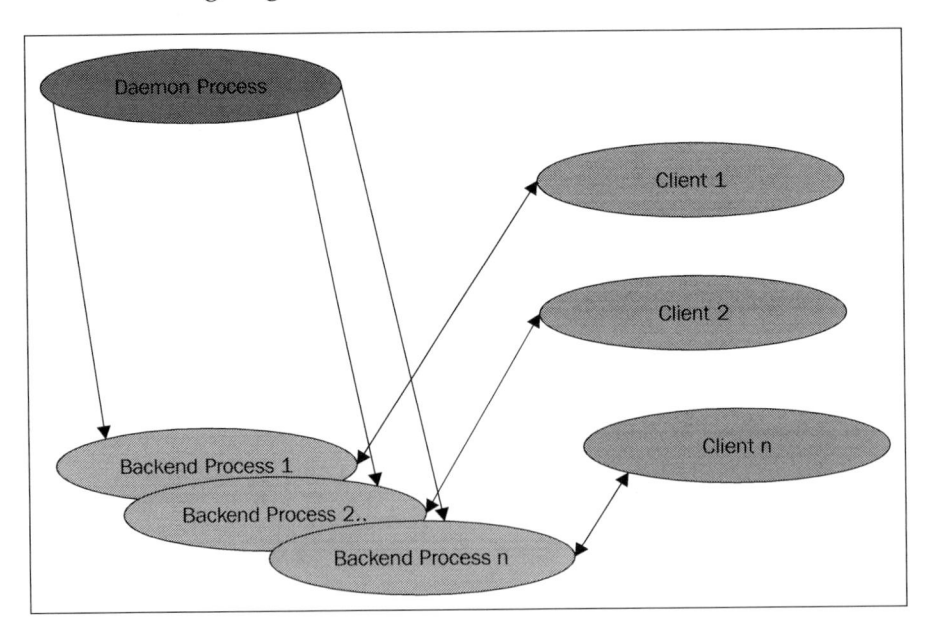

Once a user is connected to a database, the user typically wants to read (SELECT) data or write (UPDATE/DELETE/INSERT) data, not to mention making changes to table structure, adding indexes, and so on. For example, a user logs in to Amazon and searches for the latest iPad, its price, and availability. This sounds simple enough. Assuming the simplest (unbelievably simple) table structure, this search will become the query:

```
SELECT price, available_count FROM product_tbl WHERE product = 'iPad';
```

However, when we consider that there might be thousands of users who want to do this, it gets a little bit more complex. The preceding query gets executed a few thousand times concurrently. When thousands of users search for different products, the iPad gets changed to thousands of different product names. So far so good. However, what happens when there is just one of the new iPads left at Amazon and there are a few hundred users trying to add it to their shopping cart? Gets real tricky, right? That is, for the database, many users trying to write to the same record:

```
UPDATE product_tbl SET available_count =0 WHERE product = 'iPad';
```

With these possibilities at the back of our minds, let's move on with understanding the rest of the PostgreSQL processes and memory management.

Understanding the shared buffer

When there are thousands of users trying to read/write data to many different tables, reading from the directories/files (which we saw getting created when we installed PostgreSQL and created a database with a couple of tables) will result in a miserably non-scalable system. The reads and writes will result in searching for many files, opening these files, using `fseek()` for specific data records, locking, editing, and unlocking. To make this a lot more scalable and faster, the concept of shared buffers (memory area) is introduced. Now, the backend processes are no longer reading from the files and writing to the files, but dealing with buffers or RAM, with significant improvement in performance. The amount of memory to be allocated is decided by the `shared_buffers` parameter in `postgresql.conf`. This fixed-size block of shared memory is allocated when the server is started.

It's not this memory chunk alone that is responsible for improving the response times, but the OS cache also helps quite a bit by keeping a lot of data ready-to-serve. Together, these two caches result in a significant reduction in the actual number and volume of physical reads and writes. In addition to these two levels of caching, there could be a disk controller cache, disk drive cache, and so on. The bottom line is that these caches improve performance by reducing the physical I/O necessary.

Server Architecture

There are also risks associated with huge caches, such as the spikes in I/O, when large volumes of data get flushed from the buffer to disk. For a detailed understanding of the risks and benefits of caches, disks, and physical and logical I/O tuning, *PostgreSQL 9.0 High Performance*, *Gregory Smith*, *Packt Publishing*, is recommended.

Let's just consider the possible routes a simple `SELECT` statement might take, considering the shared buffer cache and OS cache alone.

The first thing the process will check is whether the data it wants is available in the database buffer cache. If it is not available in the database buffer cache, a request goes to the OS to fetch the specific file/block(s). There is a chance that the OS cache already has the file/block(s) and passes it to the database cache. In both these cases, a physical I/O is avoided. It's only when the data is not present in either of these caches (or other caches), that a user initialized read/write will really result in a physical I/O. These three possibilities are shown in the following diagram:

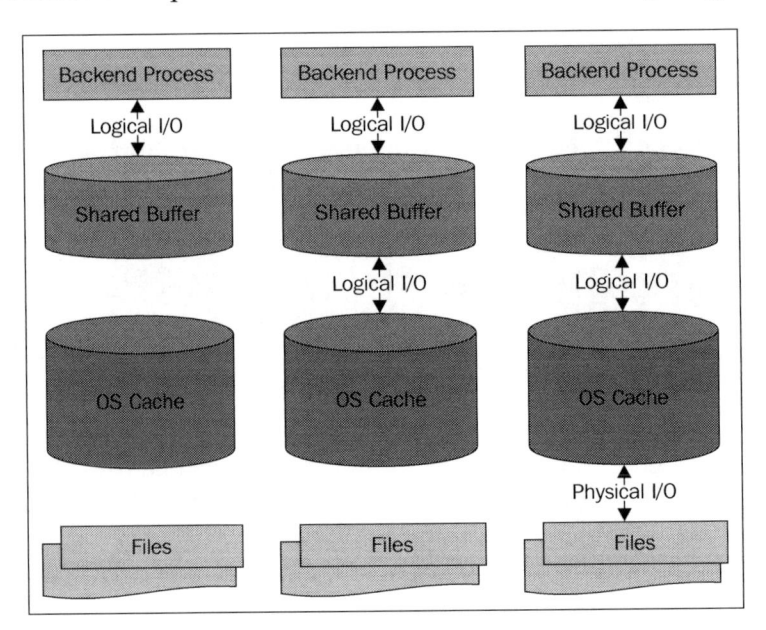

It's evident that most of the user-driven data fetches and writes will happen via buffers. Exceptions to this would be databases where the buffer is minuscule compared to the data that is usually read and written. Even in cases where the number of transactions per second is very high, the physical I/O will be limited if these transactions are mostly working with the same datasets. It's only when different transactions are accessing data from really different areas in the file system that the issue of frequent buffer flushes to disk and reads from disk will occur.

Even in a scenario where a user makes a lot of changes to table data and issues a commit, it might not immediately result in writes to the underlying data files. This might just result in ensuring that **Write Ahead Log (WAL)** files are synchronized with the WAL buffer.

WAL forms a critical component in ensuring the **Durability (D)** and, to some extent, the **Atomicity (A)** of ACID properties of transactions. However, first let's continue with the buffer and see how user-changed data finally reaches the data files.

Inspecting the buffer cache

PostgreSQL provides an extension to view what is in the buffer cache. It can be installed in a similar manner to what we did earlier. Log in to psql and create two databases:

```
CREATE DATABASE test;
CREATE DATABASE mydb;
```

Connect to the test database and execute:

```
CREATE EXTENSION pg_buffercache;
CREATE EXTENSION
```

So, what happens when we do this? We get an idea by looking at the SQL. At shell prompt, go to the /usr/local/pgsql/share/extension directory:

```
[postgres@MyCentOS ~]$ cd /usr/local/pgsql/share/extension
[postgres@MyCentOS extension]$ pwd
/usr/local/pgsql/share/extension
[postgres@MyCentOS extension]$ more pg_buffercache--1.0.sql
/* contrib/pg_buffercache/pg_buffercache--1.0.sql */

-- complain if script is sourced in psql, rather than via CREATE EXTENSION
\echo Use "CREATE EXTENSION pg_buffercache" to load this file.
\quit

-- Register the function.
CREATE FUNCTION pg_buffercache_pages()
RETURNS SETOF RECORD
AS 'MODULE_PATHNAME', 'pg_buffercache_pages'
LANGUAGE C;

-- Create a view for convenient access.
CREATE VIEW pg_buffercache AS
    SELECT P.* FROM pg_buffercache_pages() AS P
```

Server Architecture

```
    (bufferid integer, relfilenode oid, reltablespace oid,
reldatabase oid,
    relforknumber int2, relblocknumber int8, isdirty bool,
usagecount int2);

-- Don't want these to be available to public.
REVOKE ALL ON FUNCTION pg_buffercache_pages() FROM PUBLIC;
REVOKE ALL ON pg_buffercache FROM PUBLIC;
```

> One thing we need to remember is that extensions get installed in a database in the cluster. If we have to use them in another database in the cluster, we must install the extensions in this database too. In PostgreSQL, a cluster refers to a set of databases using the same configuration files, listening for requests at a common port. Clusters, databases, and related objects will be covered in detail in *Chapter 3, PostgreSQL – Object Hierarchy and Roles*.

Let's connect to the test database and see what is present in the buffer cache:

```
[postgres@MyCentOS extension]$ psql -d test
Type "help" for help.

test=# SELECT DISTINCT reldatabase FROM pg_buffercache;
 reldatabase
-------------
       12896
           0
       24741
(4 rows)
```

So, we have some part of two databases in the cache. The record with 0 represents buffers that are not used yet:

```
test=# \! oid2name
All databases:
    Oid  Database Name  Tablespace
----------------------------------
  16440           mydb  pg_default
  12896       postgres  pg_default
  12891      template0  pg_default
      1      template1  pg_default
  24741           test  pg_default
```

[26]

These are the `test` database (to which we are connected) and the `postgres` database.

We can link this with a couple of other views to get a better picture:

```
SELECT
c.relname,
count(*) AS buffers
FROM pg_class c
JOIN pg_buffercache b
ON b.relfilenode=c.relfilenode
INNER JOIN pg_database d
ON (b.reldatabase=d.oid AND d.datname=current_database())
GROUP BY c.relname
ORDER BY 2 DESC;
```

relname	buffers
pg_operator	13
pg_depend_reference_index	11
pg_depend	9

We see that it is mostly data dictionary views.

> There are many data dictionary tables and views that provide us information about various objects, object types, permissions, and so on. These together manage the book-keeping activities for the cluster; `pg_class` is one of these catalog tables. One of the columns in this table is `relname`. Although, it sounds like it will be storing relation/table names, it can also store data for other object types. We should use it along with the `relkind` column. The `relkind` column tells us what type of object the record refers to. Possible values in `relkind` include r (table), i (index), S (Sequence), v (view), and so on.

Let's remove `relname` from the preceding query and modify it slightly:

```
SELECT
c.relname,
count(*) AS buffers
FROM pg_class c
JOIN pg_buffercache b
ON b.relfilenode=c.relfilenode
JOIN pg_database d
ON (b.reldatabase=d.oid AND d.datname=current_database())
WHERE c.relname NOT LIKE 'pg%' GROUP BY c.relname
ORDER BY 2 DESC;
```

Server Architecture

```
relname | buffers
--------+--------
(0 rows)
```

We will now try populating the buffer with a user-created table. We will first create a table and insert a record:

```
[postgres@MyCentOS ~]$ psql -d test
CREATE TABLE emp(id serial, first_name varchar(50));
INSERT INTO emp(first_name) VALUES('Jayadeva');
SELECT * FROM emp;
 id | first_name
----+------------
  1 | Jayadeva
(1 row)
```

> The `serial` keyword refers to autoincrementing integer type. Using this keyword will automatically create a sequence number generator (SEQUENCE) and the column (`id` in the table `emp`) will be populated from this sequence. For more information about numeric data types, refer to http://www.postgresql.org/docs/current/static/datatype-numeric.html#datatype-numeric-table.
>
> For details about sequences, refer to http://www.postgresql.org/docs/current/static/sql-createsequence.html.

We can repeat the query to inspect the buffer and check whether the buffer contains the newly created table and its sequence:

```
relname    | buffers
-----------+--------
emp_id_seq |    1
emp        |    1
```

Let's modify the query a bit:

```
SELECT
c.relname,
b.isdirty
FROM pg_class c JOIN pg_buffercache b
ON b.relfilenode=c.relfilenode
JOIN pg_database d
ON (b.reldatabase=d.oid AND d.datname=current_database())
WHERE c.relname not like 'pg%';
```

```
    relname   | isdirty
--------------+---------
 emp_id_seq   | f
 emp          | f
```

Notice that the `isdirty` flag is `f` (false):

```
UPDATE emp SET first_name ='Newname';
UPDATE 1
```

If we repeat the query for buffers with the `isdirty` flag, we will get:

```
    relname   | isdirty
--------------+---------
 emp_id_seq   | f
 emp          | t
```

The output tells us that the buffer is dirty. Let's force a checkpoint:

```
CHECKPOINT;
CHECKPOINT
```

We will repeat the query:

```
    relname   | isdirty
--------------+---------
 emp_id_seq   | f
 emp          | f
(1 row)
```

Now the buffer is no longer dirty.

Checkpoint

Checkpoint is a mandatory process. To understand this, let's discuss blocks. PostgreSQL always reads and writes data in blocks. Consider the `emp` table. It has just one record. The data in this record should add up to a few bytes; we have the value 1 in the column `id`, and the value `Newname` in the column `first_name`. However, this table will consume 8K in the disk because PostgreSQL works with 8K blocks. A block is also referred to as a page. It is easy to verify that PostgreSQL uses blocks. Ensure that our table has just one record as follows:

```
SELECT * FROM emp;
 id | first_name
----+------------
  1 | Newname
(1 row)
```

Server Architecture

Then, we find the filename:

```
SELECT pg_relation_filepath('emp');
 pg_relation_filepath
----------------------
 base/24741/24742
(1 row)
```

Now, we check the size of the file:

```
\! ls -l /pgdata/9.3/base/24741/24742
-rw-------. 1 postgres postgres 8192 Nov 15 11:33
/pgdata/9.3/base/24741/24742
```

8192 bytes = 8K. So, a table with just one record takes up 8K.

Let's try inserting some data and see what happens:

```
INSERT INTO emp(id , first_name) SELECT
generate_series(1,5000000),
'A longer   name ';
INSERT 0 5000000
```

After executing the preceding query a few times, let's check the size of the files from the shell prompt:

```
[root@MyCentOS 24741]# ls -lh 24742*
-rw-------. 1 postgres postgres 1.0G Nov 17 16:14 24742
-rw-------. 1 postgres postgres  42M Nov 17 16:14 24742.1
-rw-------. 1 postgres postgres 288K Nov 17 16:08 24742_fsm
-rw-------. 1 postgres postgres  16K Nov 17 16:06 24742_vm
```

So, we have directories for databases and files for tables. Within the files, data is managed in blocks. In short, the physical layout of a PostgreSQL cluster can be presented as follows:

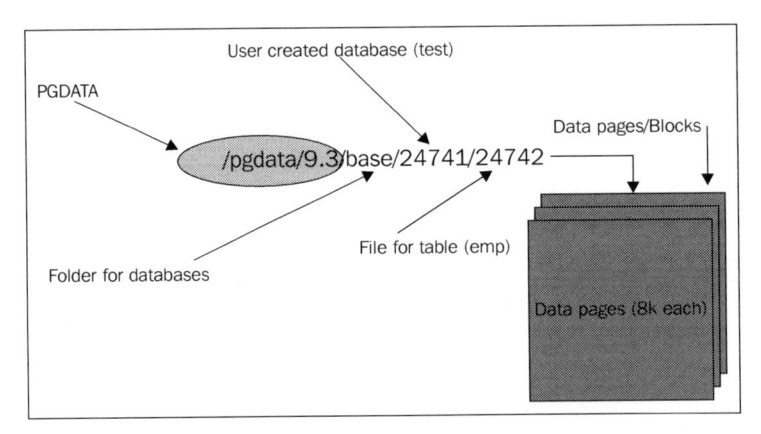

Once a user makes changes to the data (which has been made available in the buffer), that buffer is dirty. As mentioned earlier, the fact that a user has committed a change does not mean that the change has been written to the data file. It's the job of the checkpointer process to write the change to the data file. When a checkpoint happens, all dirty (modified) pages are written to the table and index files. The process also marks the pages as clean. It also marks the write-ahead log as applied up to this point.

Checkpoints are points in the sequence of transactions at which it is guaranteed that the heap and index data files have been updated with all information written before this checkpoint. At checkpoint time, all dirty data pages are flushed to disk and a special checkpoint record is written to the log file. Until now, the change records have only been written to the write-ahead log files. In the event of a crash, the crash recovery procedure looks at the latest checkpoint record to determine the point in the log (known as the redo record) from which it should start the REDO operation. Any changes made to data files before this point are guaranteed to be already on disk. Hence, after a checkpoint, log segments preceding the one containing the redo record are no longer needed and can be recycled or removed from http://www.postgresql.org/docs/current/static/wal-configuration.html.

The question now: is when does a checkpoint happen? To some extent, we decide this. There are a few parameters that decide when a checkpoint should happen: checkpoint_segments, checkpoint_timeout, and checkpoint_completion_target.

The first one is checkpoint_segments. The default value for this is 3. Once 3 WAL segments have been filled, a checkpoint occurs. Each WAL segment is 16 MB. Once 3 WAL segments of 16 MB worth of changes have been made, a checkpoint should happen. We will cover WAL in the next section.

The second parameter, checkpoint_timeout, is a timeout value, which can be set in seconds (default), minutes, or an hour. A checkpoint will occur when either:

- checkpoint_timeout period has elapsed
- checkpoint_segments number of WAL have been filled

Let's consider a server with around 16 GB shared buffer. This is a server that caters to significant load. If a significant proportion of this load consists of writes, then, most of this 16 GB buffer can become dirty in a few minutes. A low setting for checkpoint segments will result in the available segments getting filled quickly and frequent checkpoints. Similarly, a low setting for `checkpoint_timeout` will also result in frequent checkpoints. This results in excessive disk throughput. On the other hand, if we keep these values very high, this will result in infrequent checkpoints. In a write-heavy system, this can result in significant I/O spikes during checkpoints, which affects the performance of other queries. Another parameter: `checkpoint_completion_target` can be tweaked to alleviate this to some extent.

This parameter tells PostgreSQL how quickly it must try and finish the checkpointing process in each iteration. With the default value of `0.5`, PostgreSQL can be expected to complete each checkpoint in about half the time before the next checkpoint starts. When we increase this value to, say `0.9`, the writes resulting from the checkpoint get spread over a longer period. So, the I/O spikes get flattened out.

One issue with very infrequent checkpoints and a lot of dirty buffers is that time to recover might go up. In the case of database restarts, for example, a crash, it finds out the last checkpoint information. It will then replay all the transactions that happened after the last checkpoint and until the last commit. The transactions/changes are read from the WAL. If the volume of dirty data was huge when the system went down, this means a large number of transactions has to be replayed before the database is open for business. This implies a higher downtime. From this angle too, it is better to have more frequent checkpoints rather than infrequent checkpoints. The time to recover might be as high as the `checkpoint_timeout` value. An excellent post on this parameter is available at http://www.depesz.com/2010/11/03/checkpoint_completion_target/.

The checkpointer is a process started by the postmaster as soon as the startup subprocess finishes, or as soon as recovery begins if we are doing database recovery. It remains alive until the postmaster commands it to terminate.

WAL and the WAL writer process

When we make changes to the data, the changes are not written to the data files immediately, as mentioned before (probably many times). Changes are made to the blocks in the buffer and records of these changes are written to the WAL buffer (as soon as changes to data are made). The changes are flushed to the WAL segments when the changes are committed.

In the `pg_xlog` directory, the WAL segments are each 16 MB in size:

```
[postgres@MyCentOS pg_xlog]$ pwd
/pgdata/9.3/pg_xlog
[postgres@MyCentOS pg_xlog]$ ls -alrt
total 16396
drwx------.  2 postgres postgres     4096 Oct 13 13:23 archive_status
drwx------.  3 postgres postgres     4096 Oct 13 13:23 .
drwx------. 15 postgres postgres     4096 Nov 15 20:17 ..
-rw-------.  1 postgres postgres 16777216 Nov 15 20:17 000000010000000000000001
```

We can find out the segment PostgreSQL is writing to now using the `pg_current_xlog_location` function:

```
[postgres@MyCentOS pg_xlog]$ psql
psql (9.3.0)
Type "help" for help.

postgres=# SELECT pg_xlogfile_name(pg_current_xlog_location());
     pg_xlogfile_name
--------------------------
 000000010000000000000001
(1 row)
```

The name is not a random collection of digits and numbers. It's comprised of three parts of 8 characters each:

000000010000000000000001

The digits are classified as follows:

- The first 8 digits identifies the timeline
- The following 8 digits identifies the (logical) `xlog` file
- The last ones represent the (physical) `xlog` file (`Segment`)

Each segment contains blocks of 8K. Usually, PostgreSQL moves from one segment to the next when one segment is filled up, that is, all the 16 MB is filled. However, it's also possible to trigger the switch.

There are many functions related to WAL, which are useful in archival, recovery, and so on.

For example, `pg_switch_xlog` moves to the next transaction log file, allowing the current file to be archived. If there has been no transaction log activity since the last transaction log switch, `pg_switch_xlog` does nothing and returns the start location of the transaction log file currently in use. WAL is mostly written to and rarely read from. Cases when WAL is read from include:

- Recovery
- Server startup
- Replication

Let's take a look at a few uses of WAL.

Recovery

This is the primary purpose of the WAL concept. Here, we are referring to recovering transactions that have been committed, but have not found their way to the data files. All the changes made to the database will find their way into the WAL segments, irrespective of whether the changes have been reflected into the data files or not. In fact, it's mandatory that changes have been written to WAL files before they are written to the data files themselves. Loss of WAL files almost certainly means lost transactions.

Incremental backup and point-in-time recovery

We can take a snapshot of the PostgreSQL filesystem and then set up a WAL archival process. The snapshot taken need not be a consistent one. The WAL segments generated will keep getting archived and we can use the snapshot and the archived WAL segment to perform a point-in-time recovery. In this process (which will be covered in *Chapter 10, Scaling, Replication, and Backup and Recovery*), we restore the file snapshot, and then replay the WAL segments until a specific point in time or until a transaction.

Replication

WAL segments have been used for the two purposes mentioned earlier. From version 9.0, WAL segments have been used for replication also. The rationale is simple. All the changes happening in the server are being recorded in the WAL segments anyway. Why not use these and get a stand-by server ready for failover?

We will cover the steps to set these up in *Chapter 10, Scaling, Replication, and Backup and Recovery*.

WAL also reduces the number of disk writes necessary to guarantee that a transaction is committed, thus improving performance. This is achieved because WAL writes are sequential. If a number of small transactions are committed, they will appear sequentially in the log. If the database were to work without WAL, a transaction commit will immediately result in writing data out to all the data files that were affected by the transaction.

Now, let's also take a look at a few key parameters related to WAL. Change the directory to `/pgdata/9.3` and execute the following command:

```
[postgres@MyCentOS 9.3]$ grep wal postgresql.conf
wal_level = archive              # minimal, archive, or hot_standby
#wal_sync_method = fsync         # the default is the first option
#wal_buffers = -1                # min 32kB, -1 sets based on
shared_buffers
#wal_writer_delay = 200ms        # 1-10000 milliseconds
#max_wal_senders = 0             # max number of walsender processes
#wal_keep_segments = 0           # in logfile segments, 16MB each; 0
disables
#wal_sender_timeout = 60s        # in milliseconds; 0 disables
#wal_receiver_status_interval = 10s    # send replies at least this
often
#wal_receiver_timeout = 60s      # time that receiver waits for
```

The `wal_level` is an important parameter as this setting has a direct impact on what we can do with WAL, whether we can use it only for recovery from a crash, or we can use it also to archive for a point-in-time recovery, or whether we can use it to create a stand-by server. This setting determines the amount of information written to WAL. This is an enum type of value, which means that it can have one of a possible list of values. The possible values are `minimal`, `archive`, and `hot_standby`. The default value is `minimal`, which writes only the information needed to recover from a crash or immediate shutdown. The `archive` value adds logging required for WAL archiving, and `hot_standby` further adds information required to run read-only queries on a standby server. This parameter can only be set at server start.

In `minimal` level, WAL-logging of some bulk operations can be safely skipped, which can make the operations faster. Minimal WAL does not contain enough information to reconstruct the data from a base backup and the WAL logs, so either archive or the `hot_standby` level should be used to enable WAL archiving (`archive_mode`) and streaming replication.

In the `hot_standby` level, the same information is logged as with `archive`, plus the information needed to reconstruct the status of running transactions from the WAL. To enable read-only queries on a standby server, `wal_level` must be set to `hot_standby` on the primary, and a `hot_standby` setting must be enabled in the standby.

When `fsync` is on, the PostgreSQL server tries to ensure that data really gets flushed to the disk (remember the different levels of cache?). Setting `fsync` to off might result in significant gains in performance, but carries a risk. This can result in an unrecoverable data corruption in the event of a power failure or a system crash. In cases where `fsync` is turned off, `wal_sync_method` is not relevant at all. When `fsync` is on, we could choose one of many options, such as `open_datasync`, `fdatasync`, `fsync`, and so on; each one has a different way to ensure that data gets flushed to disk. A description of these methods is available at http://www.postgresql.org/docs/current/static/runtime-config-wal.html#GUC-WAL-SYNC-METHOD.

For an in-depth discussion on the `fsync` options and its impact on the performance and possibility of data loss, please refer to *PostgreSQL 9.0 High Performance, Gregory Smith, Packt Publishing*.

The `wal_buffers` memory is the amount of shared memory set aside for the WAL buffer. Setting this to `-1` will result in an automatic selection based on the `shared_buffers` setting. In automatic setting, the value can range from 64 KB to 16 MB. When set manually, the minimum possible value is 32 KB.

Another decision is how frequently the WAL writer should flush WAL to disk. What we need to remember is that this will be far more frequent than checkpoint frequency. The WAL flush interval is indicated by `wal_writer_delay`. The default value is 200 milliseconds.

There are a few more parameters relevant for replication and we will cover them in *Chapter 10, Scaling, Replication, and Backup and Recovery*.

The background writer

The background writer is responsible for writing to disk specific dirty buffers based on an algorithm, whereas checkpointer writes all dirty buffers. The process takes into consideration shared memory usage data as well as information about which blocks have been used/accessed recently (least recently used). The primary objective of this process is to ensure that free buffers are available for use. The relevant parameters are as follows:

```
#bgwriter_delay = 200ms                  # 10-10000ms between rounds
#bgwriter_lru_maxpages = 100             # 0-1000 max buffers
written/round
```

```
#bgwriter_lru_multiplier = 2.0          # 0-10.0 multiplier on
buffers scanned/round
```

As we can see, the default value for delay is 200 milliseconds. This parameter specifies how long the process should wait between successive executions. The `bgwriter_lru_maxpages` parameter specifies the maximum number of buffers that will be written by the process in each iteration. The third parameter is also used to arrive at the number of buffers that will be needed. If this value is set to 2 and the average recent need (number of buffers) is estimated to be 10, dirty buffers will be cleared until there are 20 buffers available or until `bgwriter_lru_maxpages` has been written.

The `bgwriter` function is started by the postmaster as soon as the startup subprocess finishes, or as soon as recovery begins if we are performing archive recovery. It remains alive until the postmaster commands it to terminate. A quick comparison of commits, checkpoints, and background writer can be pictured, as shown in the following diagram:

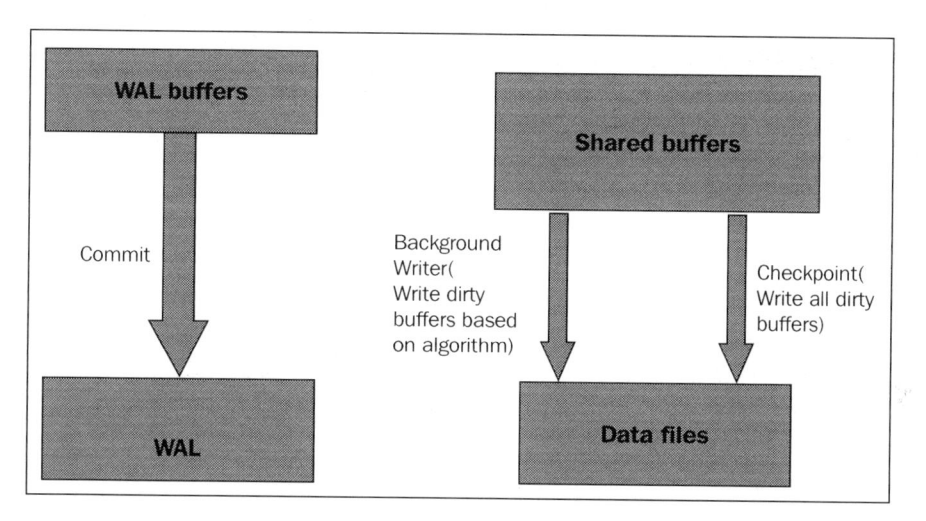

The autovacuum launcher process

This is an optional process. There is a parameter called `autovacuum` in `postgresql.conf`, with ON as default value. This process automates the execution of vacuum and analyzes commands based on a few parameters. To understand autovacuum, first, we have to understand vacuum.

Server Architecture

Assume that we delete a few records from a table. PostgreSQL does not immediately remove the deleted tuples from the data files. These are marked as deleted. Similarly, when a record is updated, it's roughly equivalent to one delete and one insert. The previous version of the record continues to be in the data file. Each update of a database row generates a new version of the row. The reason is simple: there can be active transactions, which want to see the data as it was before. As a result of this activity, there will be a lot of unusable space in the data files. After some time, these dead records become irrelevant as there are no transactions still around to see the old data. However, as the space is not marked as reusable, inserts and updates (which result in inserts) happen in other pages in the data file.

> PostgreSQL can provide different versions of the data to concurrent users. This is done so that readers do not block writers and vice versa. This is achieved via a mechanism known as **Multiversion Concurrency Control** (**MVCC**). Transactions, isolation levels, and MVCC are covered in detail in *Chapter 4, Working with Transactions*.

The vacuum process marks space used by previously deleted (or updated) records as being available for reuse within the table. There is a vacuum command to do this manually. Vacuum does not lock the table.

VACUUM FULL, in addition to marking the space as reusable, removes the deleted or updated records and reorders the table data. This requires an exclusive lock on the table.

Let's see the effect of vacuum using an example. First, we will create a new database using the `createdb` command at Command Prompt. We will then get the directory of this database using the `oid2name` command. We will then use the `cd` command to this directory. At shell prompt, execute the following command:

```
createdb vac
oid2name | grep vac
   340081                vac  pg_default
cd /pgdata/9.3/base/340081
/psql -d vac
```

The following commands are executed at psql prompt, connected to the database vac:

```
\! pwd
/pgdata/9.3/base/340081
\! ls | head -5
12629
12629_fsm
12629_vm
12631
12631_fsm
```

```
CREATE TABLE myt(id integer);
CREATE TABLE
SELECT pg_relation_filepath('myt');
pg_relation_filepath
----------------------
 base/340081/340088
(1 row)

\! ls  -lt 34*
-rw------- 1 postgres postgres 0 Aug 18 11:19 340088
```

The file created is `340088` and we can see it in the filesystem:

```
SELECT pg_total_relation_size('myt');
 pg_total_relation_size
------------------------
                      0
(1 row)

INSERT INTO myt SELECT generate_series (1,100000);
INSERT 0 100000
SELECT pg_total_relation_size('myt');
 pg_total_relation_size
------------------------
                3653632
(1 row)

vac=# \! ls -lt | head -5
total 10148
-rw------- 1 postgres postgres 3629056 Aug 18 11:23 340088
-rw------- 1 postgres postgres   24576 Aug 18 11:23 340088_fsm
-rw------- 1 postgres postgres  122880 Aug 18 11:22 12629
-rw------- 1 postgres postgres   65536 Aug 18 11:22 12658
```

The file has grown in size, as expected, because of the data inserted. Next, we delete some data from the table:

```
DELETE FROM myt WHERE id> 5 AND id <100000;
DELETE 99994
SELECT pg_total_relation_size('myt');
 pg_total_relation_size
------------------------
                3653632
(1 row)
```

Server Architecture

```
VACUUM myt;
VACUUM
SELECT pg_total_relation_size('myt');
 pg_total_relation_size
------------------------
                3661824
(1 row)
```

We can see that the size has not really gone down much. Now, we will insert data and see whether the file size goes up:

```
INSERT INTO myt SELECT generate_series (1,1000);
INSERT 0 1000
select pg_total_relation_size('myt');
 pg_total_relation_size
------------------------
                3661824
```

The table size has not gone up, although we inserted 1000 records:

```
\! ls -lt 34*
-rw------- 1 postgres postgres    8192 Aug 18 11:25 340088_vm
-rw------- 1 postgres postgres 3629056 Aug 18 11:23 340088
-rw------- 1 postgres postgres   24576 Aug 18 11:23 340088_fsm
VACUUM FULL myt;
VACUUM
SELECT pg_total_relation_size('myt');
 pg_total_relation_size
------------------------
                  40960 (1 row)
```

The size of the table has gone down significantly:

```
SELECT pg_relation_filepath('myt');
pg_relation_filepath
----------------------
 base/340081/340091
\! ls -lt | head -5
total 6588
-rw------- 1 postgres postgres      0 Aug 18 11:29 340088
-rw------- 1 postgres postgres  40960 Aug 18 11:29 340091
-rw------- 1 postgres postgres 122880 Aug 18 11:28 12629
-rw------- 1 postgres postgres  32768 Aug 18 11:28 12634
```

The file has changed from 340088 to 340091. VACUUM FULL creates a new empty file, copies over records that are not dead, and empties the original file.

Executing vacuum with the "analyze" option reads the records in the tables and generates statistics used by the query planner.

Autovacuum automates the vacuum process. It's recommended to have the autovacuum process do the cleanup of the data files unless there are specific reasons not to. In cases where the database is under heavy load for most part of the day, vacuum can be scheduled during off-peak hours. Although, there are few or no deletes/updates in the cluster, it's useful to have routine vacuuming as vacuum updates the data statistics used by the planner.

The logging process

This is an optional process and the default setting is off. We have to set the `logging_collector` parameter to on to start this process:

```
cd $PGDATA
```

Edit the `postgresql.conf` file and make a few changes:

```
log_destination = 'stderr'
logging_collector = on
log_directory = 'pg_log'
log_min_duration_statement = 0


[postgres@MyCentOS 9.3]$ pg_ctl restart
waiting for server to shut down.... done
server stopped
server starting
[postgres@MyCentOS 9.3]$ ps f -U postgres
  PID TTY        STAT   TIME COMMAND
 2581 pts/2      S      0:00 -bash
 3201 pts/2      R+     0:00  \_ ps f -U postgres
 2218 pts/1      S+     0:00 -bash
 3186 pts/2      S      0:00 /usr/local/pgsql/bin/postgres
 3187 ?          Ss     0:00  \_ postgres: logger process
 3189 ?          Ss     0:00  \_ postgres: checkpointer process
 3190 ?          Ss     0:00  \_ postgres: writer process
 3191 ?          Ss     0:00  \_ postgres: wal writer process
 3192 ?          Ss     0:00  \_ postgres: autovacuum launcher process
 3193 ?          Ss     0:00  \_ postgres: stats collector process
```

See the logger process that was kicked off. Now, logging has many parameters. Logging the activities in a PostgreSQL database provides a lot of insight into what is happening in the database, and this is one utility that should be exploited to the maximum extent. If we go to the `pg_log` directory, we can see the log files get generated and view them.

The logger will capture launching of the utility programs:

```
..
LOG:    database system is ready to accept connections
LOG:    autovacuum launcher started
..
```

Failed login attempts:

```
FATAL:  role "hacker" does not exist
```

Errors in the application:

```
ERROR:  function non_existing_function() does not exist at character 8
HINT:  No function matches the given name and argument types. You might need to add explicit type casts.
STATEMENT:  select non_existing_function();
```

If you went through the messages carefully, you will notice that the first message was marked LOG, the second FATAL, and the third one ERROR.

It's very easy to use this kind of tags (severity levels) in order to analyze what happened in the database over a period of time: how many failed login attempts were there, how many application errors were there, and so on. The complete list of severity levels are shown in the following table:

Severity	Usage
INFO	This provides information implicitly requested by the user, for example, output from VACUUM VERBOSE.
NOTICE	This provides information that might be helpful to users, for example, notice of truncation of long identifiers.
WARNING	This provides warning of likely problems, for example, COMMIT outside a transaction block.
ERROR	This reports an error that caused the current command to abort.
LOG	This reports information of interest to administrators, for example, the checkpoint activity.
FATAL	This reports an error that caused the current session to abort.
PANIC	This reports an error that caused all database sessions to abort.

Often, we use triggers to insert data into some audit table in order to audit changes to table data or to track who was trying to do what. In most cases, triggers with tables work. However, when a user attempts to, say, INSERT a record and the attempt fails, the insert to audit table also fails. A suggested workaround, as PostgreSQL does not have autonomous transactions, is to use dblink to insert the audit record. This becomes a transaction on its own and will be committed, although the insert that triggered this rolls back.

> PostgreSQL description of autonomous subtransaction is available at http://wiki.postgresql.org/wiki/Autonomous_subtransactions. A link to the discussion on how to achieve this using dblink is available at http://postgresql.1045698.n5.nabble.com/autonomous-transactions-td1978453.html. Discussion on integrating this in PostgreSQL is available at http://postgresql.1045698.n5.nabble.com/Autonomous-Transaction-WIP-td5798928.html.

Another option is to do the auditing using RAISE LOG. Connect to test database and create a function:

```
CREATE OR REPLACE FUNCTION audit_tbl()
RETURNS trigger AS
$BODY$
DECLARE
    aud_data text;
BEGIN
  aud_data =NEW.first_name;
  RAISE LOG 'Audit data  : %', aud_data;
  RETURN NEW;
END;$BODY$
LANGUAGE plpgsql;
CREATE TRIGGER emp_trg
  BEFORE INSERT
  ON emp
  FOR EACH ROW
  EXECUTE PROCEDURE audit_tbl();
INSERT INTO emp (first_name) values ('Scott');
```

Now, the log file has the following entry. The audit_data variable can have concatenated values of different "new" values, other descriptions you might want to add, and so on:

```
  time=2013-11-17 12:26:35 IST:db=test;user=postgres type=INSERT LOG:
Audit data   : Scott
```

Server Architecture

We can also use `RAISE LOG` to debug the code.

The parameters to control logging are numerous. It's classified into three groups, such as where to log, when to log, and what to log.

An excellent description of the parameters can be found, as usual, in PostgreSQL documentation at `http://www.postgresql.org/docs/current/static/runtime-config-logging.html`.

We will see a few useful options and move on:

`log_min_duration_statement = 0`

This setting causes the duration of each completed statement to be logged if the statement ran for at least the specified number of milliseconds. The default value is `-1`, which disables logging the duration of statements. Setting the value to `0` results in the duration of all statements to be logged. This approach, along with analysis using a tool such as `pgbadger` (which will be covered in *Chapter 12, PostgreSQL – Extras*), helps in tracking down slow queries quickly. However, in a system with hundreds of queries executed every second, this setting can result in log files growing pretty quickly. So, it is better to have a process in place to move the log files to another location, where a tool such as `pgbadger` can be used to mine the log files and generate user-friendly reports.

The `log_line_prefix` parameter is another one that merits attention. This parameter lets us customize the `log` statement with format code to display information about the executed statement. The information that can be captured includes which user executed the query, on which database, from which host, time of execution (with millisecond precision), and so on. We can see the value as follows:

`log_line_prefix = 'time=%t:db=%d;user=%u '`

When we have the preceding setting in the file, it will result in log entries similar to the following:

```
time=2013-11-16 20:10:00 IST:db=;user= LOG:    parameter
"log_line_prefix" changed to "time=%t:db=%d;user=%u "
time=2013-11-16 20:10:13 IST:db=postgres;user=postgres LOG:
duration: 183.970 ms   statement: select count(*) from myt;
time=2013-11-16 20:10:17 IST:db=postgres;user=postgres LOG:
duration: 0.302 ms   statement: select now();
time=2013-11-16 20:10:27 IST:db=postgres;user=postgres LOG:
duration: 2.346 ms   statement: insert into myt values(1);
```

Add `type=%i` so that the prefix looks like `time=%t:db=%d;user=%u type=%i` and this gives us the following output:

```
time=2013-11-16 20:28:57 IST:db=postgres;user=postgres type=SELECT
LOG:   duration: 0.151 ms   statement: select now();
time=2013-11-16 20:28:58 IST:db=postgres;user=postgres type=INSERT
LOG:   duration: 3.385 ms   statement: insert into myt values(1);
```

The `log_line_prefix` parameter is another very useful one that can enable logging in a customized format in great detail. We can use the log file to conduct an analysis of what has been happening in the database.

A few useful prefix options are as follows:

Option	Description
%a	Application name
%u	Username
%d	Database name
%r	Remote host and port
%h	Remote host
%p	Process ID
%t	Timestamp without milliseconds
%m	Timestamp with milliseconds
%i	Command tag
%e	SQL State error code
%c	Session ID
%l	Number of log line for that session
%s	session start timestamp

Note that the `log_line_prefix` parameter does not work with the `csvlog` option.

> Log files tend to grow pretty quickly in an active server if you are logging all the SQL statements. Having a process to compress and remove the files from the production server might be necessary if you are logging all the SQL statements. Another option is to write the logs to a separate partition, preferably on a cheap, high capacity disk.

Server Architecture

The stats collector process

This process, as the name indicates, collects statistics about the database. It's an optional process with the default value as on. The process keeps track of access to tables and indexes in both disk-block and individual row-terms. It also keeps track of record counts for tables, and tracks the vacuum and analyze actions. It's important to note that individual processes transmit new statistical counts to the collector just before going idle. As a result, many of the counters will not reflect activities of in-flight transactions.

The data gets logged in a set of tables and we can access this via a number of views provided. The views start with `pg_stat`. Type the following command:

```
\d pg_stat
```

Hitting the *Tab* key twice will list all the views, as shown in the following command:

```
postgres=# \d pg_stat
pg_stat_activity                    pg_statio_all_sequences
pg_statio_user_tables               pg_stat_user_functions
pg_stat_all_indexes                 pg_statio_all_tables
pg_statistic                        pg_stat_user_indexes
pg_stat_all_tables                  pg_statio_sys_indexes
pg_statistic_relid_att_inh_index    pg_stat_user_tables
pg_stat_bgwriter                    pg_statio_sys_sequences
pg_stat_replication                 pg_stat_xact_all_tables
pg_stat_database                    pg_statio_sys_tables
pg_stats                            pg_stat_xact_sys_tables
pg_stat_database_conflicts          pg_statio_user_indexes
pg_stat_sys_indexes                 pg_stat_xact_user_functions
pg_statio_all_indexes               pg_statio_user_sequences
pg_stat_sys_tables                  pg_stat_xact_user_tables
```

We can know where a view is getting data from using `\d+`:

```
postgres=# \d+ pg_statio_user_tables
        View "pg_catalog.pg_statio_user_tables"
   Column    |  Type  | Modifiers | Storage | Description
-------------+--------+-----------+---------+-------------
 relid       | oid    |           | plain   |
 schemaname  | name   |           | plain   |
 relname     | name   |           | plain   |
.....
View definition:
 SELECT pg_statio_all_tables.relid,
    pg_statio_all_tables.schemaname,
    pg_statio_all_tables.relname,
```

```
        pg_statio_all_tables.heap_blks_read,
        pg_statio_all_tables.heap_blks_hit,
        ...
        pg_statio_all_tables.tidx_blks_hit
   FROM pg_statio_all_tables
  WHERE (pg_statio_all_tables.schemaname <> ALL
    (ARRAY['pg_catalog'::name, 'information_schema'::name]))
    AND pg_statio_all_tables.schemaname !~ '^pg_toast'::text;
```

So, it's a subset of the data from the `pg_statio_all_tables` view. What about `pg_statio_all_tables`?:

```
postgres=# \d+ pg_statio_all_tables
            View "pg_catalog.pg_statio_all_tables"
     Column     |  Type  | Modifiers | Storage | Description
----------------+--------+-----------+---------+-------------
 relid          | oid    |           | plain   |
 schemaname     | name   |           | plain   |
 relname        | name   |           | plain   |
 heap_blks_read | bigint |           | plain   |
 ...
 tidx_blks_hit  | bigint |           | plain   |
View definition:
 SELECT c.oid AS relid,
    n.nspname AS schemaname,
    c.relname,
    pg_stat_get_blocks_fetched(c.oid) - pg_stat_get_blocks_hit(c.oid)
AS heap_blks_read,
    pg_stat_get_blocks_hit(c.oid) AS heap_blks_hit,
    sum(pg_stat_get_blocks_fetched(i.indexrelid) - pg_stat_get_blocks_
hit(i.indexrelid))::bigint AS idx_blks_read,
    sum(pg_stat_get_blocks_hit(i.indexrelid))::bigint AS
idx_blks_hit,
    pg_stat_get_blocks_fetched(t.oid) - pg_stat_get_blocks_hit(t.oid)
AS toast_blks_read,
    pg_stat_get_blocks_hit(t.oid) AS toast_blks_hit,
    pg_stat_get_blocks_fetched(x.oid) -
pg_stat_get_blocks_hit(x.oid)
AS tidx_blks_read,
    pg_stat_get_blocks_hit(x.oid) AS tidx_blks_hit
   FROM pg_class c
   LEFT JOIN pg_index i ON c.oid = i.indrelid
   LEFT JOIN pg_class t ON c.reltoastrelid = t.oid
   LEFT JOIN pg_class x ON t.reltoastidxid = x.oid
   LEFT JOIN pg_namespace n ON n.oid = c.relnamespace
```

```
        WHERE c.relkind = ANY (ARRAY['r'::"char", 't'::"char",
'm'::"char"])
        GROUP BY c.oid, n.nspname, c.relname, t.oid, x.oid;
```

In short, the stats collector process keeps track of a number of items, updates them in some tables, and we have views built on top of these tables to provide a reasonably well-formatted output regarding database activity. Keeping track of the stats view will be useful in zooming in on tables that are frequently accessed, identifying columns to be indexed and can also help in providing input on configuring the server parameters (such as `shared_buffers` and other memory areas). Some of the (`pg_stat_replication`) views provide information on the status of replication (WAL sender processes).

There are a few functions available to manage statistics. For example, `pg_stat_reset()` resets all statistics counters for the current database to zero:

```
test=# SELECT relname, n_tup_ins FROM pg_stat_user_tables;
 relname | n_tup_ins
---------+-----------
 emp     |         2
 dept    |         0
(2 rows)
```

The result says that 2 records have been inserted into the table `emp`:

```
test=# SELECT pg_stat_reset();
 pg_stat_reset
---------------

(1 row)
test=# SELECT relname, n_tup_ins FROM pg_stat_user_tables;
 relname | n_tup_ins
---------+-----------
 emp     |         0
 dept    |         0
(2 rows)
```

The counter has been reset to 0. We can insert a record:

```
test=# INSERT INTO emp(first_name) VALUES ('Scottnew');
INSERT 0 1
test=# SELECT relname, n_tup_ins FROM pg_stat_user_tables;
 relname | n_tup_ins
---------+-----------
 emp     |         1
 dept    |         0
(2 rows)
```

The counter has been incremented.

For statistics collection too, there are a set of parameters. Some of them have default values set to on and others to off. We will take a look at a few of these.

The counters that are disabled by default are: `log_statement_stats`, `log_parser_stats`, `log_planner_stats`, `log_executor_stats`, and `track_io_timing`.

The `track_activities`, `update_process_title`, and `track_counts`, settings are the ones that are on by default.

The WAL sender and WAL receiver

These are two processes introduced in the recent versions of PostgreSQL, mainly, to support the replication process. The sender process sends the WALs to the standby server and the receiver on the slave side receives it.

So far, we covered most of all the key processes and one big memory area: `shared_buffers`. However, we have a couple of important memory areas still to be covered. Let's do this before we move on to the next section.

Sorting in memory with work_mem

There are two important parameters used by PostgreSQL to allocate and use memory at session level. We can get them by executing the following command in the PostgreSQL data directory as follows:

```
grep work postgresql.conf
#work_mem = 1MB                          # min 64kB
#maintenance_work_mem = 16MB             # min 1MB
```

The first one is `work_mem`. The default value is set to 1 MB and minimum 64 KB. This is the amount of memory to be used by internal sort operations and hash tables before switching to temporary disk files. The last part is crucial (if enough memory is not allocated, it will result in physical I/O), which will certainly result in a spike in response time. So it sounds like setting this pretty high will be good. However, the issue is that this is not allocated at the server level, as is done for `shared_buffers`. This is allocated for each user. Even in a query, if there are multiple sort operations in parallel, each one might run up to the maximum set for this parameter. So, if we have kept the default `max_connections` (100) and decided to increase this to 32 MB, we might end up using more than 3 GB memory if many of the individual sessions are doing heavy sorts.

Server Architecture

A better option is to increase this at session level for cases where we know that the data volume to be handled is going to be high and still we need a short response time:

```
postgres=# INSERT INTO myt select generate_series (1,1000000);
postgres=# CREATE TABLE myt (id serial);
postgres=# SET work_mem = '64kB';
postgres=# SELECT temp_files, temp_bytes FROM pg_stat_database
WHERE
datname = 'postgres';
 temp_files | temp_bytes
------------+------------
          9 |  284303360
(1 row)

postgres=# SELECT * FROM ( SELECT * FROM myt ORDER BY id ) t
limit 1000;
 id
-----
   1
postgres=# SELECT temp_files, temp_bytes FROM pg_stat_database
WHERE
datname = 'postgres';
 temp_files | temp_bytes
------------+------------
         10 |  312320000
```

The sort operation ended up creating a temp file:

```
postgres=# SHOW work_mem;
 work_mem
----------
 64kB
(1 row)

postgres=# SET work_mem to '1MB';
SET
postgres=# SHOW work_mem;
 work_mem
----------
 1MB
(1 row)

postgres=# SELECT * FROM ( SELECT * FROM myt ORDER BY id ) t
limit 1000;
```

```
    id
  -----
      1
  .....
postgres=# SELECT temp_files, temp_bytes FROM pg_stat_database
WHERE
datname = 'postgres';
 temp_files | temp_bytes
------------+------------
         10 |  312320000
(1 row)
```

The number of temp files has not gone up.

Maintenance with maintenance_work_mem

This memory area is used by operations such as vacuum. As is the case with work_mem, the space allocated will have an impact on how quickly the maintenance activities are completed. Typical activities using this area include analyzing, vacuuming, creating an index, reindexing, and so on.

Showing the impact of this value is pretty easy, as shown in the following command:

```
postgres=# \timing on
Timing is on.
```

> It's a good idea to use the timing setting when we are at the psql prompt.

There is a one column table with a few hundred thousand records:

```
postgres=# SELECT pg_size_pretty(pg_table_size('myt'));
 pg_size_pretty
----------------
 69 MB
(1 row)

postgres=# SELECT current_database();
 current_database
------------------
 postgres
(1 row)
```

Server Architecture

```
Time: 1.152 ms
postgres=# SELECT temp_files, temp_bytes FROM pg_stat_database
WHERE datname = 'postgres';
 temp_files | temp_bytes
------------+------------
          4 |  120143872
(1 row)

Time: 17.547 ms
```

As of now, there are four temp files in this database:

```
postgres=# CREATE INDEX myindex ON myt(id);
CREATE INDEX
Time: 3477.075 ms
postgres=# SELECT temp_files, temp_bytes FROM pg_stat_database
WHERE datname = 'postgres';
 temp_files | temp_bytes
------------+------------
          5 |  160186368
(1 row)
Time: 11.900 ms
postgres=# DROP INDEX myindex;
DROP INDEX
Time: 17.686 ms
postgres=# CREATE INDEX myindex on myt(id);
CREATE INDEX
Time: 3213.370 ms
postgres=# SELECT temp_files, temp_bytes FROM pg_stat_database
WHERE datname = 'postgres';
 temp_files | temp_bytes
------------+------------
          6 |  200228864
(1 row)

Time: 11.433 ms
postgres=# DROP INDEX myindex;
DROP INDEX
Time: 17.625 ms
```

Each index creation is added to the number of temp files. Now, let's increase the maintenance work memory:

```
postgres=# SET maintenance_work_mem TO '1GB';
SET
Time: 0.359 ms
```

```
postgres=# CREATE INDEX myindex ON myt(id);
CREATE INDEX
Time: 2894.212 ms
postgres=# SELECT temp_files, temp_bytes FROM pg_stat_database
WHERE datname = 'postgres';
 temp_files | temp_bytes
------------+------------
          6 |  200228864
(1 row)

Time: 11.328 ms
```

No more temp files. Let's reset maintenance_work_mem.

```
postgres=# RESET maintenance_work_mem;
RESET
Time: 0.425 ms
postgres=# SHOW maintenance_work_mem;
 maintenance_work_mem
----------------------
 16MB
(1 row)

Time: 0.413 ms
```

As restoring the database using pg_restore usually involves index creation, it's recommended to increase maintenance_work_mem when using pg_restore.

> The pg_restore utility is the one that is used to restore a PostgreSQL database from an archive file created by pg_dump.

The default values for these two settings have been revised upward in PostgreSQL version 9.4.

Understanding effective_cache_size

This is not an allocation setting. It's not a cache or buffer similar to the ones discussed so far. This setting just gives an idea to PostgreSQL about how much disk cache is available to a single query. This area is not reserved by the database, but is used by the optimizer to arrive at the query execution plan.

Server Architecture

Most of the important buffers have been covered. There is also the **Commit Log (CLOG)** buffer to store the commit status for each transaction that has been assigned a transaction ID. Other memory areas include the freespace map to keep track of free space in data pages, catalog cache to store the system catalog information, and so on.

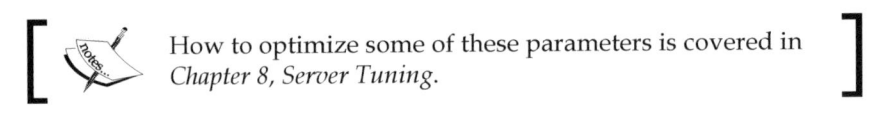

> How to optimize some of these parameters is covered in *Chapter 8, Server Tuning*.

To sum up, this is what different buffers in a system running PostgreSQL will look like:

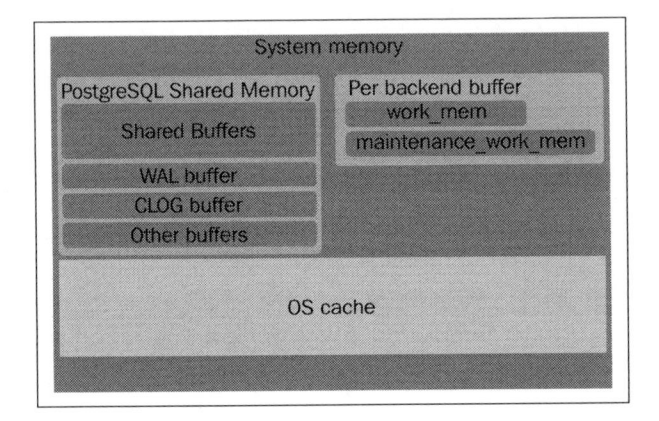

```
┌─────────────────────────────────────────────┐
│              System memory                  │
│  ┌──────────────────────┬────────────────┐  │
│  │PostgreSQL Shared Mem │Per backend buf │  │
│  │                      │   work_mem     │  │
│  │   Shared Buffers     │maintenance_work_mem│ │
│  │                      │                │  │
│  │    WAL buffer        │                │  │
│  │    CLOG buffer       │                │  │
│  │    Other buffers     │                │  │
│  └──────────────────────┴────────────────┘  │
│  ┌───────────────────────────────────────┐  │
│  │             OS cache                  │  │
│  └───────────────────────────────────────┘  │
└─────────────────────────────────────────────┘
```

Summary

In this chapter, we covered the important processes and memory structures in PostgreSQL. We also saw how some configuration settings can be effectively used to capture data about the activities in the server and use it to further optimize the database performance. In the next chapter, we will look at the concepts of tablespaces, schemas, and roles. We will also look at how these are related to each other and how we can use them to take care of security and logical separation issues.

3
PostgreSQL – Object Hierarchy and Roles

In the previous chapter, we covered the important processes and memory structures used internally by PostgreSQL. In this chapter, we will cover a few topics that will be more directly used when someone goes about initializing a cluster and creating objects in the cluster, such as tablespaces, databases, schemas, roles, and related items.

The PostgreSQL cluster

Let's start off by looking at what a cluster means in PostgreSQL. This is important because the term cluster means different things in different databases. In Oracle, it usually means **Real Application Clusters** (**RAC**), of course, there are clustered tables too, in MySQL, the term mostly refers to an in-memory database solution. In these cases, we can choose to not have a cluster. However, this is not the case with PostgreSQL. In PostgreSQL, if you have a working database, it means that you have a cluster. In PostgreSQL, a cluster refers to a set of databases, using the same configuration files, listening for requests at a common port. The databases belonging to the cluster use a common filesystem location. There is a common set of background processes and memory structures (such as shared buffers used by this set of databases). In the previous chapter, when we executed **initdb**, we initialized a PostgreSQL cluster.

It's possible to run multiple PostgreSQL clusters on a server (although not a recommended practice in production) as long as they are listening on different ports and have separate storage areas defined.

PostgreSQL does not offer any out-of-the-box ability to either limit the CPU used by a cluster or to set priorities for databases/users and queries. Each cluster will act as if it is the only entity using the resources available. Hence, it's not recommended to run multiple PostgreSQL clusters on a server, especially if one of them is mission critical.

> A useful write-up on this is available at http://wiki.postgresql.org/wiki/Prioritizing_databases_by_separating_into_multiple_clusters.

Understanding tablespaces

PostgreSQL introduced the concept of tablespaces in version 8. In PostgreSQL, a tablespace is a link to a location in the filesystem, that is, a directory. It's a container to hold all other objects, such as tables, indexes, and so on.

There are many situations in which such a feature, storing data in a location other than the default location, could be useful. One scenario when we might want to use tablespaces is when we run out of space on the partition in which we initialized the database cluster. Another scenario could be that we know the usage patterns of different databases/objects and want to move specific objects to a different disk for performance reasons. A set of frequently and heavily accessed objects could be created in a tablespace that is located on a fast disk, or a database supporting a transactional system can be on a fast disk, whereas one supporting a data warehouse/reporting system, with a more relaxed response time requirement, can be on a slower disk.

When we initialized a cluster, two default tablespaces got created, one was a tablespace called `pg_default`. All objects which are created by users without specifying a tablespace will be created in the `pg_default` tablespace. The location for the default tablespace: `pg_default` is the base directory under PGDATA. The other one: `pg_global` holds the system tables shared by all the databases in the cluster.

We will switch to the `pg_tblspc` directory, create a tablespace, and see what happens. We will then use the DROP TABLE IF EXISTS syntax to drop tables if they are already there and create the tables again. At shell prompt, change the directory with the following command:

`cd /pgdata/9.3/pg_tblspc`

Make sure `postgres` is the owner of `/pgdata` by executing:

`chown postgres /pgdata`

Then, as `postgres` user, execute:

`mkdir /pgdata/tbl1`

Then, log in to psql and execute the SQL statements, as shown here:

`CREATE TABLESPACE mytablespace LOCATION '/pgdata/tbl1';`

The following screenshot illustrates the preceding command:

```
postgres=# \! pwd
/pgdata/9.3/pg_tblspc
postgres=# \! ls -l
total 0
postgres=# CREATE TABLESPACE mytablespace LOCATION '/pgdata/tbl1';
CREATE TABLESPACE
Time: 2.256 ms
postgres=# \! ls -l
total 0
lrwxrwxrwx 1 postgres postgres 12 Sep  1 12:33 356500 -> /pgdata/tbl1
```

As you can see from the preceding screenshot, there is a link named `356500` that points to the `/pgdata/tbl1` directory. If we execute `oid2name` with the `-s` option, we can see that it is the tablespace's OID.

We can create a table and specify its tablespace. If we do not specify a tablespace, it will go to the default tablespace. Refer to the following table creation SQL statements and the files that are created:

```
DROP TABLE IF EXISTS emp;
DROP TABLE IF EXISTS dept;
CREATE TABLE emp(id int, first_name text);
CREATE TABLE dept (id int, dept_name text) tablespace mytablespace;
\! oid2name -d test
```

The following screenshot illustrates the preceding command:

```
test=# DROP TABLE IF EXISTS emp;
DROP TABLE
test=# DROP TABLE IF EXISTS dept;
DROP TABLE
test=# CREATE TABLE emp(id int, first_name text);
CREATE TABLE
test=# CREATE TABLE dept (id int, dept_name text) tablespace mytablespace;
CREATE TABLE
test=# \! oid2name -d test
From database "test":
  Filenode   Table Name
  ----------------------
    356580        dept
    356574        emp
test=# \! find /pgdata -type f \( -name 356580 -o -name 356574 \)
/pgdata/tbl1/PG_9.3_201306121/331880/356580
/pgdata/9.3/base/331880/356574
test=# SELECT pg_relation_filepath('emp');
 pg_relation_filepath
----------------------
 base/331880/356574
(1 row)

test=# SELECT pg_relation_filepath('dept');
            pg_relation_filepath
-------------------------------------------------
 pg_tblspc/356500/PG_9.3_201306121/331880/356580
(1 row)
```

PostgreSQL – Object Hierarchy and Roles

Note that we have been executing shell commands from the psql prompt by prefixing the commands with \!. This and other features of psql will be covered in *Chapter 6, Client Tools*. We also used OR, denoted by the -o option of the find command, to find files with name a or name b. The pg_relation_filepath() function can be used to get the entire path (relative to PGDATA) of any relation.

We can see that inside the physical tablespace directory, there is a subdirectory with a name that depends on the PostgreSQL server version. Within the version-specific subdirectory, there is another subdirectory for each database that has elements in the tablespace named after the database's OID. Tables and indexes are stored within this directory, using the filenode naming scheme.

Let's look at a metadata view and see what it says about the table and tablespaces:

```
SELECT tablename, tablespace  FROM pg_tables WHERE tablename IN
('emp','dept');
tablename |   tablespace
----------+---------------
emp       |
dept      | mytablespace
(2 rows)
```

The dept value is in the tablespace mytablespace and emp, which was created without specifying a tablespace, has a null value in the tablespace column. It's possible to specify default tablespaces for each database, and it is possible to set the default tablespace for a user, as follows:

```
test=# ALTER DATABASE test SET default_tablespace='mytablespace';
ALTER DATABASE
test=# CREATE USER myuser;
test=# ALTER USER myuser SET default_tablespace='mytablespace';
ALTER ROLE
```

> If we have non-default tablespaces in our PostgreSQL server, then we have an extra step during recovery on a different server; we have to ensure that the directories, which the tablespaces point to, exist on the server.

Managing temporary objects with temporary tablespaces

We will cover tables and temporary tables to set the context for temporary tablespace. PostgreSQL uses tables to store data. The tables, which can be created using the CREATE TABLE command (http://www.postgresql.org/docs/current/static/sql-createtable.html), are not different from the tables created in Oracle or SQL Server using a similar syntax. We specify the type of data that will be stored in the tables by mentioning the data type for each column. We can also specify constraints (primary key, unique, check, and others) when we create tables. PostgreSQL ensures that the data written to these tables is crash safe and uses WAL to take care of the durability of the transactions.

There might be scenarios where we do not want data written to a table in order to survive a system crash (situations where we are willing to sacrifice durability for better performance). A table storing user session data for a web application is an example. If the system crashes or reboots, we expect the users to log in again. Usually, it is okay to lose the data for sessions that were live when the system went down. Also, there might be tables that are used to store intermediate data for complex calculations (during the Transform step of the **Extract, Transform, Load (ETL)** workflow to a data warehouse, for example). In this case, we would rather redo the batch operation in the event of a failure, and the intermediate results are not going to be used in the rerun. In these situations, performance is more important than the durability of transactions. PostgreSQL provides two special types of tables to address these situations.

The first type is temporary tables. These tables are created using the TEMPORARY keyword when we create the table. For example:

```
CREATE TEMPORARY TABLE mytemp (id int);
```

From the same session, we can work with this table as we would with a non-temporary table. However, if we try querying the table from another psql session, we will get an error, as shown here:

```
ERROR:  relation "mytemp" does not exist
```

This is because the table is created in the session-private buffer. As other sessions do not access the table, a lot of synchronization overhead is avoided and this is one reason why performance is usually better when we work with temporary tables. Writes to disk for these tables are handled by the backend process for the session. We can query the schema under which the tables are created:

```
SELECT relname,relnamespace,pn.oid, pn.nspname FROM
    pg_class pc JOIN  pg_namespace pn ON
```

```
pc.relnamespace=pn.oid  where relname IN ('mytemp','emp');
 relname | relnamespace |   oid  |  nspname
---------+--------------+--------+-----------
 emp     |         2200 |   2200 | public
 mytemp  |       364778 | 364778 | pg_temp_2
```

The temporary table is created under a special schema. We can specify that such temporary objects should be created in a separate tablespace using the `temp_tablespaces` parameter. We can set this at a session or at cluster level. Let's try this. Log in as `postgres`, create a directory under `/pgdata`:

mkdir /pgdata/tmptblsp

Log in to psql and create a tablespace:

```
CREATE TABLESPACE mytmptblspc LOCATION '/pgdata/tmptblsp';
SET temp_tablespaces='mytmptblspc';
CREATE TEMPORARY TABLE mynewtbl(id int);
```

Now, create the same table from another psql session in the same database. Then, execute the query to get the tablespace names:

```
SELECT tablename, tablespace  FROM pg_tables
WHERE tablename ='mynewtbl';
 tablename | tablespace
-----------+-------------
 mynewtbl  | mytmptblspc
 mynewtbl  |
```

Now, we have two tables with the same name, but under different tablespaces. In addition to temporary tables, temporary files created to sort large datasets also go into temporary tablespaces. We can provide a comma-separated list of tablespaces to distribute the load associated with temporary objects, and PostgreSQL will choose one at random to create temporary objects.

Coming back to temporary tables, it is possible to index temporary tables. As the autovacuum daemon does not vacuum or analyze temporary tables, it's better to analyze the temporary tables after populating them. This might help speed up queries against the table.

The table will be automatically dropped once the session ends. It's also possible to use the ON COMMIT option to tell PostgreSQL to drop the table at the end of the transaction. We can also specify whether the data should be preserved or deleted at the end of the transaction using the ON COMMIT option.

The temporary table we covered is a subset of unlogged tables. Each time we need a temporary table, we would use the CREATE TEMPORARY TABLE command. However, it's also possible that we want to reuse the same table (structure) in different sessions and share data across sessions. At the same time, we want tables that are fast to insert/update and are willing to compromise on durability. We can create unlogged tables for such requirements, as shown here:

```
CREATE UNLOGGED TABLE myunloggedtbl(id int);
```

Data inserted into this table will be accessible from all sessions. The changes to the table data will survive normal restarts, but might not survive crashes.

Views

PostgreSQL provides views that are stored queries. The query used to create a view can be very simple (query a single table with a WHERE clause) or pretty complex (join a number of tables and apply many filters). Views do not store data. When we execute a query against a view, the underlying tables are queried. Views can serve quite a few useful purposes. We can use views as a security measure to ensure that users get to see only a subset of data (specific columns or records). For this, we can create views and provide users access to the views, and not to the underlying tables.

Views can also be used to make it easy to retrieve data in cases where it might be necessary to write complex queries. We can create a view using the complex query and then a simple SELECT option against the view is all it takes to get the data we want. Views are common in all relational database management systems and we are not covering them in-depth here. Refer to http://www.postgresql.org/docs/current/static/sql-createview.html for more information on views.

Databases, schemas, and search_path

As per the documentation, a database is a named collection of SQL objects. It's not possible to access objects in one database from another database directly. We can access other databases using a database link (or foreign data wrappers), which is an extension, as mentioned in the previous chapter.

PostgreSQL – Object Hierarchy and Roles

> There are two template databases: `template0` and `template1` in any PostgreSQL cluster. When we create a database using `CREATE DATABASE db1;`, a clone of the `template1` database is created. If we have a few user-created tables with some master data in `template1`, these will be copied to the new database. If we want to create a `newdb` database that is a clone of a user-created database `mydb`, we can use `CREATE DATABASE newdb TEMPLATE mydb;`.

Another important concept is the schema, which is a container or a namespace within a database. Any object that we create in a database (such as a table, an index, a view, and so on) gets created under a schema. We can use schemas to group together related objects within the same database. To some extent, these can be associated to the concept of databases in MySQL. We can access objects in different schemas from the same connection.

When we create objects without specifying the schema, they get created under a default schema called public. An exception to this is when another schema appears first in the `search_path`, more on this later. Let's see what happened to the `emp` and `dept` tables we created earlier:

```
test=# SELECT schemaname, tablename FROM pg_tables WHERE tablename IN ('emp','dept');
schemaname | tablename
------------+----------
 public     | emp
 public     | dept
(2 rows)
```

Let's create a new schema:

```
test=# CREATE SCHEMA mynewschema;
CREATE SCHEMA
```

We will create a couple of tables under this schema:

```
test=# CREATE TABLE mynewschema.emp (id integer, first_name text);
CREATE TABLE
test=# CREATE TABLE mynewschema.emp1 (id integer);
CREATE TABLE
```

Let's insert data into the `emp1` table:

```
test=# INSERT INTO emp1(id) VALUES(1);
ERROR:  relation "emp1" does not exist
LINE 1: INSERT INTO emp1(id) VALUES(1);
                    ^
```

[62]

Chapter 3

Oops, what went wrong? We must now discuss a setting critical to the visibility of objects: search_path. It's very similar to the PATH environment variable in Unix as well as Windows operating systems. When we type a command, the system searches for an executable with this name in the list of directories/folders appearing in PATH and uses the first one that is found. In a similar fashion, PostgreSQL uses a setting called search_path to figure out where it should search for the object the user is trying to access. A couple of useful Session Information Functions are provided to get information related to these values:

```
test=> SELECT current_schema;
current_schema
----------------
 public
(1 row)


test=> SELECT current_schemas(true);
current_schemas
--------------------
 {pg_catalog,public}
(1 row)
```

The current_schema function provides the schema into which objects created will go, and current_schemas provides us the list of schemas that are present in the search_path schema. We can see that the new schema we created is not there in the path:

```
test=# SHOW search_path;
search_path
----------------
 "$user",public
(1 row)
```

Let's add the new schema to search_path:

```
test=# SET search_path="$user",public,mynewschema;
SET
test=# SHOW search_path;
search_path
-------------------------------
 "$user", public, mynewschema
(1 row)

test=# INSERT INTO emp1(id) VALUES(1);
INSERT 0 1
```

[63]

PostgreSQL – Object Hierarchy and Roles

Let's also try inserting a record into the `emp` table, which we created, as there are two tables in this database by this name appearing under two different schemas:

```
test=# INSERT INTO emp(id, first_name) VALUES (1,'OldOne');
INSERT 0 1
test=# SELECT * FROM emp;
 id | first_name
----+------------
  1 | OldOne
(1 row)

test=# SET search_path="$user",mynewschema, public;
SET
test=# SELECT * FROM emp;
 id | first_name
----+------------
(0 rows)
```

It's obvious that the order in which schemas are listed matters. Let's try putting `mynewschema` first and creating a table:

```
test=# SET search_path=mynewschema, "$user", public;
SET
test=# CREATE TABLE dept( id integer, dept_name text);
CREATE TABLE
test=# SELECT tablename, schemaname FROM pg_tables WHERE tablename = 'dept';
 tablename |  schemaname
-----------+--------------
 dept      | public
 dept      | mynewschema
(2 rows)
```

The importance of `search_path` should be clear by now. Besides setting the `search_path` at runtime in the session, as in the preceding code, we can also set the default `search_path` in the configuration file. We can see the parameter in `postgresql.conf` under `/pgdata/9.3`.

```
[postgres@MyCentOS 9.3]$ grep search_path postgresql.conf
#search_path = '"$user",public'        # schema names
```

We can also use the `SET SCHEMA` command, as shown here:

```
postgres=# SHOW search_path;
 search_path
---------------
```

[64]

```
  "$user",public
(1 row)

postgres=# SET SCHEMA   'mynewschema';
SET
postgres=# SHOW search_path;
 search_path
-------------
 mynewschema
(1 row)
```

We can also use the ALTER USER command. Log in as a superuser, such as postgres:

```
test=# ALTER USER myuser SET search_path=mynewschema;
ALTER ROLE
test=# \q
[postgres@MyCentOS ~]$ psql -U myuser -d test
psql (9.3.0)
Type "help" for help.

test=> SHOW search_path;
 search_path
-------------
 mynewschema
(1 row)
```

So, search_path is the one setting that can be set in different ways (configuration file and command line) at different levels (user, database, and session).

As this parameter can be set at different levels, we might run into nasty surprises if we do not pay attention to how it is being set. For example:

- If it is being reset at the database level or server level, existing connections will not use the new value
- We can set it at the database level, but the one set at a user level (could be a different value) will be used
- Setting it at the session level will not work for other/new connections

PostgreSQL – Object Hierarchy and Roles

If we create a schema with the same name as the user, this schema will be searched first.

> For a more exhaustive list of issues we might run into when using schemas and `search_path`, refer to http://www.postgresonline.com/journal/archives/279-Schema-and-search_path-surprises.html, http://blog.endpoint.com/2012/11/postgresql-searchpath-behaviour.html, and http://petereisentraut.blogspot.in/2009/07/schema-search-paths-considered-pain-in.html.

By default, users cannot access any object in schemas they do not own. To allow users to make use of the objects in other schemas, additional privileges (for example, `SELECT` and `UPDATE` on tables) must be granted, as appropriate for the object.

Unlike databases, schemas are not rigidly separated: a user can access objects in any of the schemas in the database, assuming that the user has privileges to do so.

So, the objects in a PostgreSQL cluster can be represented, as shown in the following diagram:

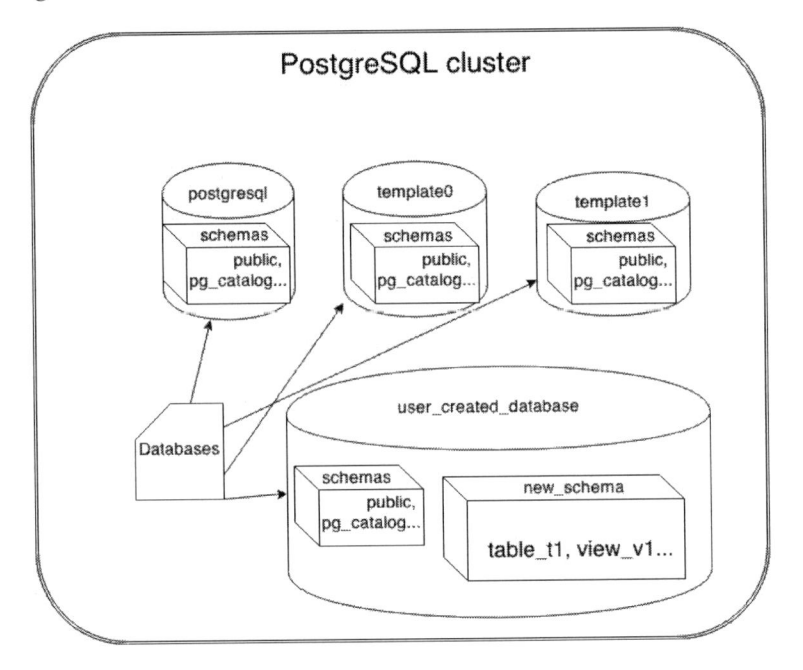

Schemas – use cases

Let's take a look at some situations where using schemas can help:

- In a system where users deal with mutually-exclusive data sets, it's possible to create one schema per user and ensure security by providing each user access to his/her schema alone.
- In a **Software as a Service (SaaS)** model, we can create a schema for each client, thus taking care of security/data-separation concerns. This also makes it possible to roll out client-specific data model changes. It also permits sharing of specific data across clients when necessary.
- In a complex system such as an **Enterprise Resource Planning (ERP)** with many hundreds or thousands of tables, using separate schemas for different modules (finance, human resources, production planning, and so on) will improve maintainability of the database.

In the preceding cases, for those who need to see a superset of the data, views can be created on a union of the tables under different schemas.

We can implement the preceding use cases using separate databases too. However, a couple of issues with this approach are as follows:

- To view a superset of data, we have to depend on foreign data wrappers that connect all these databases and it results in a complex setup.
- When we use foreign data wrappers, query execution times are also likely to become unpredictable, especially when joining local tables with remote tables, or when the data volume transferred across the link is substantial.

Roles and privileges

From clusters, databases, schemas, and objects, let's move on to people who use them, also known as users. In PostgreSQL, a role is almost the same as a user because a role can be a user or a group of users. The CREATE USER command is equivalent to CREATE ROLE except that CREATE USER implies the LOGIN privilege, whereas CREATE ROLE does not. So, if we need to create a user who can log in, we should use CREATE ROLE. Take a look at the difference in the following command:

```
postgres=# CREATE USER my_user;
CREATE ROLE
postgres=# CREATE ROLE my_role;
CREATE ROLE
postgres=# \q
[postgres@MyCentOS ~]$ psql -U my_user -d postgres
psql (9.3.0)
Type "help" for help.
```

PostgreSQL – Object Hierarchy and Roles

A user can log in:

```
postgres=> \q
[postgres@MyCentOS ~]$ psql -U my_role -d postgres
FATAL:  role "my_role" is not permitted to log in
psql: FATAL:  role "my_role" is not permitted to log in
```

A role can't log in. We have to explicitly provide login privileges:

```
[postgres@MyCentOS ~]$ psql
psql (9.3.0)
Type "help" for help.
postgres=# ALTER ROLE my_role WITH login;
ALTER ROLE
postgres=# \q
[postgres@MyCentOS ~]$ psql -U my_role -d postgres
psql (9.3.0)
Type "help" for help.
postgres=> \q
```

> Roles are shared across the cluster. They are not database-specific.

The most important role is probably the `postgres` role as it has the superuser attribute. The name of the role with the superuser attribute, as mentioned earlier, need not be `postgres`. We could use any user to initialize the cluster, and also provide the superuser attribute to a new user created after cluster initialization. The list of existing roles can be retrieved by the `du` command at the psql prompt. The + option, as usual, displays the description too:

```
postgres=# \du+
                             List of roles
 Role name |                   Attributes                    | Member
 of | Description
-----------+-------------------------------------------------+--------
---+------------
 my_role   |                                                 | {}
           |
 my_user   |                                                 | {}
           |
 myuser    |                                                 | {}
           |
```

[68]

```
 postgres     | Superuser, Create role, Create DB, Replication | {}
             |

postgres=# ALTER USER my_user WITH superuser;
ALTER ROLE
postgres=# \du+
                                  List of roles
 Role name   |                    Attributes                     | Member
 of | Description
-------------+----------------------------------------------------+--------
----+------------
 my_role     |                                                    | {}
             |
 my_user     | Superuser                                          | {}
             |
 myuser      |                                                    | {}
             |
 postgres    | Superuser, Create role, Create DB, Replication     | {}
             |
```

We assigned the superuser attribute to my_user and verified that the changes have been reflected in the system. It's important to note that the newly created users can connect to the database, but can't do anything else, such as retrieving data from a table. Log in as my_role to test:

```
psql -U my_role -d test
test=> SELECT current_user;
current_user
--------------
my_role
(1 row)

test=> \d emp
        Table "public.emp"
   Column   |   Type   | Modifiers
------------+----------+-----------
 id         | integer  |
 first_name | text     |

test=> SELECT * FROM emp;
ERROR:  permission denied for relation emp
```

PostgreSQL – Object Hierarchy and Roles

To do anything useful in the database, the users have to be provided appropriate privileges. The privileges, like in any other database, can be provided at database level or individually at the object level (table, view, function, and so on). The type of privileges can be read-only (SELECT), or read-write (DELETE/UPDATE/INSERT), or use functions (EXECUTE). The privilege to create and/or drop objects is separate from the read/write/execute privileges mentioned. Log in as postgres to the test database:

```
test=# GRANT ALL ON emp TO my_user;
GRANT
test=# GRANT SELECT ON emp TO my_role;
GRANT
test=# GRANT INSERT ON emp TO myuser;
GRANT
```

We can grant privileges to other users and then get a rather cryptic listing of privileges on a table with the command \dp+ emp; at the psql prompt, as shown in the following screenshot:

```
test=# \dp+ emp;
                              Access privileges
 Schema | Name | Type  |     Access privileges      | Column access privileges
--------+------+-------+----------------------------+--------------------------
 public | emp  | table | postgres=arwdDxt/postgres +|
        |      |       | my_user=arwdDxt/postgres  +|
        |      |       | my_role=r/postgres        +|
        |      |       | myuser=a/postgres          |
(1 row)
```

In the preceding output, my_user has arwdDxt for all privileges, my_role has a select-only privilege (r, for read) and myuser has an insert (a, for append) privilege. The possible values displayed in the output of a dp command are shown in the following table:

Value	Meaning
r	Read
w	Write (update)
a	Append (insert)
d	Delete
D	Truncate
x	References
t	Trigger
X	Execute

[70]

Value	Meaning
U	Usage
C	Create
c	Connect
T	Temporary
arwdDxt	All privileges

We can get the privileges output in an easy to understand format with the query:

```
SELECT pu.usename , pc.tbl, pc.privilege_type
     FROM pg_user pu JOIN (
       SELECT  oid::regclass tbl, (aclexplode(relacl)).grantee,
          (aclexplode(relacl)).privilege_type FROM  pg_class
WHERE
relname='emp'
          ) pc ON pc.grantee=pu.usesysid;
```

The following screenshot illustrates the preceding command:

```
test=# SELECT pu.usename , pc.tbl, pc.privilege_type
test-#      FROM pg_user pu JOIN (
test(#        SELECT  oid::regclass tbl, (aclexplode(relacl)).grantee,
test(#           (aclexplode(relacl)).privilege_type FROM  pg_class WHERE relname='emp'
test(#           ) pc ON pc.grantee=pu.usesysid ;
 usename  | tbl | privilege_type
----------+-----+----------------
 my_role  | emp | SELECT
 postgres | emp | INSERT
 postgres | emp | SELECT
 postgres | emp | UPDATE
 postgres | emp | DELETE
 postgres | emp | TRUNCATE
 postgres | emp | REFERENCES
 postgres | emp | TRIGGER
 my_user  | emp | INSERT
 my_user  | emp | SELECT
 my_user  | emp | UPDATE
 my_user  | emp | DELETE
 my_user  | emp | TRUNCATE
 my_user  | emp | REFERENCES
 my_user  | emp | TRIGGER
 myuser   | emp | INSERT
(16 rows)
```

Refer to the PostgreSQL documentation at http://www.postgresql.org/docs/current/static/sql-grant.html for all possible incarnations of the GRANT command used to provide privileges to users and roles.

Another important aspect of roles is that they can be inherited. So, we could grant SELECT on table t1 to role1, and grant role11 to role2; role2 will now have the SELECT privilege on table t1.

Let's look at a few use cases for roles and privileges. We could create a `report_user` role and give the `SELECT` permission on a set of tables to this role. We can then create users for the individuals who work in the reporting section and grant `report_user` role to these users. When one of the users moves out of the department, we can just drop the login created for that user.

Using read-only roles is safer when we opt for horizontal scaling (as discussed in *Chapter 10, Scaling, Replication, and Backup and Recovery*) with slaves used for read-only queries. When all access to slaves is via read-only roles, we can be sure that there won't be any attempts to write to the slaves.

Summary

In this chapter, we went through the concept of tablespaces (containers for other objects). We also covered views and tables, especially temporary tables, and concepts specific to PostgreSQL, such as databases, `search_path`, and schemas. We also saw how privileges and access controls are managed.

In the next chapter, we will cover transactions, and we will see how concurrency is managed in PostgreSQL.

4
Working with Transactions

Now that we have covered the installation, key objects (databases and schemas) and high-level architecture, let's look at what is probably the most important concept when it comes to working with databases: transactions. The ability to provide transaction control at different isolation levels is one reason why relational databases, whether it is PostgreSQL, Oracle, DB2, or SQL Server, still rule the roost when it comes to supporting critical applications where data integrity is important. Due to their tried and tested transaction handling capabilities, relational database management systems have managed to hold their place even in a time when NoSQL databases seem to be getting most of the attention and blogspace. In this chapter, we will learn the theoretical underpinnings of transactions. We will also see how PostgreSQL manages transactions and concurrency.

Understanding transactions

Transaction is a set of one or more SQL statements that take the database from one consistent state to another. The most common example used to explain transactions is of transferring money from one account to another. Let's use this in the following example.

Let's create a table to simulate a few possible scenarios:

```
[root@MyCentOS ~]# psql
psql (9.3.0)
Type "help" for help.

postgres=# CREATE USER bank PASSWORD 'bank';
CREATE ROLE
postgres=# ALTER USER bank WITH createdb;
ALTER ROLE
postgres=# \c test bank
You are now connected to database "test" as user "bank".
```

Working with Transactions

```
test=> CREATE DATABASE accounts;
CREATE DATABASE
test=> \c accounts;
You are now connected to database "accounts" as user "bank".
accounts=> CREATE TABLE account (id serial PRIMARY KEY ,
first_name varchar(100), last_name varchar(100), account_bal
numeric (10,2));
CREATE TABLE
```

Once this is done, we can populate the table with some data to simulate a bank with a few million customers. I used web2py framework's data generation component for this.

> web2py is a free open source framework to develop database-driven web-based applications. The link to understand how to generate dummy data with web2py is http://web2py.com/books/default/chapter/29/14/other-recipes#Populating-database-with-dummy-data.

Consider the following code:

```
accounts=> SELECT COUNT(*) FROM account;
  count
---------
 1915046
(1 row)
```

Now, let's find the richest and the poorest of the lot:

```
accounts=> SELECT * FROM account WHERE account_bal = (
SELECT max(account_bal) FROM account
)
UNION
SELECT * FROM account WHERE account_bal = (
SELECT min(account_bal) FROM account
);
    id   | first_name | last_name  | account_bal
---------+------------+------------+-------------
 1890988 | Paulina    | Coburn     |        0.00
....
 1828027 | Hyon       | Aspell     |        0.00
       2 | William    | Blake      |  7000000.00
  535889 | Riley      | Truden     |        0.00
```

[74]

We have quite a few individuals with zero account balance. Now, if we were to look at what has to be done if William Blake decides to transfer $10,000 to Riley Truden, the logic flow would be:

1. Does the account with the ID value 2 have enough funds? (a READ/SELECT statement).
2. If yes, deduct $10,000 from the account with the ID value 2 (a WRITE/UPDATE statement).
3. Add $10,000 to the balance of the account with ID 535889 (a WRITE/UPDATE statement).

For the system to move from one consistent state to another (which is what a transaction should do), either both the updates should work, or both should be rolled back. If the first update worked and the second one failed (as the server crashed), the database will be in an inconsistent state. There will be $10,000 missing in the account books. We could add $10,000 to the balance for account ID 535889 and then deduct the amount from William Blake's account in the next step. If the credit succeeds and debit fails, there will be an unaccounted $10,000 in the bank's accounts. The flowchart for the first approach will be like this:

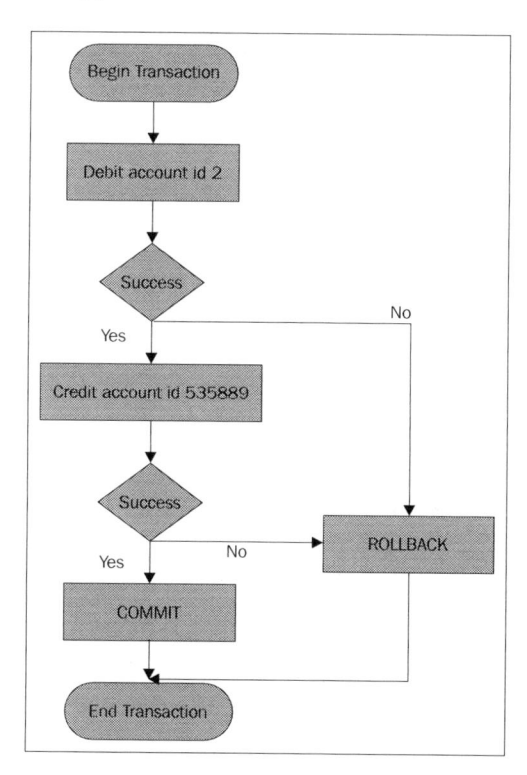

Actually, there could be more tables involved. There might be a transaction table, which keeps track of the account ID, type of transaction (debit or credit), amount, date/time of transaction, and so on, and there might be two inserts in this table, one for each of the two accounts affected.

When we deal with an e-commerce site, one business transaction might involve completely different systems, such as the e-commerce site provider's system, the actual vendor's system (think about a retailer selling via Amazon), the payment processing system, and so on. So, a transaction ends up crossing many boundaries. However, here we are getting into the realm of distributed transactions. For now, we will stick to situations where a transaction will mean one logical unit of work within the database boundaries. Let's cover the ACID properties of transactions.

ACID properties of transactions

The ACID properties are covered in the following sections:

A for atomicity

The logical unit mentioned in this heading is A(not)-TOM(piece/cut)-ic. So, either all the SQL statements get executed, or none of them does. This was what we were doing in the preceding flowchart.

C for consistency

The transaction will take the database from one consistent state (where all defined and enforced business rules hold true) to another consistent state (where the rules still hold true).

I for isolation

This one needs quite a bit of elaboration. Isolation means that no user is impacted by whatever other users do at the same time. It's as if each transaction is happening serially, one after the other; although in reality there might be hundreds of concurrent transactions. When you transfer online funds, you really feel that you are the only one using the system. In short, you are not seeing the effect of what others are doing on the system. Also, others are not seeing the impact of your actions either.

However, this is not a simple and straightforward concept like atomicity and consistency, mainly because of the business impact. Let's consider two examples. First, consider the case of only one seat left on the flight to Las Vegas for the long weekend. How should the isolation be handled? Assume that one customer has chosen the last seat available, clicked on book, and is looking at the fare details. At this point in time, the question is should everyone else see zero availability? Those seeing no availability might book tickets on another airline and the one guy who was about to grab that only seat might decide not to book it. In such situations, it's first a business decision and this can be translated into implementation via the isolation level.

Let's also consider a report to find the total account balance for a bank. Assume that the transaction to transfer $10,000 from account ID 2 to account ID 535889 starts soon after, for the table and data provided earlier. The total balance report query will be:

`SELECT SUM(account_bal) FROM ACCOUNT;`

This aggregation step scans the values row by row and keeps adding the balances. Let's call this transaction T1. Let's call the money transfer transaction T2.

In the following table, we have the points in time marked as p1, p2, p3, and so on, and the state of T1 and T2 transactions each point in time is provided in the T1 and T2 columns:

Period	T1	T2
p1	Starts summing	
p2	Adds balance of ID 2 to SUM	Starts
p3	Continues summing	Debits account ID 2
p4	...	Credits account ID 535889
p5	...	Commits
p6	Adds balance of IDs...,535889,...rest to SUM	
p6	Returns SUM	

If all committed changes are made visible to the summing query, it might end up adding $10,000 twice. Later in this chapter, we will see how PostgreSQL's **Multiversion Concurrency Control (MVCC)** handles such scenarios.

From these two examples, it's obvious that the version of data that a user/session should see depends a lot on the business context. There is no one perfect isolation level.

Keeping this in mind, let's look at the SQL standard isolation levels.

Read uncommitted

This is the most relaxed/lowest level of isolation. Changes made to data in one session will be visible to other sessions even before they are committed. This is referred to as dirty read. Let's see how dirty reads will affect the case of William Blake when he transfers $10000 to Riley Truden:

Period	T1 (William Blake)	T2 (Riley Truden)
p1	Clicks on transfer funds	Keeps refreshing account balance
p2	Chooses Riley's account and types in $10,000	
p3	Clicks on submit (database begins the transaction, changes the account balance in both accounts, and retrieves balance from account after update is executed. Changes not committed yet)	
p4	Sees a screen that says "After this transfer, your balance will be $6,990,000. Confirm/cancel?"	Refreshes his screen and sees that the balance has gone up by $10,000
p5	Changes his mind and clicks on the cancel button (database rolls back transaction)	
p6		Refreshes his screen and sees that the balance has gone down by $10,000

Read committed

In this level, changes made to data in other sessions and committed will be visible to other sessions. Changes not committed will not be visible to other sessions. So, the phenomenon of dirty reads will not happen. Still, there is no guarantee that the same SELECT statement issued twice within a transaction will fetch the same results. The second issuance might fetch different results if another session has changed the data and committed it in the meantime. This means that there could be non-repeatable reads. The locking mechanism used to implement this will be stricter than the one used for the previously described isolation level.

Repeatable reads

In this level, the issue is of phantom reads. The dataset returned by successive selects could have changed because of another session inserting records, which met the criteria and committed. These are phantom records. However, the result set, which met the SELECT criteria itself, would be locked and hence wouldn't be modified by another session. This is the key difference between read committed and repeatable read isolation. This implies that the locking level has become a bit stricter.

Let's see what phantom read means:

Period	T1	T2
p1	SELECT COUNT(*) FROM accounts where balance < 1000 and balance > 100 (returns 1500)	
p2		UPDATE accounts SET balance = 500 where ID = 123 and balance = 1500; commit;
p3	SELECT COUNT(*) FROM accounts where balance < 1000 and balance > 100 (returns 1501)	

A record, which was not there earlier (phantom), appeared in the second issuance of the query in the same transaction (T1).

To recap, a dirty read occurs when one transaction can see uncommitted data from another transaction. A non-repeatable read occurs when two fetches of the same row in one transaction obtains different data within the row. A phantom read occurs when two issuances of the same query in one transaction obtain different result sets.

Serializable

This is the strictest isolation level. Transactions occur as if they are happening serially, one after the other. In this level, phantom reads are not possible.

To recap, locking gets stricter as we move from read uncommitted to serializable levels of isolation. The inconsistencies that are allowed in each level can be summarized as follows:

Isolation level	Dirty reads	Non-repeatable reads	Phantoms
Read uncommitted	Yes	Yes	Yes
Read committed	No	Yes	Yes
Repeatable read	No	No	Yes
Serializable	No	No	No

In PostgreSQL, it's possible to set any of the four isolation levels. Internally, there are only three levels (there is no read uncommitted level and dirty reads also are not possible). Phantom reads are not possible in PostgreSQL's implementation of repeatable read. We could say that PostgreSQL's implementation is stricter than the minimum protection prescribed by SQL standard.

We will go through the levels offered by PostgreSQL and also look at a few useful functions and commands to deal with transactions.

Read committed

This is the default isolation level. In this level, a query sees a snapshot of the data with all changes that were committed before the statement began executing. We are using the word statement here, not transaction. It does see effects of changes made within it. Let's see what this means, and we will also see a couple of useful functions. The SQL statements that we will use are shown in the following screenshot:

```
accounts=# SHOW default_transaction_isolation ;
 default_transaction_isolation
-------------------------------
 read committed
(1 row)

accounts=# SELECT txid_current();
 txid_current
--------------
        50486
(1 row)

accounts=# SELECT txid_current();
 txid_current
--------------
        50487
(1 row)

accounts=# SELECT txid_current();
 txid_current
--------------
        50488
(1 row)
```

Each query we execute increases the transaction ID. This is because in PostgreSQL, if we don't explicitly start a transaction, each statement will implicitly run within its own transaction. If we plan to execute a series of SELECT statements, some of which are based on the results of the previous ones, we should execute them in a transaction. Another point to note is that SELECT is also a transaction. Let's see how we can wrap statements in a transaction.

In PostgreSQL, we use the BEGIN and COMMIT (or ROLLBACK) constructs to wrap a set of SQL statements in one transaction, as shown in the following screenshot:

```
accounts=# BEGIN;
BEGIN
accounts=# SELECT txid_current();
 txid_current
--------------
        50492
(1 row)

accounts=# SELECT now();
              now
-------------------------------
 2014-09-19 15:24:03.194696+05:30
(1 row)

accounts=# SELECT clock_timestamp();
       clock_timestamp
-------------------------------
 2014-09-19 15:25:04.637009+05:30
(1 row)

accounts=# SELECT txid_current();
 txid_current
--------------
        50492
(1 row)

accounts=# SELECT now();
              now
-------------------------------
 2014-09-19 15:24:03.194696+05:30
(1 row)

accounts=# SELECT clock_timestamp();
       clock_timestamp
-------------------------------
 2014-09-19 15:25:13.414053+05:30
(1 row)

accounts=# COMMIT;
COMMIT
accounts=# SELECT txid_current();
 txid_current
--------------
        50493
```

Note that from BEGIN to COMMIT, the transaction ID remained the same. This is what we mean when we say within the same transaction.

Another important (although unrelated) thing to note is the now() function. The result returned by now() remains the same within a transaction. It does not return the actual current time. If we want to use the current timestamp, we can use clock_timestamp().

> Pay attention to the functions you use to get date/time values. Very often, you would expect the values returned to change over time, but they do not. This is because they mark the date/time at the beginning of the current transaction. Although the names of the functions might be a bit confusing, the documentation clearly states this.

Repeatable read

In this level, a query sees data as it existed at the beginning of the transaction. Note that the key term here is transaction. So, if we execute the same SELECT multiple times within a transaction, the results will be consistent. In the read committed level, the snapshot as it existed at the time of execution of the SQL statement (not transaction) within the transaction is used. In repeatable read, the snapshot as it existed at the beginning of the transaction is used.

Let's see how we can change the isolation level:

```
accounts=> BEGIN;
BEGIN
accounts=> SHOW transaction_isolation;
transaction_isolation
----------------------
 read committed
(1 row)

accounts=>SET transaction isolation level repeatable read;
SET
accounts=> SHOW transaction_isolation;
transaction_isolation
----------------------
 repeatable read
(1 row)

accounts=>COMMIT;
COMMIT
accounts=> SHOW transaction_isolation;
transaction_isolation
----------------------
 read committed
(1 row)
```

If we have only reads from a session, we get the same dataset. It will always present data as it existed at the beginning of the transaction. If we have writes and try to change data that has been modified by another session, we will get an error. Let's see how this works. Take two psql sessions and set the isolation level in both sessions. Delete all the records, except a couple of records from the account table or just delete all data and insert the one record:

```
accounts=> INSERT INTO account (first_name,last_name, account_bal)
values ( 'Jane', 'Adam', 1000);
```

Then, at psql, execute:

```
SET default_transaction_isolation = 'repeatable read';
```

Take one more psql session (marked T2). The following table illustrates the SQL commands in the two sessions:

Period	T1	T2
p1	BEGIN;	
p2	SELECT * FROM account;	
p3		BEGIN;
P3		SELECT * FROM account;
p4		UPDATE account SET account_bal = 2000 WHERE id = 2;
p5		COMMIT;
p6	UPDATE account SET account_bal = 2000 WHERE id = 2;	

We will get the following error:

```
ERROR: could not serialize access due to concurrent update
```

If we executed the SELECT statement instead of attempting an update, we would see the data as it existed at the beginning of T1. Make sure that you are replacing the ID in the SQL statements with a value that exists in the table.

Serializable level

This is the strictest level available. The PostgreSQL documentation says "To guarantee true serializability, PostgreSQL uses predicate locking, which means that it keeps locks that allow it to determine when a write would have had an impact on the result of a previous read from a concurrent transaction, had it run first. In PostgreSQL, these locks do not cause any blocking and therefore cannot play any part in causing a deadlock."

In short, PostgreSQL does not block any transaction. It will, at serializable isolation level, detect conflicts and abort transactions to avoid anomalies. It's up to the developer to decide whether the transaction should be retried or not when a rollback is detected.

We will see how the same set of statements behaves under different isolation levels. The data in the account table after deleting all but a few records looks like this:

```
SELECT first_name, sum(account_bal)
    FROM account GROUP BY first_name;
 first_name |  sum
------------+--------
 Jane       | 100.00
 John       | 200.00
```

We will set the isolation level to serializable in two psql sessions. We will then insert data for two individuals in the account table from these sessions:

`SET default_transaction_isolation = 'serializable';`

The following table illustrates the account table:

Period	T1	T2
p1	BEGIN;	
p2	SELECT first_name, sum(account_bal) FROM account GROUP BY first_name;	
p3	INSERT INTO account (first_name,last_name,account_bal) values ('Jane','Doe',100);	
P3		BEGIN;
p4		SELECT first_name, sum(account_bal) FROM account GROUP BY first_name;
p5		INSERT INTO account (first_name,last_name, account_bal) values ('John','Doe',100);
p6		COMMIT;
p7	SELECT first_name, sum(account_bal) FROM account GROUP BY first_name;	
p8	COMMIT;	

This will result in an error, as shown in the following command:

```
ERROR:  could not serialize access due to read/write dependencies
among transactions
DETAIL:  Reason code: Canceled on identification as a pivot,
during commit attempt.
HINT:  The transaction might succeed if retried
```

The sequence of actions in the preceding table can be tried after setting isolation level to repeatable read in both sessions, and then to read committed in the sessions to see how it affects the data returned within transactions.

Refer to http://wiki.postgresql.org/wiki/SSI and https://wiki.postgresql.org/wiki/Serializable for detailed information about the serializable snapshot isolation and the serializable isolation level.

> Serializable or repeatable read transactions use one snapshot for the entire transaction, whereas a read committed transaction uses a new snapshot for each statement.

Choosing the right isolation level is not a simple process. We can decide to set different isolation levels to cater to different situations in the same system. For example, we can decide to opt for a default isolation level of read committed for most use cases that involve user interaction. However, we might need to execute background jobs in parallel and to ensure that there are no anomalies, set the serializable isolation level for these jobs. PostgreSQL documentation about transaction isolation can be found at http://www.postgresql.org/docs/current/static/transaction-iso.html.

From isolation, let's move to the last property of ACID.

D for durability

Durability refers to the level of certainty that can be offered once a transaction is committed; it will remain so, irrespective of power failures, operating system failures, hardware failures, and so on. One way in which PostgreSQL achieves this is using **Write Ahead Logs (WAL)**, which was discussed in a previous chapter.

PostgreSQL and MVCC

PostgreSQL uses MVCC to provide different views of the database to different sessions, which are based on the isolation level setting. With MVCC, high levels of concurrency are achieved without sacrificing performance. The key rule is that readers should not block writers and writers should not block readers. MVCC is used by many other databases (for example, Oracle and Berkeley DB).

PostgreSQL uses the concept of transaction ID to achieve MVCC. In the previous section, we saw the transaction ID being retrieved using the `txid_current()` function. Each transaction will see the effect of all transactions that were started and committed before the current transaction started. This is the most basic rule followed to get consistent views of the data in a transaction.

In the following figure, P0 is a point in time. **T1, T2, T3** up to **T13** are transactions that begin one after the other. **P1** is the point in time when transaction **T10** started.

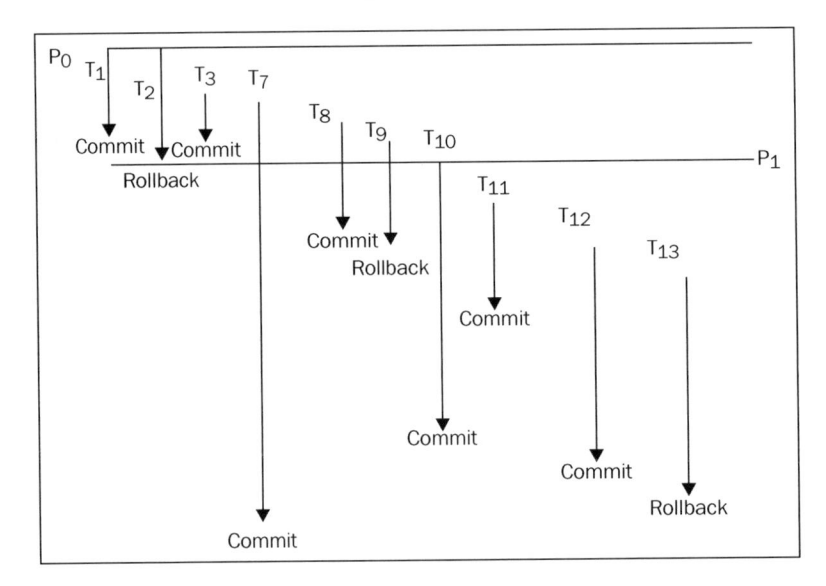

All the statements in T10 will see the effect of transactions T1, T3, and other transactions that were started and committed before T10 started. No statement in T10 will see the effect of T7 since it was committed after T10 ended. Some statements in T10 will see the effect of T8 if the isolation level is read committed. Some statements in T10 will see the effect of T11 if the isolation level is read committed. No statement in T10 will see the effect of T13.

PostgreSQL uses a few system columns to manage this. There are quite a few system columns present in all the tables in PostgreSQL. The two most relevant columns to generate snapshots of data are:

- `xmin`: This column holds the identity of the transaction, which created the specific version of the row. Note that we are saying version of the row. When we update a record, as mentioned in the section on vacuuming, the existing record is not overwritten. A new version is created.
- `xmax`: This column holds the identity of the transaction, which deleted the specific row. Again, the record is not really removed from the database, it's just marked as deleted. If the record is no longer useful, as there are no transaction with IDs less than the `xmax` column of a row, vacuum will take care of the record and see to it that the space gets reused for new inserts.

Let's see a few examples:

```
accounts=> BEGIN;
BEGIN
accounts=> CREATE TABLE emp(id integer, first_name varchar,
last_name varchar);
CREATE TABLE
accounts=> INSERT INTO emp(first_name, last_name) VALUES
('SCOTT','TIGER');
INSERT 0 1
accounts=> SELECT xmin,xmax, *  FROM emp;
xmin | xmax | id | first_name | last_name
------+------+----+------------+----------
 6644 |    0 |    | SCOTT      | TIGER
(1 row)

accounts=> SELECT txid_current();
txid_current
--------------
         6644
(1 row)

accounts=>COMMIT;
COMMIT
```

> In PostgreSQL, the DDL statements (such as CREATE TABLE) are also part of the transactions. We can the ROLLBACK DDL statements.

Working with Transactions

We can see that the `xmin` column is populated and `xmax` is not, as no transaction has deleted the record yet. The `xmin` column is the same as the current transaction ID. We will try deleting and updating the record. Try the following command in one session:

```
accounts=> BEGIN;
BEGIN
accounts=> SELECT txid_current();
txid_current
--------------
        6645
(1 row)

accounts=> UPDATE emp SET last_name = 'TGR';
UPDATE 1
accounts=> SELECT xmin, xmax, * FROM emp;
 xmin | xmax | id | first_name | last_name
------+------+----+------------+-----------
 6645 |   0  |    |   SCOTT    |    TGR
(1 row)
```

We only see the new record created by the current transaction.

Hold! Don't type `COMMIT`. Take another session and try, as shown here:

```
accounts=> SELECT xmin,xmax, * FROM emp;
 xmin | xmax | id | first_name | last_name
------+------+----+------------+-----------
 6644 | 6645 |    |   SCOTT    |   TIGER
(1 row)
```

We can see that there is an expired version of the record with `TIGER` as `last_name`. Now, we can go to the first session and type the following command:

```
accounts=>COMMIT;
COMMIT
```

In both these sessions, we will get:

```
accounts=> SELECT xmin,xmax, * FROM emp;
 xmin | xmax | id | first_name | last_name
------+------+----+------------+-----------
 6645 |   0  |    |   SCOTT    |    TGR
(1 row)
```

Chapter 4

Now, we see the new version of the record, which was created by the transaction ID 6645. The original record that was inserted and its transaction ID is history.

> Records might have non-zero xmax values and still be valid and visible. This happens when DELETE/UPDATE is rolled back. The status of the transactions is recorded in pg_clog.

Let's look at the example of a transaction that started during the lifetime of a current transaction (that is, the example of the transaction ID 10 mentioned earlier):

```
accounts=# DELETE FROM emp;
DELETE 1
accounts=> BEGIN;
BEGIN
accounts=> SELECT txid_current();
txid_current
--------------
        6649
(1 row)

accounts=> SELECT xmin, xmax, * FROM emp;
xmin | xmax | id | first_name | last_name
------+------+----+------------+----------
(0 rows)
```

In another session, insert a record:

```
accounts=> INSERT INTO emp(first_name, last_name) VALUES
('SCOTT','TIGER');
```

Then, in the first session:

```
accounts=> SELECT xmin, xmax, * FROM emp;
xmin | xmax | id | first_name | last_name
------+------+----+------------+----------
 6650 |    0 |    | SCOTT      | TIGER
(1 row)

accounts=>COMMIT;
COMMIT
```

[89]

Working with Transactions

> **Downloading the example code**
> You can download the example code files for all Packt books you have purchased from your account at http://www.packtpub.com. If you purchased this book elsewhere, you can visit http://www.packtpub.com/support and register to have the files e-mailed directly to you.

Now, a SELECT statement in the transaction ID 6649 can see the effect of transaction ID 6650. This does depend on the isolation level set for the transaction. Try this with the isolation level set to repeatable read and check whether the behavior is the same.

For an excellent discussion of MVCC in PostgreSQL, refer to http://momjian.us/main/writings/pgsql/mvcc.pdf.

Summary

In this chapter, we covered some more theory about transactions and their ACID properties, isolation levels, and how PostgreSQL's isolation levels map to SQL standards. We covered the basics of PostgreSQL's MVCC. Along the way, we also had a look at a few system functions and columns that can be used both to understand the theory and to study system behavior in real life. In the next couple of chapters, we will focus on tools, one that can be used to design a database for PostgreSQL and another that can be used to work with the PostgreSQL cluster.

5
Data Modeling with SQL Power Architect

We spent the last few chapters understanding PostgreSQL concepts and architecture and the important ACID properties and how they are managed.

In this chapter, we will cover data modeling with **SQL Power Architect**. Data modeling is a vast topic and involves many steps. It helps in understanding business requirements to design and implement a database to meet the requirements. The process involves, typically, generating conceptual, logical, and physical schemas or data models. Understanding the requirements and translating them to a good database design is critical to the implementation of a secure and scalable system. The data models capture a lot of information, which includes the business entities involved, their attributes, the rules (also known as constraints) applicable to the entities and attributes, the relationships between the entities, and so on.

SQL Power Architect is a tool that aids in creating the physical model, generating the SQL, actually a subset of SQL - **Data Definition Language** (DDL), implementing the models for different types of databases, and also visualizing the data models.

Before we cover these features, let's first quickly cover a few tools that are used with PostgreSQL and other databases.

Tools for databases and their uses

There are many tools that are used with databases, each one with a focus on some capabilities. To interact with a database to execute queries, make changes to the database, observe what is happening in the database, and so on, there are client tools such as psql and pgAdmin (pgAdmin III). These do not have a web interface and need to be installed on the machine from which the database will be accessed. Similar capabilities are provided by phpPgAdmin, which provides a web interface.

Then, there are products such as **TOra** (http://torasql.com/). The key difference here is that TOra is a tool that works with a few databases, whereas pgAdmin has a focus on PostgreSQL.

Some tools focus on database administration activities (taking backups, restoring from backups, monitoring performance, killing sessions, monitoring memory usage, and space utilization). Some others focus on executing queries or scripts, describing tables (mostly developer activity).

However, these tools are not helpful when it comes to version control. This is not the problem they are trying to solve. Database version control involves many activities such as:

- Merging changes to the database structure when there are multiple developers working on database design
- Figuring out the changes made to the database in the latest release
- Rolling back the changes if necessary

Most database tools are not really focused on version control. One can generate scripts and use a tool (such as SVN) to track the changes. Again, the scripts to roll back changes have to be prepared more or less manually. Liquibase (http://www.liquibase.org/) is a tool that focuses on version control and should be given serious consideration if we make frequent changes to the database schema.

Then, of course, there are the database design tools. So, choosing a tool means answering some questions like:

- What is the tool mainly used for (development, administration, version control, or design)?
- Do you want a thick client tool to be used by a couple of users, or are you looking for a tool to be used by many people from various locations, and hence prefer a web-based tool?
- Will you be working with just one database (PostgreSQL) or multiple databases (PostgreSQL, MySQL, and Oracle)?

Of course, the important considerations of cost and licensing cannot be overlooked.

Database design tools

Let's see why we need a database design tool.

Although the number of tables in your database will definitely depend on the type of product you are working on, it's highly unlikely that there will be a system doing serious work with less than 10-20 tables. By the time we add tables to manage users, roles, and privileges, we will have 4-5 tables. Add a few tables to audit user actions and we will have double digits. Then, of course, there will be tables to support the core business.

We might have a system that deals with products, customers, and warehouses. Or, we can design a system that deals with flights, routes, inventory, and fare classes. Also, we can build a Facebook-killer system with friends, connections, blog posts and groups, and so on. In short, we end up with a number of tables (ranging from ten to maybe many hundreds). When writing scripts and keeping all the details about the tables and columns and their attributes in Excel work, and that might be the practice followed by many teams, using a data modeling tool helps a lot in visualizing the maze of tables we end up creating. It's also very helpful if we export or publish our tables and their relationships as images or HTML files and explain them to others using these images. Reverse engineering or generating a data model from an existing database is another useful feature of many database design tools.

Although there are many database design tools, many of them work only in a Windows environment. There are other free tools that are free, but not yet in version 1.0. We will use SQL Power Architect available under GPL, which is free and definitely stable. The GPL Community Edition version has almost all the necessary key features (such as data modeling, data profiling, reverse and forward engineering). SQL Power Architect is Java based and runs on Windows, Unix, Linux, and Mac OS platforms. We will cover the most basic steps that are necessary to design a few tables, generate the SQL, and export the model in various formats. We will also cover how to reverse engineer an existing database using the tool.

SQL Power Architect – downloading and installing

The software can be downloaded at `http://www.sqlpower.ca/page/architect_download_os`.

The downloaded file for the Unix/Generic environment is around 22 MB. Once the file is downloaded, we can extract it with the following command:

```
$tar xvf ../Downloads/SQL-Power-Architect-generic-jdbc-1.0.7.tar.gz
architect-1.0.7/LICENSE
```

```
...
architect-1.0.7/lib/xercesImpl-2.9.1.jar
architect-1.0.7/README.generic
```

> Ensure that Java is installed and working on your computer.

Then, we can change the directory with the `cd` command, set a variable, and launch the application:
```
$cd architect-1.0.7/
$pwd
/home/jayadevan/sw/architect-1.0.7
$export ARCHITECT_HOME=/home/jayadevan/sw/architect-1.0.7
$java -jar $ARCHITECT_HOME/architect.jar
```

Now, you see a window with two panes. The database pane will be where we add new connections. The playpen pane is where we can add new objects, create relationships, and so on:

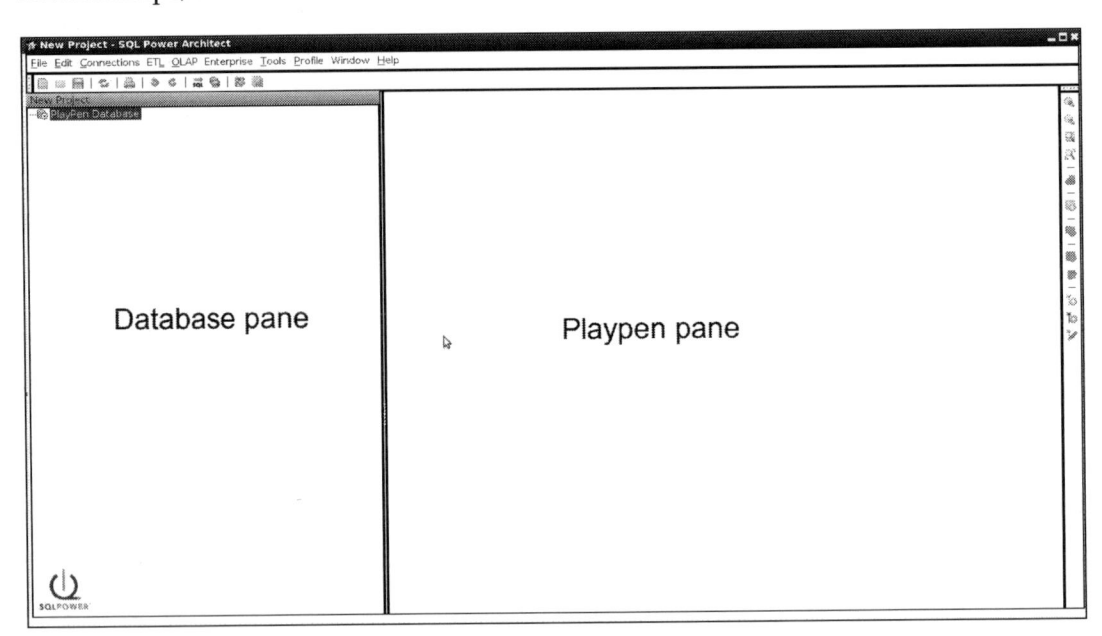

In the top-left corner, below the menu icons, we have **New Project**. Each data model is a separate project. Below this, we have Playpen Database. Playpen is the work area where we can add new objects, manipulate objects, and so on. As of now, we don't have any objects here.

Creating tables

Let's create a few tables (a customer table, an account table, and a transaction table).

Right-click in the right-hand side pane and click on **New Table**. Now, give the same logical and physical name `customer_master`, and name the primary key as `customer_master_pk`.

Then, click on **Save**, choose **Project**, and enter `banking_system` as the project name.

Now, add a few columns to the table. Right-click on the table, choose **New Column**, and enter `cust_id` as the column name. Also, select **In Primary Key** and **bigint** as the data type. Select **Yes** for auto increment. In a similar manner, add a few columns (such as `first_name` and `last_name`). These are not primary keys and are of the `VARCHAR` data type. Add another column called `dob` of type `date`. You can see that these additions also appear in the left-hand side pane under **Playpen**. Whether primary keys should be intelligent or a meaningless auto-incrementing integer is a debatable topic. For now, we will focus on the features of the design tool. Let's use an auto-incrementing integer.

In a similar manner, add a table `customer_accounts` with `account_id` as the primary key. We will add a few more columns: `cust_id` (type `bigint`), `branch_id` (type `bigint`), and `account_type` (`VARCHAR`). We can keep `branch_id` as `INT`, assuming the number of branches will not cross the limits of integer. Now let's try creating a relationship between the two tables. A simple rule will be that we cannot open an account until we capture the basic information of the customer. This means that every `cust_id` in the `customer_accounts` table should have an entry in the `customer_master` table.

Click on **New Identifying Relationship** in the right-hand side pane. Then, click on `customer_master` and then on `customer_accounts`. The column `cust_id` automatically gets added to the primary key box. We can always go and change this later by editing the column's properties.

Data Modeling with SQL Power Architect

If we click on **Relationship**, we can see the properties, as shown in the following screenshot:

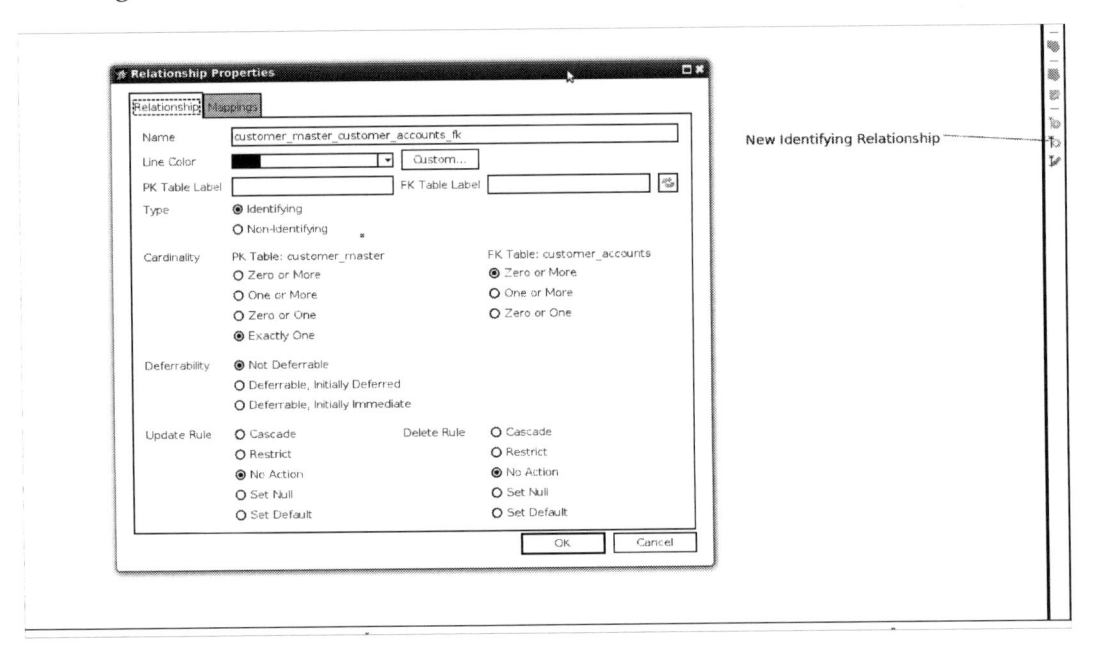

Now, try adding a new table for transactions. It can have the columns: `transaction_id` as primary key, `account_id` linking it to account table, `date_of_transaction`, amount and type of transaction (debit or credit) as other columns.

> The ability to add domains and custom data types is available in the Enterprise Edition.

[96]

Generating SQL

Next, let's try generating SQL for the two tables we just created. Click on **Tools** and select **Forward Engineer**. Then, choose **Create** in the Playpen Database and **PostgreSQL** as the **Database Type**. You will also notice the **Liquibase** option, mentioned earlier as a version control tool for databases. Once you click on **OK**, you can see the SQL generated for PostgreSQL. The SQL generated will vary depending on the database we choose. The SQL generated for PostgreSQL and Liquibase XML generated is shown in the following screenshot:

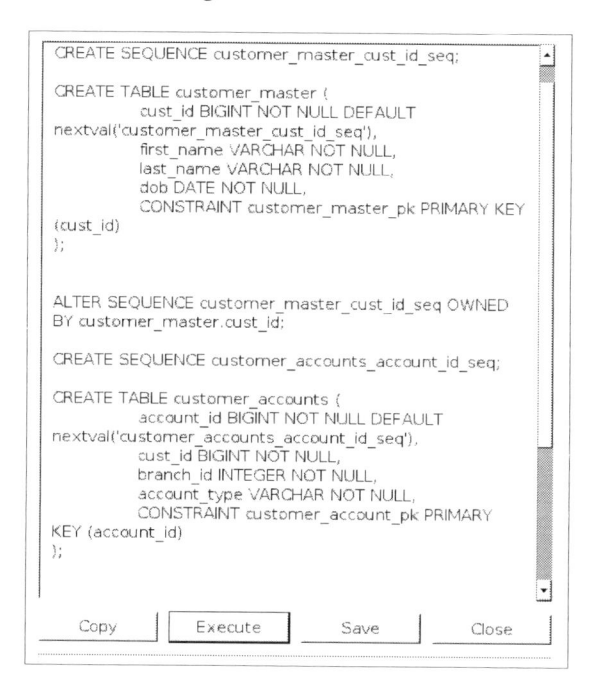

```
CREATE SEQUENCE customer_master_cust_id_seq;

CREATE TABLE customer_master (
        cust_id BIGINT NOT NULL DEFAULT nextval('customer_master_cust_id_seq'),
        first_name VARCHAR NOT NULL,
        last_name VARCHAR NOT NULL,
        dob DATE NOT NULL,
        CONSTRAINT customer_master_pk PRIMARY KEY (cust_id)
);

ALTER SEQUENCE customer_master_cust_id_seq OWNED BY customer_master.cust_id;

CREATE SEQUENCE customer_accounts_account_id_seq;

CREATE TABLE customer_accounts (
        account_id BIGINT NOT NULL DEFAULT nextval('customer_accounts_account_id_seq'),
        cust_id BIGINT NOT NULL,
        branch_id INTEGER NOT NULL,
        account_type VARCHAR NOT NULL,
        CONSTRAINT customer_account_pk PRIMARY KEY (account_id)
);
```

Copy | Execute | Save | Close

The XML generated is as follows:

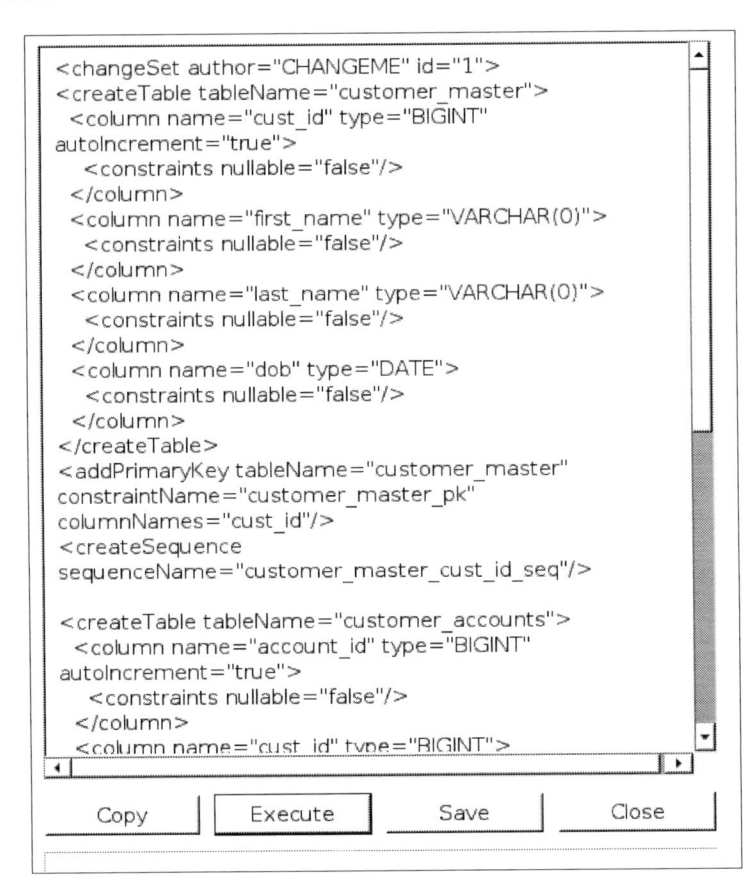

```
<changeSet author="CHANGEME" id="1">
<createTable tableName="customer_master">
  <column name="cust_id" type="BIGINT" autoIncrement="true">
    <constraints nullable="false"/>
  </column>
  <column name="first_name" type="VARCHAR(0)">
    <constraints nullable="false"/>
  </column>
  <column name="last_name" type="VARCHAR(0)">
    <constraints nullable="false"/>
  </column>
  <column name="dob" type="DATE">
    <constraints nullable="false"/>
  </column>
</createTable>
<addPrimaryKey tableName="customer_master" constraintName="customer_master_pk" columnNames="cust_id"/>
<createSequence sequenceName="customer_master_cust_id_seq"/>

<createTable tableName="customer_accounts">
  <column name="account_id" type="BIGINT" autoIncrement="true">
    <constraints nullable="false"/>
  </column>
  <column name="cust_id" type="BIGINT">
```

Now let's connect to a database to create the tables.

Navigate to **Connections | Add Source Connection | New Connection**. Fill in the appropriate values and click on **Test Connection**. If all is well, you should see **Connection test successful**, as shown in the following screenshot:

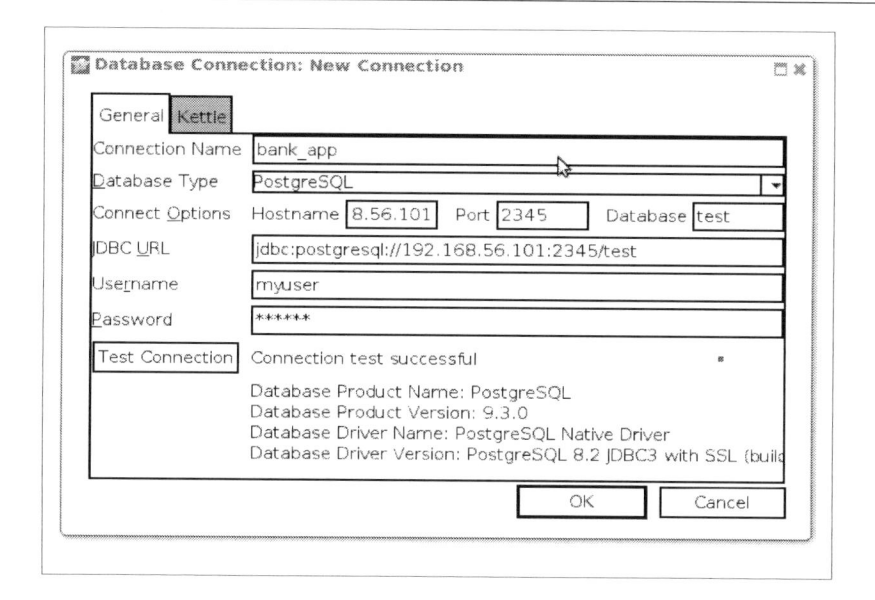

Now, we can again use the **Forward Engineer** option and create the tables in the newly added database. The option of saving the SQL is also there.

We can also use the **Forward Engineer** option to copy the data structure from one database to another. Assuming that the source database is MySQL and target is PostgreSQL, the steps will be as follows:

1. Add a connection for the source database (MySQL).
2. Add a connection for the target database (PostgreSQL).
3. Click on **Expand All Children** under the source connection in the database pane.
4. Drag and drop the objects you want to migrate in the object browser.
5. Use the **Forward Engineer** option and choose the PostgreSQL connection.
6. Inspect the script generated and select **Execute**.

7. We can use the **Copy Table Data** under **Tools** to move data from one database to another, as shown here:

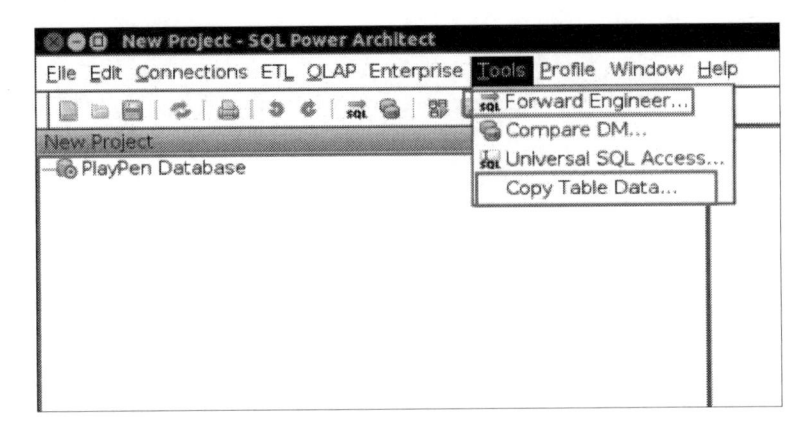

Reverse engineering and making changes

Let's try to reverse engineer from the database in which we created objects just now.

Click on **File** and select **New Project**. Then, in the left-hand side pane, right-click on **Add source connection** and choose the connection used in the previous step.

Right-click on the connection and choose **Expand All Children**.

Now, you can choose and drag and drop the objects you want in the right-hand side pane. When you do this, you will also see them in the left-hand side pane under **Playpen**. Now, changes can be made to the objects in the workspace. Once these changes are made, click on **Tools** to select **Compare DM**. Choose these options, as shown in the following screenshot. Ensure that **public** is chosen in the **schema** option (`information_schema` can be default), and the output format chosen is **PostgreSQL**. You get the SQL output, which can be either saved or executed:

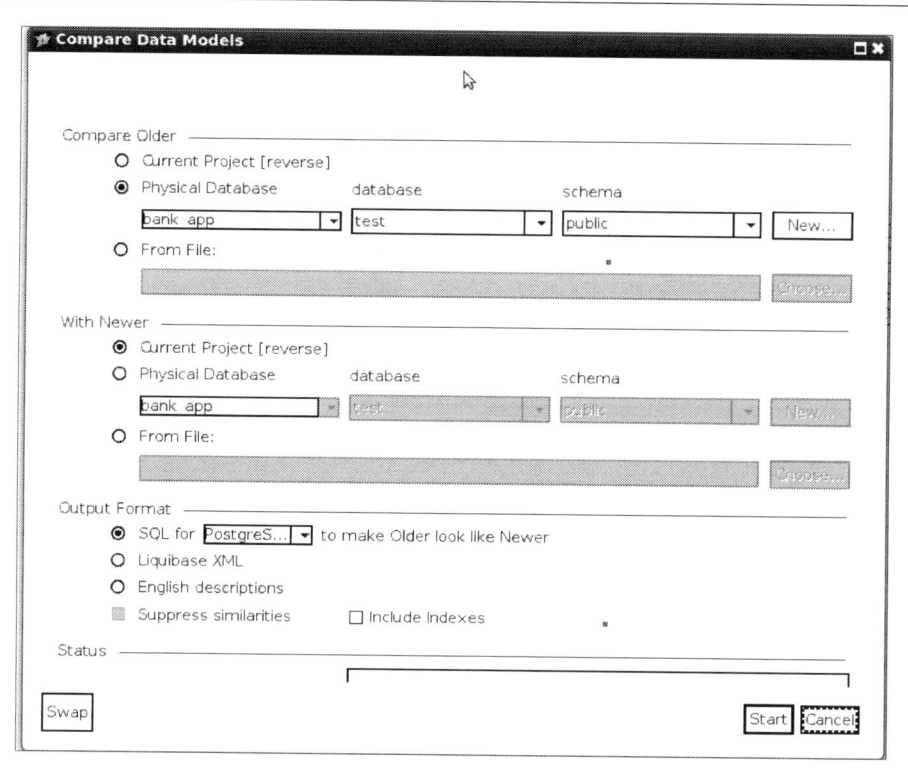

Exporting the data model

Now, we will see how we can export the data model we created. Click on **File** and you will see the **Export Playpen to PDF** and **Export as HTML** options. Choose **Generate HTML report**, select **Use built-in report** format, and choose a folder to save the file. An HTML file with the list of tables, proper links between the parent and child tables, and so on is generated.

> In *Chapter 12, PostgreSQL – Extras*, quite a few interesting data types such as RANGE, JSON, and HSTORE, and so on are covered. Go through them before you begin database design.

Profiling

Yet another useful feature of the tool is profiling. This feature is useful when you want to get an idea about the number of tables, columns, data types, and even data content in these tables. One word of caution: if the number of tables is big and/or the number of records runs into many thousands, the tool might take a long time. As the scanning process results in some load on the database server, it's better to use profiling in a development or staging environment rather than the production environment.

The profiling step itself is simple. In the left-hand side pane, right-click and choose **Add Source Connection**. Next, right-click on the database connection in the left-hand side pane and click on **Profile**. The output shows a list of tables. Choose the one you are interested in studying further, and click on **View** selected. This gives a detailed view of the table, columns, and data distribution, as shown in the following screenshot. Note that there is a Graph view, Table view, and Column view with different details. The graph view lets you choose any column and provides the values and their percentages, as shown in the following screenshot. The table values provide information (such as max length, min length, average length, max value, min value, and similar metrics). Here too, we have the option to **Export as PDF**, **Export as HTML**, and so on.

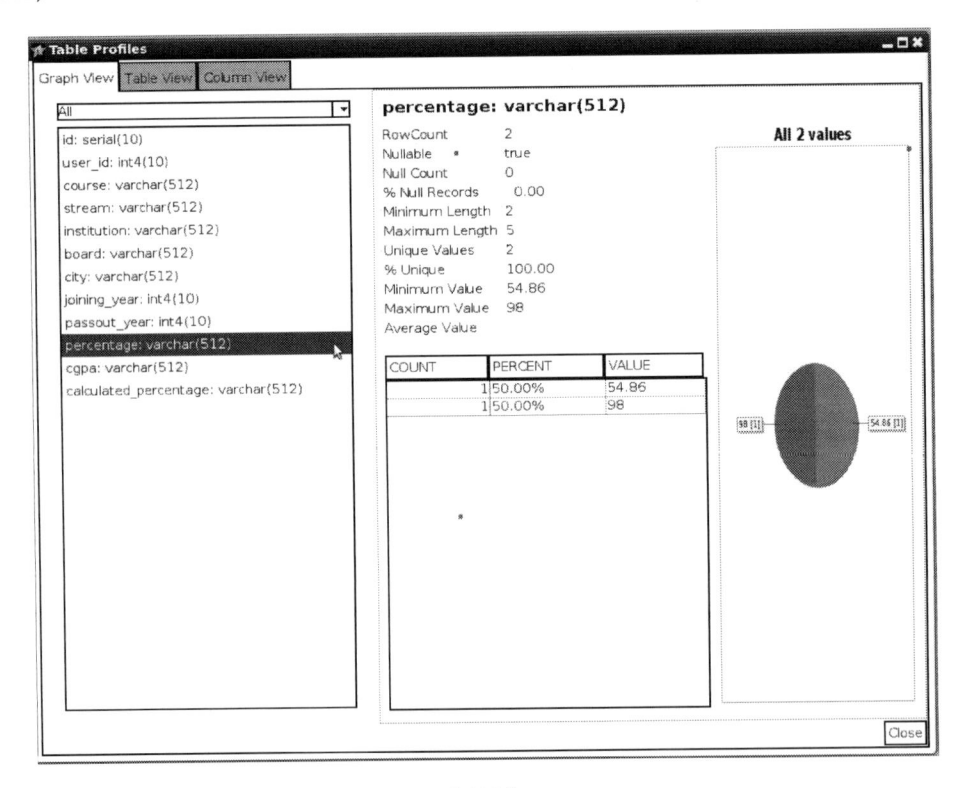

> Demo videos, some of which are relevant for the Community Edition also, are available at `http://www.sqlpower.ca/page/architect-demos`.

Summary

In this chapter, we covered the basic steps to be followed to design tables using SQL Power Architect. We also saw how to make changes and generate SQL to be applied to an existing database to sync it with the data model. Also, we covered the export options available for the data model. We also saw that we can profile an existing database with Power Architect.

In the next chapter, we will cover two client tools that can be used to work with a PostgreSQL database: pgAdmin3 and psql.

6
Client Tools

In the previous chapter, we looked at a tool that is used to design databases. Now, let's cover a few tools that are used with PostgreSQL to manipulate data, create, drop, and alter objects, find out what is happening on the server, and so on. In this chapter, we will cover one GUI and one command-line tool that are used to work with PostgreSQL. We will see how database connections are made, how SQL statements are executed, and how database objects and related metadata can be viewed. We will also look at a couple of advanced use cases (such as generating the plan for queries and changing configuration parameters).

GUI tools and command-line tools

psql is probably the most favored client tool to work with PostgreSQL, and pgAdmin is the popular GUI tool. We will cover a couple of basic features of pgAdmin and also have a look at a few not-so-basic features. To cover the tool exhaustively with screenshots, it will consume many pages and probably not add much value. There are other options such as phpPgAdmin and TOra, (toolkit for Oracle, but supports many databases) which you could explore.

pgAdmin – downloading and installation

The URL http://www.pgadmin.org/download/ provides links to various options to get the tool, including downloading and compiling from source. Compiling from source might not be easy, as there are quite a few dependencies and getting all of them to behave is a bit tough, unless you have been installing quite a bit of Linux- or Unix-based software via the compile-from-source option. For Windows, the tool can be installed using the point and click installer. For Linux-based systems, http://yum.postgresql.org/ and http://wiki.postgresql.org/wiki/Apt should provide the setup instructions.

Client Tools

> When you use the commands provided in the links to install pgAdmin, pay attention and ensure that you install only the pgAdmin software. If you just copy/paste the commands, you might end up overwriting your PostgreSQL installation.

Adding a server

The first thing we want to do once pgAdmin has been installed and started is set up a connection. For this, we use the **Add Server** option.

Click on **File** and choose **Add Server**. We get a dialog box with various options, as shown in the following screenshot:

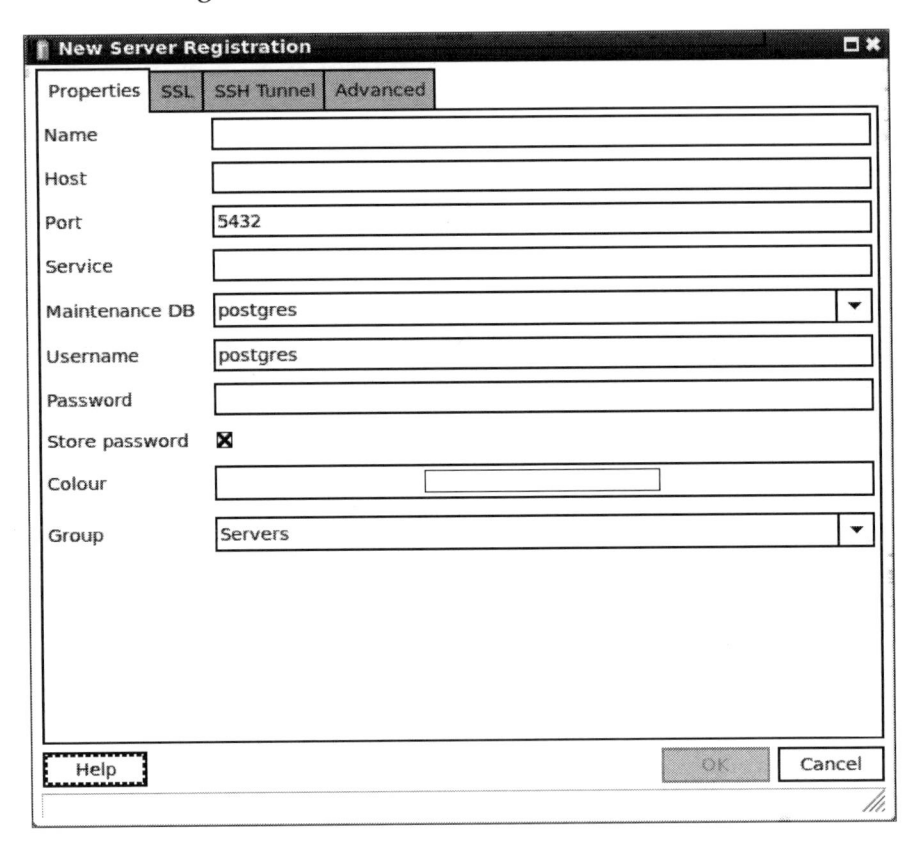

Let's look at these options in detail:

- **Name**: This can be anything that we want to use for reference. It could be `MyProductionServer1`. It's just an identifier to help us figure out which server we are looking at, if we work with many servers.
- **Host**: This is the IP address of the machine where our cluster is running. It can also be the fully qualified hostname.
- **Port**: This is the port where the cluster listens for requests.
- **Maintenance DB**: This is used to specify the initial database that pgAdmin connects to. It's the database where pgAdmin will check for optional but useful modules and extensions (such as `pgAgent` and `adminpack`).
- **Service**: This refers to the name of a service configured in the `pg_service.conf` file. We will not be using it. Detailed documentation about the file is available at http://www.postgresql.org/docs/current/interactive/libpq-pgservice.html.
- **Username**: This is the user that you will be connecting as. We could choose to save the password. If we do this, the password will be stored in a password file named `.pgpass` in the `home` directory if we are working in a Unix/Linux environment. In Windows, the password file will be under `%APPDATA%\postgresql\`, and the file will be named `pgpass.conf`. We can use the option under the **File** menu to edit the password file.

This covers the basic options. The other tabs have the not-so-basic settings. For example, we can use the **SSH Tunnel** option if the server does not allow direct connections from the client machine. This is useful when we are working for a client. Only a few machines in the client's network are allowed access from an external network. The machines on which databases are hosted will definitely not be among the machines exposed to external networks.

If you are working with the database cluster on a different machine, check whether you have modified the `postgresql.conf` (`listen_addresses` entry) and `pg_hba.conf` files on the server so that you can connect from a remote machine. The documentation links are http://www.postgresql.org/docs/current/static/runtime-config-connection.html and http://www.postgresql.org/docs/current/static/auth-pg-hba-conf.html.

Client Tools

The pgAdmin main window

Once we are connected to a server, we can go ahead and see what else is possible with pgAdmin. The main window has three panes, as shown in the following screenshot:

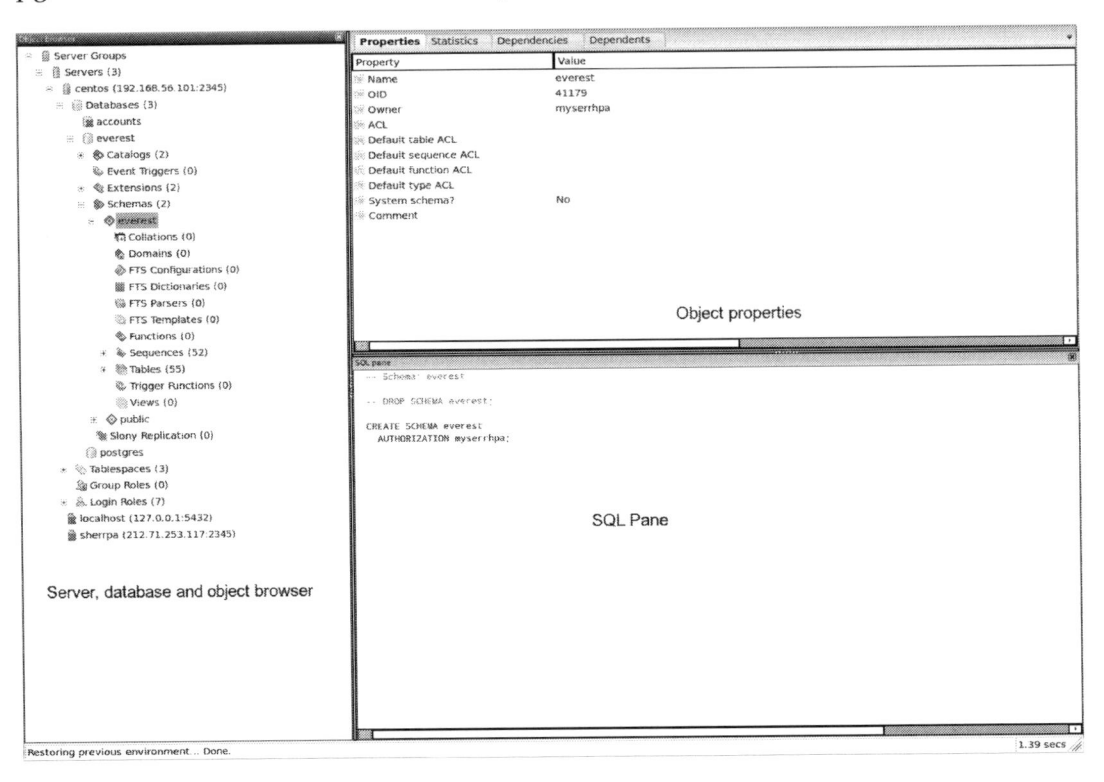

In the left-hand side pane, we have the **Object Browser** pane that shows all objects in a hierarchical manner. At the top of the hierarchy, we have **Server Groups** and then **Servers**. This is where choosing a good name for the server helps. At the next level and the levels below is the rest of the hierarchy is visible.

The top right-hand side pane provides quite a lot of very useful information. The first tab provides information such as name of the object, object identifier, estimated rows, and comment. Even more important, in many cases, is the next tab: **Statistics**. This provides information regarding reads, sequential scans, index scans, and other information that will be useful when we are trying to optimize database queries or having another look at the table design. The data shown in the **Statistics** tab as well as the other tabs in the right-hand side pane changes depending on the type of object we select in the object browser.

Chapter 6

The bottom right-hand side pane has the SQL for the object selected. Right-clicking on a table in the **Object Browser** pane gives you a few options. One of the options is the data viewer. In the data viewer menu, we can edit existing data, add new records, and delete records. The data viewer menu also lets us apply filters and select specific records.

In the case of a table, the right-click options lets us take a backup of the table, import data, restore from a backup, and so on, as shown in the following screenshot:

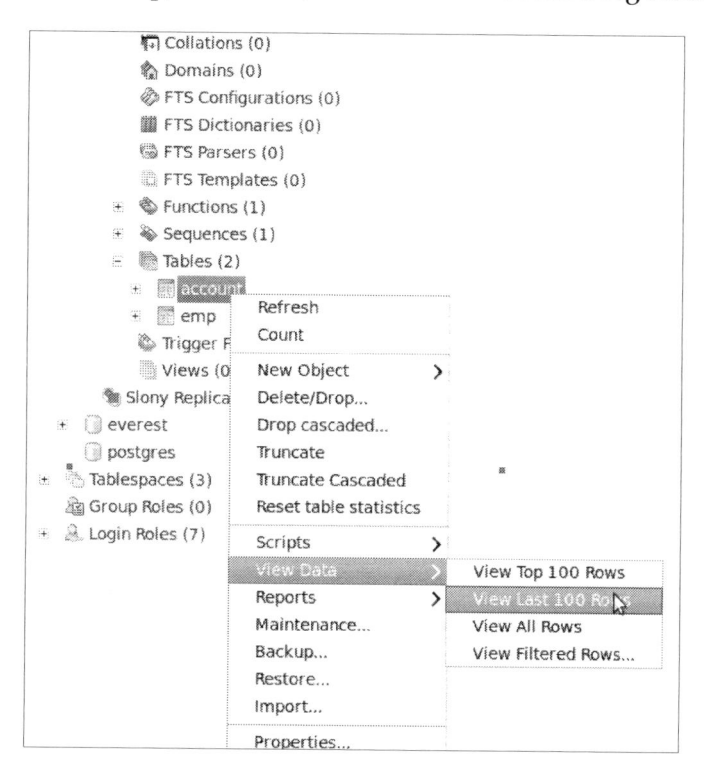

Client Tools

The **Tools** menu provides many useful options as well. The important ones are listed next. The **Server Configuration** option lets us see the current settings, edit them, and reload the parameter values, as shown in the following screenshot. Some of the settings need a server restart. So, the effect might not be visible immediately. The user must have appropriate permissions to use this feature.

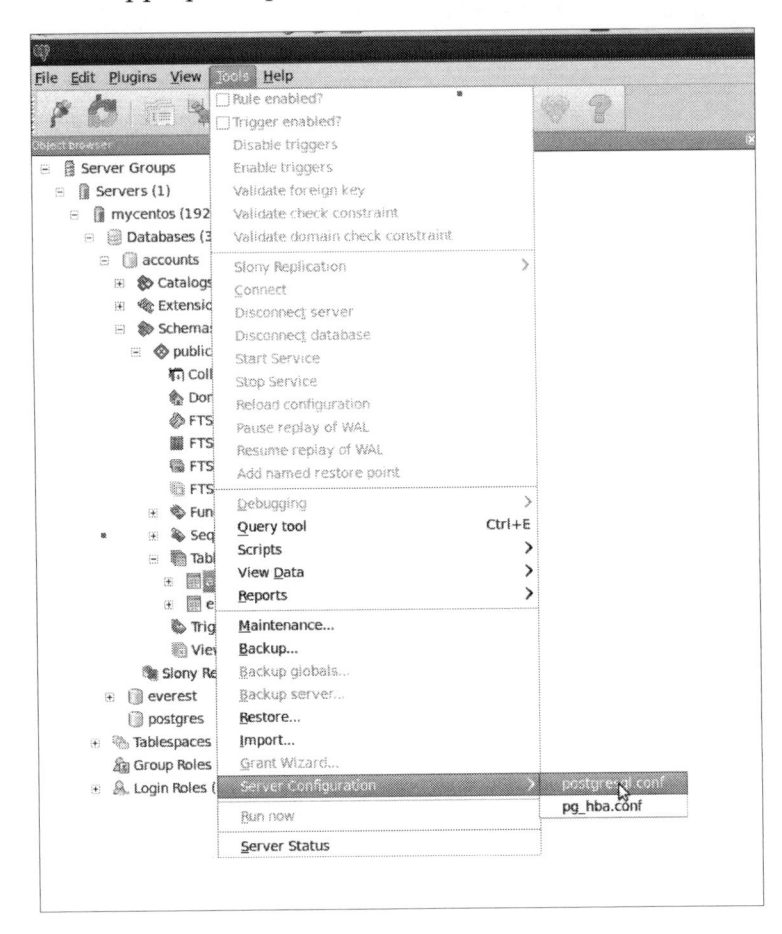

The **Server Status** option lets us see what is happening at the server. It lists the current activity, transactions, locks, and the information getting logged in to the log file. If you are not comfortable with the command-line tool and the PostgreSQL views, which store database activity data, this option can be used to retrieve pretty much the same information that you could get from these views. In addition, we can also retrieve past log files, as shown in the following screenshot:

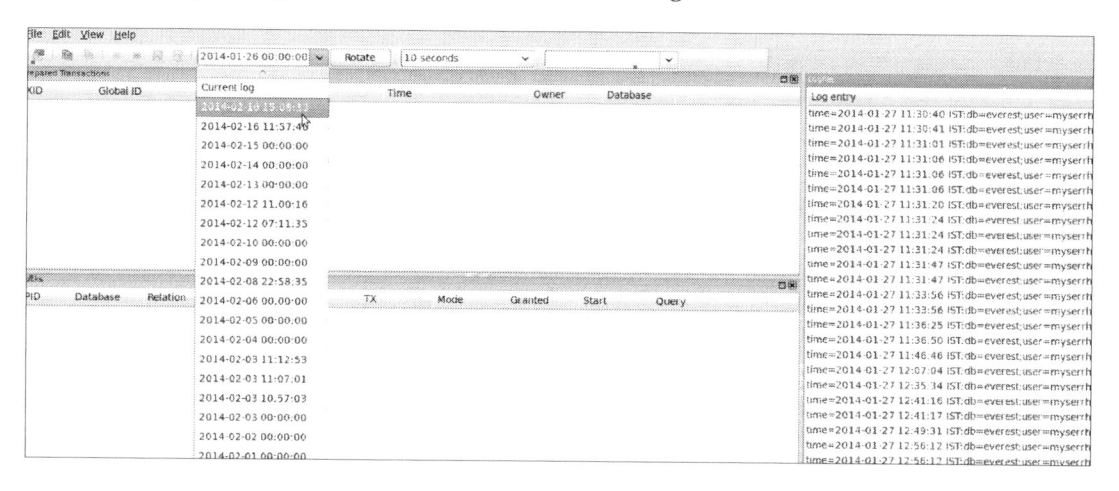

The Query tool

Once a database with the important tables is in place, we are likely to spend quite a lot of time querying the tables, manipulating the data, writing functions, and so on. For this, the **Query** tool can be used. The **Query** tool is one of the options we get when we choose the **Tools** option. The **Query** tool option gets activated only after we are connected to a database.

Client Tools

In the **Query** tool, writing and executing a SQL statement is a straightforward thing to do. It also has a graphical query builder, which is intuitive for simple queries. As shown in the following screenshot, we can choose the tables and columns we need, join tables by choosing the columns from one table and then drag it to the column to be joined within the other table:

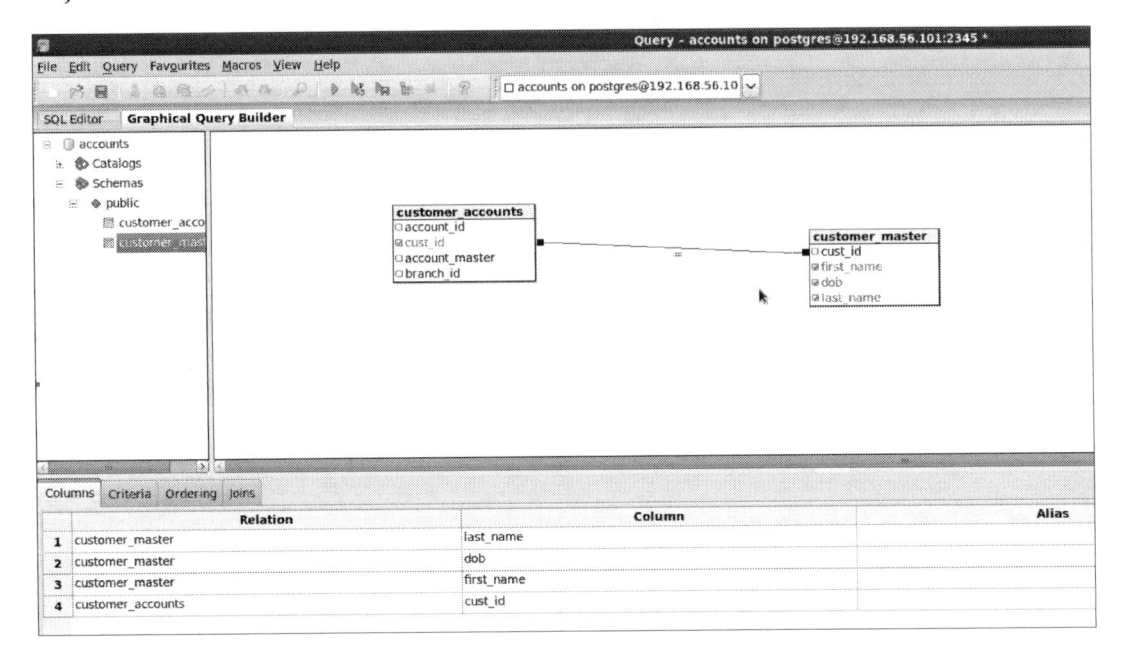

The query generated is provided here:

```
SELECT
    customer_master.last_name,
    customer_master.dob,
    customer_master.first_name,
    customer_accounts.cust_id
FROM
    public.customer_accounts,
    public.customer_master
WHERE
    customer_accounts.cust_id = customer_master.cust_id;
```

[112]

Chapter 6

Another useful feature is the **Explain** pane. We can select a query and use *Shift + F7* to generate a graphical query execution plan. The plan for the preceding query is displayed as follows:

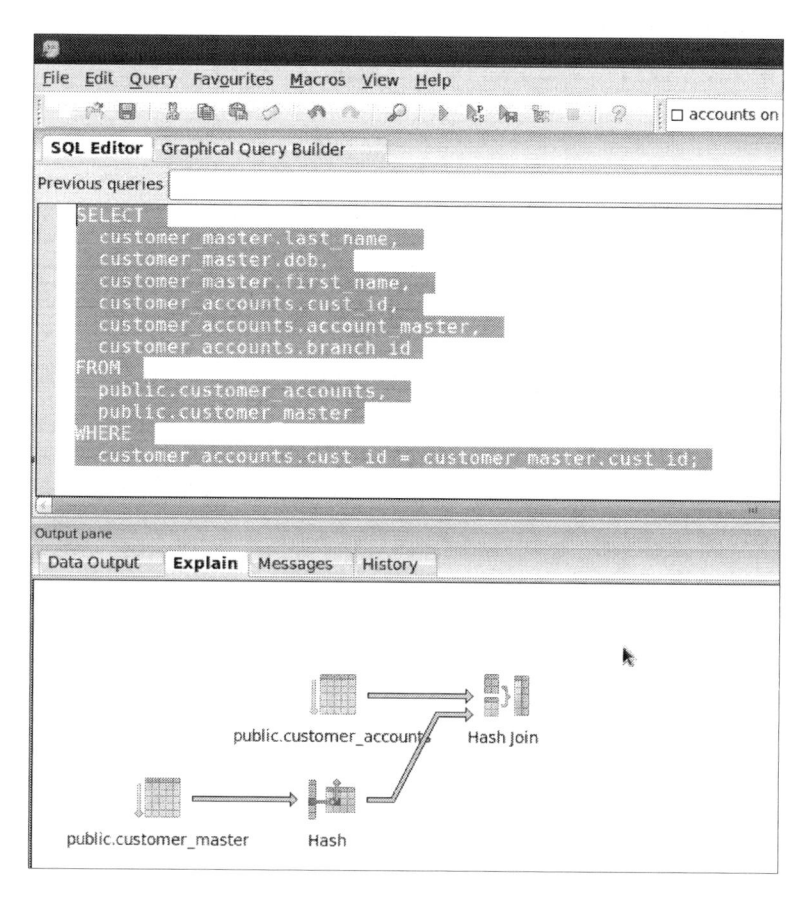

pgAdmin does provide us with many more features. We can click on **File** and then select **Options** to set which object types should be displayed in the **Object Browser** pane. The right-click options in **Database** or **Tables** lets us carry out maintenance activities (such as vacuuming and analyzing). Right-clicking on **Tables** provides a **Script** menu that can be used to generate scripts for the CREATE, SELECT, INSERT, UPDATE, and DELETE statements. We can also generate reports from the database.

> It's necessary to install the adminpack extension for some of the features to work. This can be done using the CREATE EXTENSION command.

[113]

Client Tools

This covers the features one will use most frequently in pgAdmin. Next, we will cover psql—the command-line utility to work with PostgreSQL clusters.

psql – working from the command line

psql is a very powerful command-line tool and is superior to similar utilities available with other databases. For example, if we are not sure about the name of a table (did I name it emp, employee, or employees?), the only option available in Oracle's SQL* Plus is to query a data dictionary view (such as user_tables or tab) with a LIKE filter. In psql, we can just type \dt e and hit *Tab* twice to get the list of tables starting with e. In short, psql supports tab completion—a nifty feature that is a great productivity booster. Now that it sounds interesting, let's look at more.

psql – connection options

The psql --help command lists all possible options that can be used with psql. We might want to use psql to execute a command, or to connect to a database and remain at the psql prompt to carry out many activities, execute queries, describe tables, create users, alter objects, and so on. Either way, psql needs to know:

- the host on which the PostgreSQL cluster is running
- the port at which the cluster is listening
- the database to which connection is to be made
- the user ID and password (depends on the authentication method)

Each of these options can be provided in a one letter form or in a detailed manner. For example, we could say which database to connect to use -d mydatabase or --dbname=mydatabase, as shown here:

```
psql --host=localhost --dbname=test
psql (9.3.0)
Type "help" for help.

test=# \q


psql  -h localhost -d test
psql (9.3.0)
Type "help" for help.

test=# \q
```

[114]

Chapter 6

It makes sense to use the long option initially to get familiar with the possible options. In the case of options (such as port) `--port` is pretty clear, but if we type `-P`, the error appears because `-P` is to specify printing options, not port. We use `-p` to specify port:

```
psql -h localhost -d test -U postgres -P 5432
\pset: unknown option: 5432
psql: could not set printing parameter "5432"
```

While we can definitely execute queries once we are at the psql prompt, it's the rich set of meta-commands that deserve more attention. To say that we can execute SQL is to state the obvious.

The power of \d

Any command that starts with a backslash is referred to as a meta-command. Among the numerous meta-commands, it's likely that you will find `\d` to be most useful. `\d` has a number of options. In its simplest form, without any options, it lists all user-created objects in the database, as shown here (first, create a database `myobjects` and a few objects of different types if you want to follow along, or you could try it on the database you have created):

```
myobjects=# \d
             List of relations
 Schema |    Name    |   Type   |  Owner
--------+------------+----------+----------
 public | mysequence | sequence | postgres
 public | mytable    | table    | postgres
 public | myview     | view     | postgres
(3 rows)
```

If you want to just see the tales, use `\dt` (`t` for table):

```
myobjects=# \dt
          List of relations
 Schema |  Name   | Type  |  Owner
--------+---------+-------+----------
 public | mytable | table | postgres
(1 row)
myobjects=# \ds
             List of relations
 Schema |    Name    |   Type   |  Owner
--------+------------+----------+----------
 public | mysequence | sequence | postgres
(1 row)
```

Client Tools

```
myobjects=# \dv
           List of relations
 Schema |  Name  | Type | Owner
--------+--------+------+----------
 public | myview | view | postgres
(1 row)

myobjects=# \df
                              List of functions
 Schema |  Name  | Result data type | Argument data types |  Type
--------+--------+------------------+---------------------+--------
 public | myfunc | integer          | integer, integer    | normal
(1 row)
```

We can use s for sequence, v for view, f for function, and so on. For schemas, we have to use n, which denotes namespace. A + sign at the end will give us some more information (such as comments for tables and additional information for functions), as shown in the following screenshot:

```
myobjects=# \df+
                                                    List of functions
 Schema |  Name  | Result data type | Argument data types |  Type  | Security | Volatility |  Owner   | Language | Source code  | Description
--------+--------+------------------+---------------------+--------+----------+------------+----------+----------+--------------+-------------
 public | myfunc | integer          | integer, integer    | normal | invoker  | immutable  | postgres | sql      | select $1 + $2; |
(1 row)
myobjects=# \dt+
                        List of relations
 Schema |  Name   | Type  |  Owner   | Size    | Description
--------+---------+-------+----------+---------+-------------
 public | mytable | table | postgres | 0 bytes | My table
(1 row)
myobjects=# \dt
           List of relations
 Schema |  Name   | Type  |  Owner
--------+---------+-------+----------
 public | mytable | table | postgres
(1 row)
```

The + sign is very useful when we want to see a view or function definition. \d without any letter after it is interpreted as \dtvsE. In this, E stands for foreign tables. We have already covered the rest.

By the way, we can also use patterns, as shown here:

```
myobjects-# \dt my*
           List of relations
 Schema |  Name   | Type  |  Owner
--------+---------+-------+----------
 public | mytable | table | postgres
 public | mytbl   | table | postgres
(2 rows)

myobjects-# \dt myta*
           List of relations
 Schema |  Name   | Type  |  Owner
--------+---------+-------+----------
 public | mytable | table | postgres
(1 row)

myobjects-#
```

We can use psql with the -E option. This will display all the SQL statements used by PostgreSQL internally when we execute a \d command or other backslash commands. In the following example, the setting is turned ON from psql:

```
test=# \dx
                     List of installed extensions
      Name      | Version |   Schema   |             Description
----------------+---------+------------+--------------------------------------
 pg_buffercache | 1.0     | public     | examine the shared buffer cache
 pgpool_recovery| 1.0     | public     | recovery functions for pgpool-II
 plpgsql        | 1.0     | pg_catalog | PL/pgSQL procedural language
(3 rows)

test=# \set ECHO_HIDDEN
test=# \dx
********* QUERY *********
SELECT e.extname AS "Name", e.extversion AS "Version", n.nspname AS "Schema", c.description AS "Description"
FROM pg_catalog.pg_extension e LEFT JOIN pg_catalog.pg_namespace n ON n.oid = e.extnamespace LEFT JOIN pg_catalog.pg_description c ON c.objoid = e.oid AND c.classoid =
'pg_catalog.pg_extension'::pg_catalog.regclass
ORDER BY 1;
*************************

                     List of installed extensions
      Name      | Version |   Schema   |             Description
----------------+---------+------------+--------------------------------------
 pg_buffercache | 1.0     | public     | examine the shared buffer cache
 pgpool_recovery| 1.0     | public     | recovery functions for pgpool-II
 plpgsql        | 1.0     | pg_catalog | PL/pgSQL procedural language
(3 rows)
```

After the setting is turned ON, we can see the query executed:

psql rocks!

More meta-commands

The \h command provides help. So does \?. The first one provides help for SQL commands, whereas the second one provides help for psql commands (for example, meta-commands).

In previous chapters, we saw that many host commands can be executed from the psql prompt in the following manner. The example also shows how output can be redirected to a file. Note that in the first command where we redirect output, there is no ! after \:

```
test=# \o out.txt
test=# show data_directory;
test=# \! cat out.txt
 data_directory
----------------
 /pgdata/9.3
(1 row)

test=# \! ls
out.txt
test=# \o
test=# \! rm out.txt
test=# \! ls
```

Client Tools

The file is gone. Now, we will see how we can execute SQL statements in a file from psql. We use the \i option for this:

```
test=# \! echo "SELECT 1; " > a.sql
test=# \i a.sql
 ?column?
----------
        1
(1 row)

test=# \! cat a.sql
SELECT 1;
```

Another important command is to change the setting for timing. How much time the query is taking is something we want to know when we are trying to optimize a query. To enable this, we can use the following code:

```
postgres=# \timing
Timing is off.
postgres=# \timing
Timing is on.
postgres=# select now();
              now
-------------------------------
 2014-02-19 03:06:53.785452+00
(1 row)

Time: 0.202 ms
```

Timing is a toggle option. It makes sense to have this on by default. In addition to timing, there can be other non-default settings that we want to use. These can be set using the .psqlrc file. Let's see how it works. psql will look for the system-wide startup file (psqlrc) and the user-specific startup file (.psqlrc) and execute commands in these files before accepting user input. If these files are not found, psql will go ahead with the default settings. In Windows, the personal startup file will be %APPDATA%\postgresql\psqlrc.conf. We can create these files if they are not present, which is likely. We will create a file with two non-default settings and see how they work. We will change the timing option and psql prompt to non-default values. In the home directory, create a file named .psqlrc, and make these two entries:

```
\set PROMPT1 '%n@%/   '
\timing
```

The following screenshot illustrates the effect of the settings:

```
[postgres@MyCentOS ~]$ more .psqlrc
\set PROMPT1 '%n@%/ '
\timing
[postgres@MyCentOS ~]$ psql -d test
Timing is on.
psql (9.3.0)
Type "help" for help.

postgres@test select 1;
 ?column?
----------
        1
(1 row)

Time: 2.001 ms
postgres@test \q
[postgres@MyCentOS ~]$ mv .psqlrc .psqlrcb
[postgres@MyCentOS ~]$ psql -d test
psql (9.3.0)
Type "help" for help.

test=# select 1;
 ?column?
----------
        1
(1 row)
```

The prompt has changed to include the user (%n), the symbol (@), and database name (%/). The file was renamed to .psqlrcb just to see what the prompt looked like if there was no .psqlrc file. We can try renaming the .psqlrcb file to .psqlrc so that it's used by psql. Add an entry in the file, as shown here:

```
\set HISTFILE ~/history-:DBNAME
```

If we connect to a couple of databases and exit, for each database we connected to, there will be a separate history file.

> Executing \conninfo at the psql prompt gives us information (such as user, database connected to, and port).

By now, we have covered most of the commands that can be used to get information about the environment, switch between databases, read from and write to files, and so on. For an exhaustive listing of the possibilities, we can get help for meta-commands at the psql prompt by typing \?. The commands are neatly grouped together into different sets: general, query buffer, input/output, and so on. Also, refer to http://www.postgresql.org/docs/current/static/app-psql.html for more options and explanation.

Client Tools

Setting up the environment

We will usually work with a specific set of servers and databases. Typing in the information regarding the database name, user, host, port, and so on, can get tedious. With pgAdmin, we can store the information for different environments. What about psql? This is where environment variables help. The following list covers a few important variables (there are more):

- PGHOST: This is the address of the host where the cluster is running
- PGPORT: This is the port at which the server is listening
- PGDATABASE: This is the database to connect to
- PGUSER: This is the database that the user can connect to

Now, we can create a few environment files and source them as required. There can be better options, but this is one. Let's create a file named .mylocalenv. Its entries are as follows:

```
$ more .mylocalenv
export PGHOST=localhost
export PGPORT=5432
export PGUSER=postgres
export PGDATABASE=myobjects
```

We can source the file as follows:

```
$ source ./.mylocalenv
```

Ensure that the values have been set as:

```
$ env | grep PG
PGPORT=5432
PGUSER=postgres
PGDATABASE=myobjects
PGHOST=localhost
```

Now, try connecting:

```
$ psql
Password:
psql (9.3.0)
Type "help" for help.

myobjects=# SELECT current_database();
 current_database
------------------
 myobjects
(1 row)
```

One item that we left out is the password. It's not a good idea to set this as an environment variable. For this, we use the `.pgpass` file in our `home` directory. A reference to this file was made in the pgAdmin section.

The `.pgpass` file contains entries in `host:port:database:user:password` form; for example:

```
more ~/.pgpass
localhost:5432:myobjects:postgres:tcc123
```

If we try to connect to the default database (`myobjects`, that is, the database set in the `env` file), it does not ask for a password. However, if we try to connect to another database, the password prompt appears:

```
$ psql
psql (9.3.0)
Type "help" for help.

myobjects=# \q
postgres@jayadevan-Vostro-2520:~$ psql -d postrges
Password:
```

> The password is stored as plain text in the `.pgpass` file. This is not the recommended method to store passwords.

History of commands

The `\s` command lists all the commands you have executed so far. The data is stored in `~/.psql_history`, that is, `.psql_history` under the `home` directory of the Linux user under which we are connecting to psql.

Summary

In this chapter, we covered two PostgreSQL tools: one GUI tool and one command-line tool. While the GUI tool might be easier to learn than the other one, it's better to learn the command-line tool because it provides you with a lot of flexibility. For example, you could create SQL files, call them from shell scripts and schedule them in cron. For such automated batch jobs, psql usually proves to be more powerful than a GUI tool. Also, for efficiency, it's better to work from command line. Typing \d and hitting *Enter* is faster than moving the mouse around; click on an icon and wait for the data to be displayed. In some cases, such as the execution plan for a query, the visual display might be easier to understand than text. Choosing between a point-and-click option and a command-line option is definitely a matter of personal preference. You can take your pick.

In the next chapter, we will take a look at the PostgreSQL optimizer and see how queries can be optimized with this information.

7
SQL Tuning

Having covered how to access PostgreSQL using client tools, it's time to focus on queries and query optimization. First, we will cover a few facts before looking at the decisions the optimizer has to take. Finally, we will cover a few optimization strategies and a few rules of thumb to be followed.

We need to realize that query optimization does not always mean rewriting queries. It might involve changing table definitions, creating indexes, and sometimes even dropping indexes. It's also necessary to understand what information the optimizer needs to arrive at optimal plans. Let's cover a few facts about how databases are used and how do they work.

Understanding basic facts about databases

Let's understand a few facts about databases.

Fact 1 – databases are more frequently read from than written to

In almost all applications, except in the rarest of rare cases, a piece of data is read many times and written to or changed a few times. It's important to keep this fact in mind when we try to optimize queries. Let's look at a few examples.

First, let's consider a site http://www.expedia.com. The flight fares for a specific route get updated a few times at most for a specific class of seats and a specific date range. However, these sets of data will be queried many, many times by users around the world before a booking (a set of writes) eventually happens. This is often referred to as look to book ratio. It can range from 10:1 to a really high ratio like 50:1 or more in some cases.

SQL Tuning

Let's consider banking applications. We very often check our account balances. Even when we use an online platform with the sole purpose of transferring money to another account, there is the account balance page coming up, resulting in a read. In addition, there will be the numerous reads happening against each account (for transactions and balances) to generate daily reports to meet the banks' internal as well as mandatory/legal reporting requirements. When we consider social networking and blogging sites, most of us read more than write. If the content is served by databases (even otherwise), this means more reads than writes.

Then, there are the cases of systems that are possible candidates for big data or NoSQL solutions. An example could be data read from thousands or millions of sensors/devices in a city and written to a data sink. The data can be displayed in huge screens in a command center for a few seconds (that is, data is read and displayed). The data will be read again to aggregate thousands of records to form one of many points used to plot trends in a chart, depicting power consumption for the city across time periods and seasons.

In short, databases are more frequently read from than written to. Why is this relevant? Very often, something we do to improve the performance of a read query, such as creating an index, can result in a minor increase in the time to write to the table. The index also needs to be updated, right? So, we need to consider the impact on writes, but also remember the fact that the benefit from improved read performance usually outweighs the slightly deteriorated write performance.

Fact 2 – data is always read in blocks or pages, not as individual records or columns

When we ask a PostgreSQL database to fetch one column from a record in a table with 30 columns and millions of records, PostgreSQL fetches one block of 8 KB. Similarly, when we change the value of a column in a record, PostgreSQL will read and then write an 8 KB block. If we look at database/query optimization techniques, we will realize that most of them are focused on a couple of items:

- Reduce the number of read/written blocks. The focus here is not on physical reads/writes but the number of blocks accessed.
- Reduce physical I/O.

These two together cover probably most of the techniques we adopt to reduce database bottlenecks. There are other possibilities such as using disks with higher RPM or moving to Solid State Disks. We also try to reduce CPU utilization.

Approaches to reducing the number of blocks read/written

Let's see how the most common approaches to optimization eventually end up reducing the number of blocks accessed:

- **Indexing**: When a SELECT, UPDATE, or DELETE query affecting a few records out of a big dataset takes time, we create an index on the column or columns on which filters are applied. What creating an index does is reduce the number of blocks that have to be scanned to return the relevant records. The term SELECTIVITY is used to refer to the proportion of records that will be retrieved.

- **Normalization**: When we split one fat table into smaller tables by applying the rules of normalization, the number of columns goes down in the resultant tables. As a consequence, each of the resultant tables occupies fewer blocks compared to the original table. When data from one of the new tables is to be fetched or updated, fewer blocks have to be read.

- **Partitioning**: Often, we split a table with a really huge number of records into many smaller pieces or partitions. While normalization reduces the number of columns in the resultant tables, partitioning splits the table horizontally. When data is fetched based on filters applied on the partition key, the optimizer is able to figure out that the data resides in one or more specific partitions and is able to avoid scanning the entire table. In effect, there is a dip in the number of blocks to be fetched. Partitioning mostly helps in the case of very large tables and not in the case of small tables.

Keeping this in mind, let's move on and cover the query execution process in PostgreSQL.

Query execution components

PostgreSQL query execution involves the following four key components:

- **Parser**: This performs syntax and semantic checking of the SQL string
- **Rewriter**: This changes the query is some cases; for example, if the query is against a view, the rewriter will modify the query so that it goes against the base tables instead of the view
- **Planner**: This key component comes up with a plan of execution
- **Executor**: This executes the plan generated by the planner

Planner

The planner's job is to come up with a plan of execution. A plan is a tree consisting of one or more nodes. Each node, on execution, returns zero or more tuples. These tuples are used by the parent nodes in the tree until we reach the root node, which returns the results to the client. The planner has to make a few decisions, which we will cover now.

Access methods

Consider a simple query:

```
SELECT FIRST_NAME, LAST_NAME FROM EMP WHERE DEPT_NAME = 'HR'
```

A crucial decision the optimizer has to take is how to get the data that the user wants. Should it:

- Fetch the data from a table, or
- Go to an index, and
- Stop here because all the columns required are there in the index (PostgreSQL Version 9.2 and higher only), or
- Get the location of the records and go to the table to get the data

The first method, fetching data directly from table, is called **Sequential Scan** (**Seq Scan**). This works best for small tables.

In the second set of options, if there is no need to access the table, we have an **Index Only Scan**.

On the other hand, if it's necessary to access the table after accessing the index, there are two options. A bitmapped index scan where a bitmap is created representing the matching tuples. Then, the records are fetched from the table (also referred to as heap). This is a two-step process; executed one after the other sequentially. The second approach is to read the index and then the table sequentially. These steps can be repeated one after the other many times until all records of interest are fetched.

The preceding section just covered a single table and index scenario. What about scenarios where we join quite a few tables? We could have INNER JOINs, OUTER JOINs (LEFT, RIGHT, or FULL), or CROSS JOINs, among others. In these cases, PostgreSQL has to decide the join strategy.

> The words INNER and OUTER are optional. PostgreSQL assumes INNER as default. If we specify LEFT, RIGHT, or FULL, an OUTER join is implied.

Join strategies

Join strategies refer to how the tables are to be joined. The possible strategies are as follows:

In the nested loop approach, each record from one table is taken and then there is a loop where it's compared with each record in the other table. If there is a match, the record is emitted:

- For each outer tuple
- For each inner tuple
- If the join condition is met
    - Emit result row

The cost is proportional to the product of the number records in the tables.

Another join strategy is to sort the datasets from both tables and then scan through the sorted sets, matching the values and returning the records when there is a match. This is called the sort-merge join.

The third option called the hash join is used in equi joins. In this approach, each row from one of the tables is hashed to create a hash table. Typically, this is done for the smaller table. Then, each row from the other table is hashed and the hash table created is probed to find a match.

In addition to the preceding decisions, there are decisions about sorting, aggregating, and/or pipelining the data. We can represent the important categories of plan nodes and decisions, as shown in the following diagram:

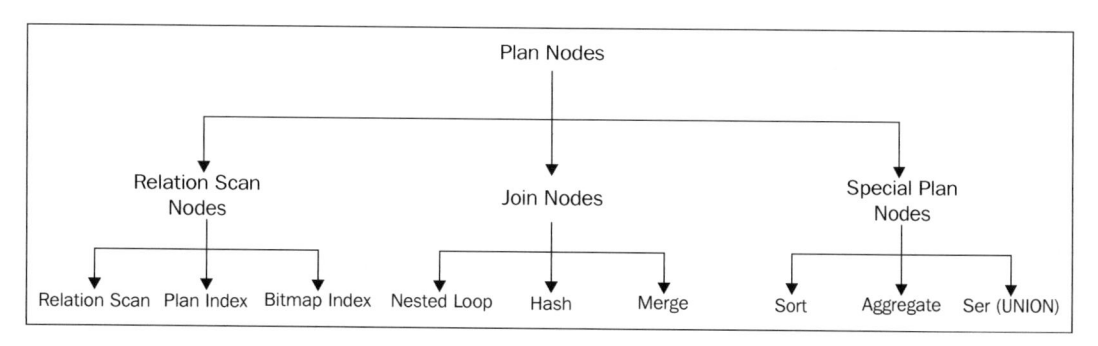

```
                            Plan Nodes
                                │
        ┌───────────────────────┼───────────────────────┐
        ▼                       ▼                       ▼
   Relation Scan            Join Nodes            Special Plan
      Nodes                                          Nodes
        │                       │                       │
   ┌────┼────┐             ┌────┼────┐            ┌─────┼─────┐
   ▼    ▼    ▼             ▼    ▼    ▼            ▼     ▼     ▼
Relation Plan Bitmap    Nested  Hash Merge       Sort Aggregate Ser (UNION)
 Scan   Index Index      Loop
```

[127]

SQL Tuning

> For a detailed look at the planner, refer to http://www.postgresqlconference.org/sites/default/files/The%20PostgreSQL%20Query%20Planner.odp, and for planner internals, refer to https://www.pgcon.org/2011/schedule/attachments/188_Planner%20talk.pdf.

Finding the execution plan

Now, we know that the planner has quite a few decisions to make and that these decisions will ultimately decide the execution time as well as consumption of resources (CPU, memory, and disk I/O). How do we know what decision the planner will take? We can use the EXPLAIN command to find out the possible (note that it's possible) execution plan. To use EXPLAIN, we have to just prefix the EXPLAIN word to the SQL statement we want to execute, as shown here:

```
EXPLAIN SELECT first_name FROM customer_master
WHERE first_name = 'Carolee';
                    QUERY PLAN
-----------------------------------------------------------------
Seq Scan on customer_master  (cost=0.00..271.62 rows=3 width=6)
   Filter: ((first_name)::text = 'Carolee'::text)
(2 rows)
```

The query plan should be read from most indented to least intended: from bottom to top. Each line with cost/rows/width is a node. The inner (child) nodes feed the outer (parent) nodes. In the preceding plan, there are no child nodes. Let's look at each word/number and see what it means.

The first part in the second line says `Filter`, meaning a filter is being applied. The data type is also mentioned. The first part of the first line says `Seq Scan on customer_master`. The table will be scanned in a sequential manner to get the relevant records. Then, we have cost. Costs are estimates of the effort a node will take. It's calculated in terms of a few variables (such as page reads and operator evaluations), based on the total data size and estimates of the number of rows that will be fetched.

Each cost entry has two parts: a startup cost and a total cost. Unless it's a really heavy query, startup costs for the innermost nodes are likely to be zero or close to zero. Startup cost is the work to be done to get the first row. For parent nodes, the startup cost will be close to the total cost of the child nodes, implying that the child node has to finish for the parent node to start processing data. This also means that the total cost of a parent node will be the total cost of the child nodes plus the node-specific cost of the parent itself.

The next entry: rows is an estimate of the number of records the node will return. The third entry: width is the estimated average width (in bytes) of each row.

Using EXPLAIN provides estimates. If we add ANALYZE, PostgreSQL executes the query and then provides the following output:

```
EXPLAIN ANALYZE SELECT first_name FROM customer_master where first_name = 'Carolee';
                              QUERY PLAN
-----------------------------------------------------------------
-------------------------------------------------
Seq Scan on customer_master  (cost=0.00..271.62 rows=3 width=6)
(actual time=87.598..119.012 rows=2 loops=1)
   Filter: ((first_name)::text = 'Carolee'::text)
   Rows Removed by Filter: 14208
 Total runtime: 119.051 ms
(4 rows)
```

Quite a bit of extra information is available now: actual time, rows, loops, Rows Removed by Filter, and Total runtime. The terms by themselves are self-explanatory. What we should pay attention to is whether the estimates and actual differ from each other. For example, the rows value is 3 in the estimate and 2 in actual. If there is a big difference between estimates and actual, we know that either the optimizer does not have the up-to-date information or the optimizer's estimates are off for some other reason.

Two other useful options available with EXPLAIN are FORMAT and BUFFERS.

If you execute the same query more than twice in succession, you might find that the Total runtime comes down significantly. This is the effect of data being read from buffer. This can be seen if we use the buffers option.

The output of EXPLAIN can be provided in different formats: TEXT, XML, JSON, or YAML. Let's see parts of the output form and understand these two options:

```
EXPLAIN (ANALYZE,buffers,format yaml) SELECT first_name FROM
customer_master WHERE first_name = 'Carolee';
```

When we execute this after a database restart, we get the following output (only a few lines displayed):

```
       Shared Hit Blocks: 0                               +
       Shared Read Blocks: 94                             +
  Total Runtime: 2.061
```

SQL Tuning

The next time, we get this:

```
Shared Hit Blocks: 94                    +
Shared Read Blocks: 0                    +
Total Runtime: 1.462
```

The difference is obvious: reads went down, hits went up, and runtime went down, implying that the data to be fetched was available in the buffer.

For a complete list of options available with `EXPLAIN`, refer to http://www.postgresql.org/docs/current/static/sql-explain.html.

> `EXPLAIN` can be also used for the `UPDATE`, `DELETE`, and `INSERT` statements. To avoid data changes when you do this, use the following command:
> **BEGIN;**
> **EXPLAIN ANALYZE ...;**
> **ROLLBACK;**

> To get a formatted output of `EXPLAIN` (along with color-coding of output) to mark nodes that need close investigation and a lot of other useful information, you can post the output of `EXPLAIN` at http://explain.depesz.com/.

Optimization guidelines and catches

We had a very brief and quick look at the decisions taken by the planner. We now know how to find out what decisions were taken by the planner using `EXPLAIN ANALYZE`. Now, let's look at a few rules of thumb to be followed to ensure that SQL statements fetch results in a reasonable amount of time. Some of the rules deal with creating indexes, whereas others deal with avoiding certain types of queries.

Indexing foreign keys

When we create a foreign key, we have a parent-child relationship between the tables. For example, there is an order header table and an order line table, which will have multiple rows for each entry in the order header table. The child tables will usually have many more records than the parent table. It's always a good idea to create an index on the foreign key column in the child table.

There are two reasons why this is useful. First, we will be always joining the parent and child table on this column. Creating an index improves performance when we join the indexed column. Second, when we make changes to the parent record, such as deleting a record, having an index improves the speed of execution of the delete statements. Often, we have batch jobs that delete/purge records from production tables to keep the production database lean. Not having indexes on foreign key columns can make such processes take forever.

Refer to the following SELECT and DELETE examples. The assumption is that there are on an average 4 records in the child table for each record in the parent table. The data output is not displayed fully:

```
CREATE TABLE order_header(
order_no serial PRIMARY KEY, order_date date
);

CREATE TABLE order_lines (
line_no serial NOT NULL, order_no integer, product_name varchar,qty
 integer,descr varchar, created_ts timestamp, modified_ts timestamp
, CONSTRAINT fk_order_lines FOREIGN KEY (order_no)
REFERENCES order_header (order_no)
MATCH SIMPLE ON UPDATE CASCADE ON DELETE CASCADE );

WITH rws AS (
INSERT INTO order_header(order_no, order_date )
SELECT   GENERATE_SERIES(1,5000000) T , now()
RETURNING order_no
)
INSERT into order_lines(line_no , order_no,product_name,qty, descr, created_ts, modified_ts)
SELECT generate_series(1,4) line_no, order_no, 'Theproduct',
100 , repeat('The description for the product',10), now(), now()
  FROM rws;

SELECT * FROM order_header oh
JOIN order_lines ol ON oh.order_no=ol.order_no
WHERE oh.order_no= 60;
(4 rows)
```

SQL Tuning

```
Time: 97875.951 ms
CREATE INDEX  ol_idx ON order_lines(order_no);
CREATE INDEX
Time: 109942.137 ms


SELECT * FROM order_header oh
JOIN order_lines ol ON oh.order_no=ol.order_no
WHERE oh.order_no= 90000;
 (4 rows)
Time: 169.059 ms
```

The drop in execution time is evident. If we explain the query and look at the output before and after creating the index, we will see a difference. Without the index on `order_lines`, there was a Seq Scan on the table. Once we added the index, this changed to an index scan. Other than this, the steps remain more or less the same. We will also see a significant drop in the total cost and time once the index is in place.

Using SELECT *

We should not use SELECT * unless we really need all the columns from the tables. While explicitly mentioning the columns we need is a good programming practice; it can also improve response time. Consider the following example. In both cases, indexes were being used. However, in one case where SELECT * was used, the index scan was followed by heap fetch. In the other case, PostgreSQL was able to get the data it wanted from the index and did not have to access the table. The plan clearly mentions Index Only Scan, as shown in the following screenshot:

```
test=# EXPLAIN ANALYZE   SELECT   order_no  FROM order_lines WHERE order_no= 10;
                                               QUERY PLAN
---------------------------------------------------------------------------------------------------------------
 Index Only Scan using ol_idx on order_lines  (cost=0.44..6.03 rows=91 width=4) (actual time=31.011..31.011 rows=4 loops=1)
   Index Cond: (order_no = 10)
   Heap Fetches: 0
 Total runtime: 32.012 ms
(4 rows)
test=# EXPLAIN ANALYZE   SELECT   *  FROM order_lines WHERE order_no= 10;
                                               QUERY PLAN
---------------------------------------------------------------------------------------------------------------
 Index Scan using ol_idx on order_lines  (cost=0.44..14.03 rows=91 width=353) (actual time=48.017..48.017 rows=4 loops=1)
   Index Cond: (order_no = 10)
 Total runtime: 49.017 ms
(3 rows)
```

It might be necessary to vacuum analyze the table to ensure that index-only scans work as expected. Refer to https://wiki.postgresql.org/wiki/Index-only_scans, especially the section under *Why isn't my query using an index-only scan?* for more specifics.

Using ORDER BY

Sometimes data output has to be ordered on one or more columns. The transactions page we see when we access our bank accounts online is one example. The data is usually sorted on the transaction date. However, there are cases when the data need not be sorted on any particular column; the results page displayed when we search for a product is an example. After seeing the results, the user can decide to sort according to the price or popularity. When we sort the results of SELECT *, the entire dataset that was selected has to be shuffled, not just the columns on which we are sorting by. Typically, this happens in memory and in cases where memory is not sufficient, this will happen on disk with a huge performance penalty. So, we should not use ORDER BY unless we have to.

If it's not possible to avoid ORDER BY, having an index on the ORDER BY columns can reduce the sort overhead, as the data will be retrieved in the sorted order from the index.

> PostgreSQL creates a B-tree index if we don't specify an index type while creating the index. The index entries are sorted in ascending order. We can change the sort order by specifying the DESC clause.

In the example, there is no index on last_name. However, there is an index on first_name. In the first query, we use ORDER BY on last_name. As expected, PostgreSQL does a Seq Scan. In the second case, PostgreSQL uses the index, although we are not filtering on any column:

```
EXPLAIN SELECT first_name, last_name
FROM customer_master
ORDER BY last_name LIMIT 10;
                            QUERY PLAN
-------------------------------------------------------------------
Limit   (cost=543.17..543.20 rows=10 width=13)
   ->  Sort   (cost=543.17..578.70 rows=14210 width=13)
        Sort Key: last_name
        ->Seq Scan on customer_master   (cost=0.00..236.10 rows=14210 width=13)
(4 rows)
CREATE INDEX cust_mst_idx1 ON customer_master (first_name);

EXPLAIN SELECT first_name, last_name
FROM customer_master
```

SQL Tuning

```
ORDER by first_name  limit 10;
          QUERY PLAN
----------------------------------------------------------------------
Limit   (cost=0.29..0.82 rows=10 width=13)
   ->  Index Scan using cust_mst_idx1 on customer_master
(cost=0.29..765.42 rows=14210 width=13)
(2 rows)
```

Using DISTINCT

Sometimes, we are not sure about the joins and filters we have used. So, we add `DISTINCT` just to ensure that there are no duplicates. However, this adds quite a bit of overhead. When we add `DISTINCT` to a query, the actual time goes up significantly and there is an extra node in the plan:

```
Unique   (cost=0.29..402.33 rows=2 width=6) (actual
time=0.030..44.960 rows=1 loops=1)
   Output: first_name
```

Using `DISTINCT` to avoid duplicates might be just hiding a problem (that of missing joins). The right approach is to check whether there are duplicates and ensure that the joins are properly formed.

Using UNION ALL instead of UNION

`UNION` does a distinct after fetching the relevant records. `UNION ALL` does not do this. Often, we miss the `ALL` construct when it does not really matter whether we get duplicates or not. However, this adds a bit of overhead.

Using functions in the FILTER clause

When we use functions on a column where filter is applied, indexes will not be used:

```
EXPLAIN SELECT first_name FROM customer_master
WHERE first_name ='Julia';
                              QUERY PLAN
----------------------------------------------------------------------
-------
 Bitmap Heap Scan on customer_master   (cost=4.31..14.74 rows=3
width=6)
   Recheck Cond: ((first_name)::text = 'Julia'::text)
```

```
       ->  Bitmap Index Scan on cust_mst_idx1   (cost=0.00..4.31 rows=3
width=0)
            Index Cond: ((first_name)::text = 'Julia'::text)
(4 rows)

EXPLAIN SELECT first_name FROM customer_master
WHERE UPPER(first_name) ='Julia';
                             QUERY PLAN
-----------------------------------------------------------------
Seq Scan on customer_master   (cost=0.00..307.15 rows=71 width=6)
   Filter: (upper((first_name)::text) = 'Julia'::text)
(2 rows)
```

In the second case, the use of the UPPER function prevented the index from being utilized. There are a couple of workarounds. The first approach would be to ensure that the data is always stored in uppercase and during display, the case conversion is taken care of. The value will be converted to uppercase before it's used by the query. Another approach is to use indexes based on expressions. See the following example:

```
CREATE INDEX ON customer_master(UPPER(FIRST_NAME));

CREATE INDEX

EXPLAIN select first_name from customer_master where
UPPER(first_name) ='Julia';
                             QUERY PLAN
-----------------------------------------------------------------
--------------------
 Bitmap Heap Scan on customer_master   (cost=4.84..97.87 rows=71
width=6)
   Recheck Cond: (upper((first_name)::text) = 'Julia'::text)
   ->  Bitmap Index Scan on customer_master_upper_idx
(cost=0.00..4.82 rows=71 width=0)
         Index Cond: (upper((first_name)::text) = 'Julia'::text)
```

Note that this is a resource-intensive approach. The function gets executed many times, when we create the index (once for each record) and whenever the column gets updated. The function also gets executed when we apply it on the variable in the filter.

> The module cited is worth a look if we want case-insensitive text; refer to http://www.postgresql.org/docs/current/static/citext.html.

SQL Tuning

Another case is when we use functions in the filter clause to convert the data type. In the case of a bank transaction table, the transaction timestamp is usually captured. When we generate a report for all the transactions that occurred during a specific day, the query (with its plan) can end up like this:

```
EXPLAIN SELECT  account_id, trans_amtFROM account_trans
WHERE date(trans_date)='2008-07-15';
                        QUERY PLAN
---------------------------------------------------------------
Seq Scan on account_trans  (cost=0.00..705.15 rows=121 width=10)
Filter: (date(trans_date) = '2008-07-15'::date)
```

Although there is an index on `trans_date`, it will not be used. It's always possible to rewrite the query as follows:

```
explain select  account_id, trans_amt  from account_trans
where  trans_date>='2008-07-15' and trans_date< '2008-07-16';

QUERY PLAN
---------------------------------------------------------------
---------------------------------------------------------------
------------------------------
 Bitmap Heap Scan on account_trans  (cost=4.88..157.38 rows=58 width=10)
   Recheck Cond: ((trans_date>= '2008-07-15 00:00:00'::timestamp without time zone) AND (trans_date< '2008-07-16 00:00:00'::timestamp without time zone))
   ->  Bitmap Index Scan on account_trans_idx2   (cost=0.00..4.87 rows=58 width=0)
         Index Cond: ((trans_date>= '2008-07-15 00:00:00'::timestamp without time zone) AND (trans_date< '2008-07-16 00:00:00'::timestamp without time zone))
```

What we did here was change `date(trans_date)='2008-07-15'` to `trans_date>='2008-07-15'` and `trans_date< '2008-07-16'`.

By rewriting, we avoided the `date()` function. With the function out of the way, PostgreSQL used the index. The estimated cost went down from `705.15` to `157.38`.

In the cases described previously, a functional transformation was applied to the data when we fetched it from the table. The result was not the same as the value in the table. For example, `UPPER('Julia')` is not the same as `'Julia'`. A B-tree index, the default index created, is a data structure that stores column values and pointers to the records, which have these values. In the specific case where we searched for `UPPER('Julia')`, the index has the value `'Julia'` and pointers to locations of corresponding records in the table. PostgreSQL won't know if `f(x)` is the same as `x`. So, it decides not to use the index.

Reducing the number of SQL statements

Let's assume that we want to generate a report for bank transactions. The report should categorize transactions into various amount groups and show us how many transactions were there for amounts ranging from 0 to 100, how many transactions were there for amounts ranging from 101 to 1000, and so on. One option to get the data is to write multiple SQL statements with different filter criteria, as shown here:

```
select count(id) from account_trans where trans_amt> 1000 and
trans_amt< 10000
..
select 'GT_100', count(id) from account_trans where trans_amt> 100
and trans_amt< 1000..
```

If we want to group the transactions into three brackets, we end up with three queries. While this approach fetches the data we want, it involves scanning the table thrice, once for each query. We can avoid this by writing the following code:

```
SELECT COUNT(CASE WHEN trans_amt< 100 THEN 1 ELSE null END)
LT_100,
       COUNT (CASE WHEN trans_amt BETWEEN 101 AND 1000 THEN 1
ELSE null END) GT_100,
       COUNT (CASE WHEN trans_amt> 1000THEN 1 ELSE null END)
GT_1000
   FROM account_trans;
```

The output from the queries from a sample dataset and execution plans are shown here:

```
accounts=# SELECT COUNT(*), trans_amt FROM account_trans GROUP BY trans_amt;
 count | trans_amt
-------+-----------
    60 |   500.0000
    29 |   100.0000
    11 | 20000.0000
(3 rows)

Time: 1.000 ms
accounts=# SELECT 'LT_100', count(id) FROM account_trans
accounts-#         WHERE   trans_amt <= 100
accounts-# UNION
accounts-# SELECT 'GT_100', count(id) FROM account_trans
accounts-#         WHERE   trans_amt > 100 AND trans_amt < 1000
accounts-#         UNION
accounts-# SELECT 'GT_1000', count(id) FROM account_trans
accounts-#         WHERE   trans_amt >= 1000 AND trans_amt < 100000;
 ?column? | count
----------+-------
 LT_100   |    29
 GT_100   |    60
 GT_1000  |    11
(3 rows)

Time: 2.001 ms
accounts=# SELECT COUNT(CASE WHEN trans_amt <= 100 THEN 1 ELSE null END) LT_100,
accounts-#        COUNT (CASE WHEN trans_amt BETWEEN 101 AND 1000 THEN 1 ELSE null END) GT_100,
accounts-#        COUNT (CASE WHEN trans_amt > 1000 THEN 1 ELSE null END) GT_1000
accounts-#    FROM account_trans;
 lt_100 | gt_100 | gt_1000
--------+--------+---------
     29 |     60 |      11
(1 row)
```

SQL Tuning

Here, we can see that the counts have been retrieved correctly in both cases. We can see the plans in the following screenshot:

```
accounts=# EXPLAIN SELECT 'LT_100', count(id) FROM account_trans
        WHERE  trans_amt <= 100
UNION
SELECT 'GT_100', count(id) FROM account_trans
        WHERE  trans_amt > 100 AND trans_amt < 1000
        UNION
SELECT 'GT_1000', count(id) FROM account_trans
        WHERE  trans_amt >= 1000 AND trans_amt < 100000;
                                QUERY PLAN
--------------------------------------------------------------------------------
 HashAggregate  (cost=10.57..10.60 rows=3 width=4)
   ->  Append  (cost=3.32..10.56 rows=3 width=4)
         ->  Aggregate  (cost=3.32..3.33 rows=1 width=4)
               ->  Seq Scan on account_trans  (cost=0.00..3.25 rows=29 width=4)
                     Filter: (trans_amt <= 100::numeric)
         ->  Aggregate  (cost=3.65..3.66 rows=1 width=4)
               ->  Seq Scan on account_trans account_trans_1  (cost=0.00..3.50 rows=60 width=4)
                     Filter: ((trans_amt > 100::numeric) AND (trans_amt < 1000::numeric))
         ->  Aggregate  (cost=3.53..3.54 rows=1 width=4)
               ->  Seq Scan on account_trans account_trans_2  (cost=0.00..3.50 rows=11 width=4)
                     Filter: ((trans_amt >= 1000::numeric) AND (trans_amt < 100000::numeric))
(11 rows)

Time: 2.001 ms
accounts=# EXPLAIN SELECT COUNT(CASE WHEN trans_amt <= 100 THEN 1 ELSE null END) LT_100,
    COUNT (CASE WHEN trans_amt BETWEEN 101 AND 1000 THEN 1 ELSE null END) GT_100,
    COUNT (CASE WHEN trans_amt > 1000 THEN 1 ELSE null END) GT_1000
    FROM account_trans;
                              QUERY PLAN
--------------------------------------------------------------------------------
 Aggregate  (cost=4.75..4.76 rows=1 width=5)
   ->  Seq Scan on account_trans  (cost=0.00..3.00 rows=100 width=5)
```

The query with the `CASE` construct had to scan the table only once, and the cost went down.

Reducing function executions

We often use user-defined functions or system-provided functions such as `date()`. While the functions might be as optimized as they could be, they do invariably introduce an overhead. Sometimes, it's possible to reduce the number of function executions by rewriting queries.

First, let's enable function tracking. The setting used to track user-defined function executions is called `track_functions`. This takes a value of `none`, `pl`, or `all`. We will set it to `all`:

```
SHOW track_functions;
track_functions
-----------------
none
(1 row)
```

[138]

```
SET track_functions='all';
SET
SHOW track_functions;
track_functions
-----------------
all
(1 row)
```

Next, we will create a function that doesn't do much, except return a substring. The main objective of creating this function is to be able to track function executions:

```
CREATE OR REPLACE FUNCTION test_exec (str text)
RETURNS text AS $$
DECLARE
    ac_type text;
BEGIN
    SELECT substring(str,1,1) into ac_type;
    RETURN ac_type;
END;
$$ LANGUAGE plpgsql;
```

Consider a case where we are selecting data from two tables: customer_accounts and account_trans with a one-to-many relation between the two. We apply the function on one of the columns selected from customer_accounts.

Let's first write the query in the simplest manner possible:

```
SELECT
test_exec(account_type) acc_type , trans_amt
FROM
account_trans at JOIN customer_accounts ca
on at. cust_id =ca.cust_id
WHERE ca.cust_id = 95;
```

The query returns 11 records, as shown here:

```
SELECT * FROM pg_stat_user_functions;
funcid | schemaname | funcname  | calls | total_time | self_time
--------+------------+-----------+-------+------------+-----------
 192232 | public     | test_exec |    11 |      0.379 |     0.379
```

The function was executed 11 times. Let's rewrite the query:

```
WITH t AS (SELECT cust_id,
test_exec(account_type) acc_typeFROM customer_accounts ca
WHERE ca. cust_id = 95)
SELECT t.acc_type, trans_amt
FROM
```

SQL Tuning

```
        account_trans at JOIN  t on at.account_id=t.id
;
SELECT * FROM pg_stat_user_functions;
 funcid | schemaname | funcname  | calls | total_time | self_time
--------+------------+-----------+-------+------------+-----------
 192232 | public     | test_exec |    12 |      0.461 |     0.461
```

The output has the same 11 records and the function was executed just once. Consider the impact when this is done for a result set with hundreds or thousands of records.

We used a `WITH` query also known as **Common Table Expression (CTE)**. CTEs allow us to write named queries, which can be used in a way similar to using tables. We could say they are temporary tables that exist for the duration of the SQL statement. It's a very useful feature that anyone working with PostgreSQL should be aware of.

This feature also lets us write recursive queries. Let's look at a scenario where recursive queries might be useful. Consider a table that stores employee information. There will be one record for each employee. Each employee has a manager. The manager's employee ID is stored in a `manager_id` column in the same table. The manager will also have a record with his data, his manager's ID in the `manager_id` column. If we want to see all employees reporting directly or indirectly (that is, if Scott reports to Smith who reports to Adam, Scott is indirectly reporting to Adam) to an employee, recursive queries can be used. Recursive queries can be used to fetch hierarchical data, traverse graphs, and so on. The links `http://en.wikipedia.org/wiki/Hierarchical_and_recursive_queries_in_SQL` and `http://www.postgresql.org/docs/current/static/queries-with.html` provide a lot of useful information on PostgreSQL's `WITH` clause and recursive queries.

One important aspect of CTEs in PostgreSQL is the way they are processed. PostgreSQL always materializes the query in the `WITH` clause. The `WITH` clause is an optimization fence. The filters we use in the CTE will not be pushed down to the main query or vice versa. It helps to be aware of this when we are working with CTEs. The link `http://blog.2ndquadrant.com/postgresql-ctes-are-optimization-fences/` explains this concept in detail.

Not using indexes

Although we have created an index on a column and this column is used in the filter clause, it's not necessary that the index will be used. PostgreSQL decides whether to use an index or not depending on the selectivity of the result set as well as cardinality. Let's cover these two concepts.

Cardinality is an indicator of the uniqueness of values in a column. Low cardinality implies a high number of duplicate values (a column used to store the gender is an example), and a high cardinality means that there are many distinct values (primary key column is an example). If a column has low cardinality, it's likely that even after applying an equality filter on this column, a large portion of the table data will be retrieved. Sequential scan of the table might be more efficient in such cases in comparison to index scans followed by random reads from the table.

Selectivity is a measure of the fraction of rows that will be retrieved by the query. This is influenced by, among other things, the operators used in the filter clauses in the query. Refer to `http://www.postgresql.org/docs/current/static/row-estimation-examples.html` to understand how selectivity is estimated in specific cases.

Let's look at a couple of examples.

Refer to the following plans and data:

```
EXPLAIN ANALYZE SELECT first_name, last_name FROM customer_master
 WHERE first_name ='Sylvia';
                                  QUERY PLAN
-----------------------------------------------------------------
 Seq Scan on customer_master  (cost=0.00..775.75 rows=41100 width=12)
(actual time=0.000..17.006 rows=40000 loops=1)
   Filter: ((first_name)::text = 'Sylvia'::text)
   Rows Removed by Filter: 1001
 Total runtime: 23.008 ms
(4 rows)


Time: 26.009 ms
EXPLAIN ANALYZE SELECT first_name, last_name FROM customer_master
 WHERE first_name ='John';
                                  QUERY PLAN
-----------------------------------------------------------------
 Index Scan using cust_mst_idx1 on customer_master  (cost=0.29..4.31
rows=1 width=12) (actual time=0.000..1.000 rows=1000 loops=1)
   Index Cond: ((first_name)::text = 'John'::text)
 Total runtime: 2.000 ms
(3 rows)
SELECT count(*), first_name FROM customer_master GROUP BY first_name;
count | first_name
-------+------------
 40000 | Sylvia
  1000 | John
```

SQL Tuning

As we can see here, a majority of the people in this table are named `Sylvia`. As such, this match is a bad candidate for index use. Why? If we had used the index, PostgreSQL would have to perform a number of random reads, which is far more expensive than reading the entirety of a medium-sized table.

Partial indexes

While we usually create indexes for all records, in PostgreSQL, it's possible to create an index for a subset of records. For example:

```
CREATE index nm_idx1 on nms_rnd(first_name ) WHERE
first_name='Jonathan';
SELECT
pg_size_pretty(pg_relation_size('nm_idx')),pg_size_pretty(pg_relat
ion_size('nm_idx1'));
 pg_size_pretty | pg_size_pretty
----------------+----------------
 120 kB         | 48 kB
```

The `nm_index` class was created without any filter. The advantage is that the index created on a subset of data will be smaller than one created without a filter. This will result in an improvement in performance when the index has to be scanned. For a use case, consider a table that stores a number of records to be processed, such as e-mail IDs to which e-mails are to be sent in a nightly-batch job. Records for which e-mails are to be sent will be flagged `'N'`. Those which are being processed will be marked `'P'`. If the process fails, the record will be flagged `'F'`. Once the e-mail is sent, the flag will be set to `'Y'`. After a few days, the number of records with flag set to `'N'` will form a really small subset of the total dataset. Most records will have the flag set to `'Y'`. The process will mostly be querying records with flag `'N'` to process. Creating an index for these records where the flag is `'N'` will be better than creating an index for the entire dataset. The SQL to create the table and index will be:

```
CREATE TABLE email_process (
recipient_idint, e_mail_sentvarchar, sent_date date );
CREATE INDEX idx_eml_pcs_1 ON email_process(recipient_id)
   WHERE e_mail_sent = 'N';
```

Optimizing functions

We can write user-defined functions in a number of languages; refer to http://www.postgresql.org/docs/current/static/xfunc.html for details. Our focus here is not on how to write functions, but on a couple of aspects of functions, which can have a significant impact on performance.

The functions in PostgreSQL have a volatility classification. The classifier is an indicator of the type of the function, what it will and will not do. PostgreSQL uses this information while deciding the execution plan; hence the classification has an impact on the performance of the queries, which uses the function. There are three possible classifications:

- VOLATILE: These functions can modify the database and return different results on successive calls with the same arguments. The function will be re-evaluated for each row in the result set in a query.
- STABLE: These functions cannot modify the database. For each row returned by a query, they will return the same results, assuming the arguments remain the same. Note that the results are bound to be the same for a single statement, not forever.
- IMMUTABLE: These functions will return the same results forever for the same arguments. This is the strictest volatility category.

For better performance, we should define functions with the strictest volatility category possible,. Let's modify the function we used earlier a bit and try the two categories: VOLATILE and IMMUTABLE:

```
CREATE OR REPLACE FUNCTION test_exec(str text)
   RETURNS text AS
$BODY$
DECLARE
ac_type text;
BEGIN
   FOR i in 1..1000
   LOOP
   SELECT substring(str,1,1) INTO ac_type;
   END LOOP;
   RETURN ac_type;
END;
$BODY$
   LANGUAGE plpgsql VOLATILE
   COST 100;
ALTER FUNCTION test_exec(text)
   OWNER TO postgres;
```

SQL Tuning

When we create a function without mentioning the category, the `VOLATILE` category is assumed. We will enable `track_functions` and also keep track of the time taken for the query execution:

```
accounts=# SELECT pg_stat_reset();
 pg_stat_reset
---------------

(1 row)

Time: 2.001 ms
accounts=# SELECT * FROM pg_stat_user_functions ;
 funcid | schemaname | funcname | calls | total_time | self_time
--------+------------+----------+-------+------------+-----------
(0 rows)

Time: 13.004 ms
accounts=# SELECT test_exec('a'), generate_series(1,5);
 test_exec | generate_series
-----------+-----------------
 a         |               1
 a         |               2
 a         |               3
 a         |               4
 a         |               5
(5 rows)

Time: 30.010 ms
accounts=# SELECT * FROM pg_stat_user_functions ;
 funcid | schemaname | funcname  | calls | total_time | self_time
--------+------------+-----------+-------+------------+-----------
 504148 | public     | test_exec |     6 |      29.01 |     29.01
(1 row)

Time: 14.005 ms
accounts=# SELECT test_exec('a'), generate_series(1,5);
 test_exec | generate_series
-----------+-----------------
 a         |               1
 a         |               2
 a         |               3
 a         |               4
 a         |               5
(5 rows)

Time: 10.003 ms
accounts=# SELECT * FROM pg_stat_user_functions ;
 funcid | schemaname | funcname  | calls | total_time | self_time
--------+------------+-----------+-------+------------+-----------
 504148 | public     | test_exec |     7 |     37.013 |    37.013
(1 row)

Time: 14.005 ms
```

The function category was changed from VOLATILE to IMMUTABLE between the successive executions. The time taken for execution went down from 30 ms to 10 ms, when the function category was changed from VOLATILE to IMMUTABLE. The drop in the number of executions of the functions is also seen.

This does not mean that we can just define all functions to be IMMUTABLE. If we add an UPDATE statement to the function and then execute, we will get the following error:

```
ERROR:   UPDATE is not allowed in a non-volatile function
CONTEXT:   SQL statement "UPDATE account SET id = id"
```

Refer to the guidelines provided at http://www.postgresql.org/docs/current/static/xfunc-volatility.html for tips on deciding the volatility of your function.

Summary

In this chapter, we covered basic facts about databases, the PostgreSQL query execution process, and a few tips on how to optimize PostgreSQL queries. Performance optimization strategies (such as modifying parameters and making use of materialized views) will be covered in the next chapter.

8
Server Tuning

In the previous chapter, we saw how the PostgreSQL optimizer works. We also saw how making changes to a query, creating an index, avoiding functions, and so on change the way queries are executed by PostgreSQL. These minor changes often have a significant impact on performance and response time. In this chapter, we will see the parameters that affect query performance, and how to use two special data structures: materialized views and partitions.

Server-wide memory settings

We will look at two parameters related to buffers, the first parameter is an allocation and the second parameter is a pointer to the optimizer. Both have a significant impact on performance.

shared_buffers

This parameter decides how much memory will be dedicated to PostgreSQL to cache data. When multiple sessions request the same data from the same table, `shared_buffers` ensure that there is no need to have many copies of the datasets in memory. This approach reduces the necessary physical I/O. The buffers are allocated at database startup. The default value set by initdb in newer versions of PostgreSQL (9.3 and higher) is 128 MB. It was 32 MB in older versions. This parameter has a significant impact on the performance because this setting directly affects the amount of physical I/O on the server.

In versions earlier than 9.3, kernel settings adjustment (`shmmax`) would be necessary to set a value higher than 32 MB for `shared_buffers`.

Server Tuning

Considering that even desktops and laptops come with 4 GB RAM or more, it makes sense to change the setting from the low value of 128 MB. If memory is available, and if the dataset is small enough (a few GB), it will help to keep the value at something close to the volume of the dataset. About 25 percent of RAM is a reasonable starting point, assuming that the server is not one with hundreds of GBs of RAM. Large values of `shared_buffers` can result in a drop in performance in older versions of PostgreSQL. Large buffers in a write-heavy system result in a lot of dirty data waiting to be flushed. Checkpoints take care of this flushing. During checkpoints, there will a big spike in the system I/O if there is a large volume of data to be flushed. Later versions of PostgreSQL added parameters to spread out the checkpoint process and thus reduce the spikes.

In cases where the server has lots of RAM, starting with something like 8 GB of `shared_buffers` and testing to see how much cache hit we are getting might be the right approach. After the allocation of memory for shared buffers, there must be enough memory available for session-level usage, for example, sorting data. The memory used for such activities is not allocated from the shared buffers. The requirements for the operating system and other processes on the server also need to be considered while setting the value for `shared_buffers`. On the other end, an upper limit of 40 percent of RAM is usually recommended.

effective_cache_size

This value tells PostgreSQL approximately how much memory is available for all cache purposes (`shared_buffers` plus filesystem cache). Unlike `shared_buffers`, this memory is not allocated. The value is used for estimation purposes by the query planner. Concurrent queries will share the available space. The default setting of 128 MB can be too low in most cases, as is the case with `shared_buffers`. Let's see the impact of this value on PostgreSQL's estimates:

```
test=# CREATE TABLE myt (id int);
CREATE TABLE
test=# INSERT INTO myt
test-#              SELECT generate_series(1,1000000) ;
INSERT 0 1000000
test=# CREATE INDEX idx_myt ON myt(id);
CREATE INDEX
test=# SET effective_cache_size='1 MB';
SET
test=# EXPLAIN SELECT * FROM myt ORDER BY id LIMIT 20;
                                   QUERY PLAN
-------------------------------------------------------------------------------
 Limit  (cost=0.42..79.52 rows=20 width=4)
   ->  Index Only Scan using idx_myt on myt  (cost=0.42..3954572.42 rows=1000000 width=4)
(2 rows)

test=# SET effective_cache_size='100 MB';
SET
test=# EXPLAIN SELECT * FROM myt ORDER BY id LIMIT 20;
                                   QUERY PLAN
-------------------------------------------------------------------------------
 Limit  (cost=0.42..1.30 rows=20 width=4)
   ->  Index Only Scan using idx_myt on myt  (cost=0.42..43680.43 rows=1000000 width=4)
(2 rows)
```

Note the cost numbers PostgreSQL estimates for the two cases. The numbers went down significantly once `effective_cache_size` was increased. Now, PostgreSQL estimates that it costs much less to retrieve the data. This example is provided just to prove that `effective_cache_size` has an impact on the cost estimate. When we actually execute the query, there might not be any difference for the two cases shown.

Let's see why this parameter has an impact. When we increase the `effective_cache_size`, the planner assumes that more pages will fit in memory. This makes using indexes better than sequential scans. If the setting is too low, PostgreSQL might decide that sequential scans will be efficient. In short, a high setting increases the likelihood of the use of indexes, whereas a low setting increases the chances of sequential scans.

Managing writes, connections, and maintenance

Now, we will look at a few other parameters that can impact performance:

The `checkpoint_segments` parameter was covered in *Chapter 2, Server Architecture*. When we increase `shared_buffers`, it might be necessary to increase this value too. In a busy system with a lot of changes being made to the data, a low value will result in frequent checkpoints. We can increase this number and spread out the process of writing a relatively larger volume of data at each checkpoint (resulting from fewer checkpoints) using `checkpoint_completion_target`. The default value of 3 is usually too low for any system with frequent writes.

We can limit the maximum number of connections allowed on the server using the `max_connections` parameter. This parameter by itself does not have an impact on performance. However, there is the `work_mem` parameter, which we covered earlier. If the maximum number of connections is kept high and work memory is also high, the memory requirements for the database cluster might shoot up. A conservative figure for `work_mem` can be arrived at by a formula, as shown in the following code:

```
work_mem = (available_ram * 0.25) / max_connections
```

Here, we are ensuring that the total memory used by working memory areas of all connections will be limited to roughly one-fourth of the RAM. As `work_mem` can be set at session level, we can always allocate more memory for individual connections when there is an obvious need to, such as in the case of batch processes, which will sort the data in a big table.

End-of-day processes in transactional systems and **Extract, Transform, and Load** (**ETL**) processes for data warehouses might benefit from higher settings of work_mem. In data warehouses, there are also jobs that refresh standard reports. These jobs are executed on completion of the ETL process. As many reports have data sorted on a number of columns, these jobs too might require higher settings for work_mem. We can set this value for the logins used to execute ETL jobs and report refresh jobs at the user level with the following code:

```
ALTER USER etluser SET work_mem = '50MB';
```

The default value of max_connections is 100. If we set it to a couple of hundred and still run into an error as follows:

```
FATAL:  sorry, too many clients already
```

The right approach would be to:

- Check whether connections are getting closed properly at the application tier
- Check whether connections are being reused
- Explore the possibility of using a connection pool

Raising maximum_connections to a value more than a few hundred should be considered only after exhausting these possibilities. Each connection consumes some system resources and increasing maximum_connections can even lead to a drop in performance. This is discussed in detail at https://wiki.postgresql.org/wiki/Number_Of_Database_Connections.

> There is a parameter called superuser_reserved_connections. This is the number of connection slots that are reserved for PostgreSQL superusers. The default value is 3. If max_connections is 100 and superuser_reserved_connections is 3, once the number of concurrent connections is 97, only superusers can connect.

The maintenance_work_mem parameter was also covered in *Chapter 2, Server Architecture*. This parameter will be used by the autovacuum process, indexing, and a few alter table statements. This can be set at a session level, thus overriding the default value set in postgresql.conf. One key difference between this and the work_mem parameter is that it is okay to set this to a value higher than the work_mem parameter because not too many maintenance activities will be happening in the server concurrently.

> For an interesting discussion on how these parameters work and which aspects need to be considered before choosing the values, refer to http://postgresql.1045698.n5.nabble.com/Auto-tuning-work-mem-and-maintenance-work-mem-td5773852.html.

Seek/scan cost and statistics parameters

Now, we will look at a few other parameters that can impact the query plan and performance.

The `default_statistics_target` parameter tells PostgreSQL how much data should be sampled to populate tables that store metadata. The default value is 100. PostgreSQL will consider (300* value) pages. This means, with the default value of 100, PostgreSQL will read 30,000 pages (or the entire table, if the table is not that big) to do random sampling of rows. From these samples, it will populate the `pg_statistic` catalog. The type of data collected include the number of distinct non-null values, most common values, most common frequencies for the values, and so on. These values will be used by the planner to decide the execution plan. Details of columns in `pg_statistic` are provided at http://www.postgresql.org/docs/current/static/catalog-pg-statistic.html.

If `EXPLAIN ANALYZE` for a query shows a significant variation between the actual and estimates, we should consider increasing the statistics target. It can be set at the `COLUMN` level for individual tables. The following code shows how to find the existing default value, how to change it for a table, and how to see the values for tables:

```
accounts=# SHOW default_statistics_target ;
 default_statistics_target
---------------------------
 100
(1 row)
accounts=# SELECT attstattarget,attname FROM   pg_attribute
WHERE   attrelid = 'customer_accounts'::regclass;
 attstattarget |    attname
---------------+--------------
             0 | tableoid
             0 | cmax
             0 | xmax
             0 | cmin
             0 | xmin
             0 | ctid
            -1 | account_id
            -1 | cust_id
```

Server Tuning

```
                  -1 | account_type
                  -1 | branch_id
(10 rows)

accounts=# ALTER TABLE customer_accounts ALTER cust_id SET
STATISTICS 200;
ALTER TABLE
accounts=# SELECT attstattarget,attname FROM  pg_attribute
WHERE   attrelid = 'customer_accounts'::regclass;
 attstattarget |    attname
---------------+--------------
             0 | tableoid
             0 | cmax
             0 | xmax
             0 | cmin
             0 | xmin
             0 | ctid
            -1 | account_id
           200 | cust_id
            -1 | account_type
            -1 | branch_id
(10 rows)
accounts=# ALTER TABLE customer_accounts ALTER cust_id SET
STATISTICS -1
;
ALTER TABLE
```

A value of `-1` indicates the default setting. Note that increasing the value results in more sampling, which translates to more resource consumption. It's better to set this in a session, see how much time analyzing the tables takes, see how much we gain in terms of query performance, and then decide whether the new value should be retained. With a higher value, the planner now has more data available and a little more work to do to come up with an optimal plan. However, this might be more than offset by improved response times for many queries. If we know that the data distribution is uneven for specific attributes, it makes sense to check the plans for queries that use the non-standard values in the WHERE clause.

There are a few cost constants that can be tweaked to influence the planner:

- `seq_page_cost`
- `random_page_cost`

These two settings are related to each other. The `seq_page_cost` is a measure of the resource cost when the server fetches pages from the data blocks sequentially (Seq Scans). In *Chapter 7, SQL Tuning*, we saw that pages can be fetched in a sequential or random manner. In a sequential access plan, data will be read one block after the other. If the blocks are numbered `1` to `100`, block number `1` will be fetched, then `2`, `3`, and so on, until all the data is fetched (except in cases where there is a `LIMIT` clause). In such cases, reads stop once the requested numbers of rows have been fetched. In the random page fetch, the database can request for block number `7`, `28`, `49`, and so on.

The default settings of `4` for `random_page_cost` and `1` for `seq_page_cost` imply that random seeks are four times as expensive as sequential access. Changing the default ratio of 4:1 to a lower ratio 2:1, increases the chances that the planner will decide to use indexes.

Let's cover a few considerations that have gone into the default setting of 4:1 and its relevance. The first one is that a random seek is far more expensive than a sequential scan. This holds true for spinning disks, but not for **Solid State Disks** (**SSDs**). If you are using a hosted server, it's likely that it's using SSDs. Digital Ocean, a new player in the **Virtual Private Server** (**VPS**), launched their services with all SSD storage in 2011. Over the past couple of years, almost all the big players, including Amazon Web Services, Rackspace, and Linode have started providing SSDs. So, it might be a good idea to alter the ratio a bit from 4:1 to a lower ratio for SSDs.

The next consideration is that while random disk seeks are expensive, most of the fetches might never result in disk I/O at all. A server with sufficient memory and proper cache settings will mean that most of the reads occur from cache. This is factored in the default setting of 4:1. Refer to http://www.postgresql.org/docs/current/static/runtime-config-query.html.

> "*The default value can be thought of as modeling random access as 40 times slower than sequential, while expecting 90% of random reads to be cached.*"

If we use spinning disks, and if most of the fetches result in physical I/O, it might be necessary to adjust the ratio in the other direction to a value higher than 4:1. Let's see the impact with some sample data and settings:

```
accounts=# CREATE TABLE myt (
            id integer primary key , txt varchar(50));
CREATE TABLE
accounts=# INSERT INTO myt SELECT
generate_series(1,100000), ' some text to ensure the table takes
many blocks';
INSERT 0 100000
accounts=# ANALYZE myt;
ANALYZE
```

Server Tuning

```
accounts=# SHOW random_page_cost ;
 random_page_cost
------------------
 4
(1 row)

accounts=# SET random_page_cost TO 400;
SET
accounts=# EXPLAIN SELECT id,txt FROM myt WHERE id IN (1,2);
                              QUERY PLAN
-----------------------------------------------------------------------
 Index Scan using myt_pkey on myt  (cost=0.29..1200.62 rows=2 width=53)
    Index Cond: (id = ANY ('{1,2}'::integer[]))
(2 rows)

accounts=# SET random_page_cost TO 4000;
SET
accounts=# EXPLAIN SELECT id,txt FROM myt WHERE id IN (1,2);
                      QUERY PLAN
--------------------------------------------------------
 Seq Scan on myt  (cost=0.00..2281.00 rows=2 width=53)
    Filter: (id = ANY ('{1,2}'::integer[]))
(2 rows)
```

The plan shifted from Index Scan to Seq Scan because indexes involve random seeks; we just told the optimizer that random seeks are very expensive. Let's see what will happen if we raise the `seq_page_cost` also:

```
accounts=# SET seq_page_cost TO 400;
SET
accounts=# EXPLAIN SELECT id,txt FROM myt WHERE id IN (1,2);
                              QUERY PLAN
------------------------------------------------------------------------
 Index Scan using myt_pkey on myt  (cost=0.29..12000.62 rows=2 width=53)
    Index Cond: (id = ANY ('{1,2}'::integer[]))
(2 rows)
```

It's not a good idea to set `random_page_cost` to a value less than `seq_page_cost`. We should also remember that it's not the individual values of random and sequential page costs, but their ratio that will influence the query planner.

CPU costs

From disk and disk access costs, let's move on to CPU. Also, let's recollect that the costs related to scans (sequential and random) were 1 and 4 respectively. Compared to these values, the default CPU-related cost settings are pretty small.

- `cpu_operator_cost` (0.0025): This value represents the CPU cost to perform an operation (such as hash or aggregation)
- `cpu_tuple_cost` (0.01): This number represents the cost to process each row
- `cpu_index_tuple_cost` (0.005): This number represents the cost of processing each index entry

These values are low because of the assumption that processing records incur fewer costs compared to fetching records. In other words, if we set the value of all these settings to 1, it's highly likely that we will run into a nasty bottleneck at the I/O side. As the impact of CPU costs are pretty small in the total cost computation (as a result of the low default settings), minor changes to these CPU cost settings are not likely to make an impact on the query plans or response times.

Let's see how these costs add up to arrive at the total cost. We will take a case where we have a straight sequential scan, no indexes involved, and no random accesses. We have no index tuples or operators and hence no CPU costs involved for these:

```
postgres=# EXPLAIN ANALYZE SELECT * FROM myt;
                                    QUERY PLAN
-----------------------------------------------------------------
 Seq Scan on myt  (cost=0.00..28850.00 rows=2000000 width=4)
(actual time=0.000..339.130 rows=2000003 loops=1)
 Total runtime: 626.217 ms
(2 rows)

postgres=# SELECT
relpages * current_setting('seq_page_cost')::decimal +
reltuples * current_setting('cpu_tuple_cost')::decimal
as total_cost FROM pg_class WHERE relname='myt';
 total_cost
------------
      28850
(1 row)
```

The number 28850 appears in the cost we computed as well as in PostgreSQL's cost estimates. The formula used to calculate the total cost can be simplified as follows:

TC = n1*c1+n2*c2+n3*c3+....

Server Tuning

Here, TC represents the total cost: n1, n2, n3, and so on represent the number of pages or tuples as the case may be: c1, c2, c3, and so on represent the respective cost constants/parameter settings.

> There is a list of Boolean settings related to the query planner configuration. By default, these are turned on. The exhaustive list is available at http://www.postgresql.org/docs/current/static/runtime-config-query.html.

As mentioned in the documentation, disabling one or more of these settings is, at best, a temporary solution. Modifying the planner cost constants, which we saw, is the right approach. We will have a look at a couple of these to see how they work. enable_indexscan and enable_bitmapscan are the two settings we will try changing. These settings, as the names suggest, enable or disable the index and bitmap scans. The default value is on for both:

```
accounts=# SHOW enable_indexscan ;
 enable_indexscan
------------------
 on
(1 row)


accounts=# EXPLAIN SELECT id,txt FROM myt WHERE id IN (1,2);
                          QUERY PLAN
-----------------------------------------------------------------
 Index Scan using myt_pkey on myt  (cost=0.29..12.62 rows=2 width=53)
    Index Cond: (id = ANY ('{1,2}'::integer[]))
(2 rows)


accounts=# SET enable_indexscan TO false;
SET
accounts=# SHOW enable_indexscan ;
 enable_indexscan
------------------
 off
(1 row)


accounts=# EXPLAIN SELECT id,txt FROM myt WHERE id IN (1,2);
                          QUERY PLAN
-----------------------------------------------------------------
 Bitmap Heap Scan on myt  (cost=8.60..16.36 rows=2 width=53)
    Recheck Cond: (id = ANY ('{1,2}'::integer[]))
```

```
        ->  Bitmap Index Scan on myt_pkey  (cost=0.00..8.60 rows=2
 width=0)
            Index Cond: (id = ANY ('{1,2}'::integer[]))
(4 rows)

accounts=# SHOW enable_bitmapscan;
 enable_bitmapscan
-------------------
 on
(1 row)

accounts=# SET enable_bitmapscan TO false;
SET
accounts=# EXPLAIN SELECT id,txt FROM myt WHERE id IN (1,2);
                        QUERY PLAN
---------------------------------------------------------
 Seq Scan on myt  (cost=0.00..2281.00 rows=2 width=53)
   Filter: (id = ANY ('{1,2}'::integer[]))
(2 rows)
```

By disabling these settings, we are forcing the planner to choose an expensive plan. As a result, the cost keeps going up.

In most cases, rather than trying to fiddle with these settings, we should ensure that the planner has up-to-date statistics available (by executing `ANALYZE`) and that it has enough of it available (by tweaking the statistics target).

While there are a few more settings that can be adjusted to influence the planner, the ones already covered should be enough in most of the cases where the optimizer seems to choose a suboptimal plan.

Now, we will look at two special objects that can be used to improve response times. One uses precalculated or prepared datasets to improve the response time, while the second one involves breaking down a big table into many smaller ones to improve performance.

Materialized views

Materialized views are similar to views because they also depend on other tables for their data, although there are a couple of differences. SELECTs against views will always fetch the latest data, whereas SELECTs against materialized views might fetch stale data.

Server Tuning

The other key difference is that materialized views actually contain data and take up storage space (proportionate to the volume of data), whereas views do not occupy significant space on disk.

Materialized views are used mostly to capture summaries or snapshots of data from base tables. Some latency/staleness is acceptable. Consider the case of a report for average branch-wise balances for a bank at the end of business day. Typically, the report will be sent after close of business for the day, implying that the averages, once calculated, are not likely to change for that particular day. In addition, no one is likely to request the report before close of business.

For a website, reports displaying average and peak traffic across different time periods in a day could be another typical use case.

There are other use cases for materialized views. Let's see one more. We can use PostgreSQL's foreign data wrappers to access data from various data sources including:

- Relational databases (such as Oracle and MySQL)
- NoSQL databases (such as MongoDB, Redis, and CouchDB)
- Various types of files

Queries against such sources do not have predictable performance. We can create materialized views on the foreign tables created on such data sources.

When we use materialized views to store precalculated aggregates, there are two advantages. First, we avoid the overhead of doing the same calculation multiple times (there may be multiple requests for the reports, right?). Materialized views that provide summaries tend to be small compared to the base tables. So, we will save on the cost of scanning big tables. This is the second advantage.

When we use materialized views to store data from foreign tables, we make the query performance more predictable. We also eliminate the data transfer that occurs when we access foreign tables multiple times.

> Foreign data wrappers will be covered in *Chapter 12, PostgreSQL – Extras*.

Here is how we can create and refresh a materialized view:

```
accounts=# CREATE TABLE myt (id integer primary key, amt numeric);
CREATE TABLE
accounts=# INSERT INTO myt SELECT generate_series(1,10000), 100;
INSERT 0 10000
accounts=# CREATE MATERIALIZED VIEW mv_myt AS
                SELECT avg(amt) FROM myt;
SELECT 1
accounts=# ANALYZE myt;
ANALYZE
accounts=# ANALYZE mv_myt;
ANALYZE
accounts=# EXPLAIN SELECT avg(amt) FROM myt;
                        QUERY PLAN
-------------------------------------------------------------
 Aggregate  (cost=180.00..180.01 rows=1 width=5)
   ->  Seq Scan on myt  (cost=0.00..155.00 rows=10000 width=5)
(2 rows)

accounts=# EXPLAIN SELECT *  FROM mv_myt;
                     QUERY PLAN
-------------------------------------------------------------
 Seq Scan on mv_myt  (cost=0.00..1.01 rows=1 width=5)
(1 row)
```

We can see the difference in cost:

```
accounts=# INSERT INTO myt VALUES (90000,200);
INSERT 0 1
accounts=# explain select avg(amt) from myt;
                     QUERY PLAN
-------------------------------------------------------------------
 Aggregate  (cost=180.00..180.01 rows=1 width=5)
   ->  Seq Scan on myt  (cost=0.00..155.00 rows=10000 width=5)
(2 rows)


accounts=# SELECT avg(amt) FROM myt;
         avg
---------------------
 100.0099990000999900
(1 row)


accounts=# SELECT *   FROM mv_myt;
         avg
---------------------
 100.0000000000000000
(1 row)
```

Server Tuning

The data is stale now. So, let's refresh the materialized view and update its contents:

```
accounts=# REFRESH MATERIALIZED VIEW mv_myt ;
REFRESH MATERIALIZED VIEW
accounts=# SELECT *  FROM mv_myt;
        avg
---------------------
 100.0099990000999900
(1 row)


accounts=# DROP TABLE myt;
ERROR:  cannot drop table myt because other objects depend on it
DETAIL:  materialized view mv_myt depends on table myt
HINT:  Use DROP ... CASCADE to drop the dependent objects too.
```

PostgreSQL is smart enough to tell us that there are dependent objects. Also, we can look up all our materialized views as follows:

```
accounts=# SELECT matviewname ,definition FROM pg_matviews;
  matviewname |          definition
--------------+-----------------------------
  mv_myt      |   SELECT avg(myt.amt) AS avg+
              |     FROM myt;
```

Partitioned tables

We saw that materialized views can be used to capture summary or preaggregated data so that instead of scanning large volumes of data in huge tables, we can scan a small table to get the data we want.

Table partitioning involves breaking a huge table into a number of small tables so that fewer blocks need to be scanned to retrieve data. When we create partitions, we use constraints to ensure that only specific datasets are stored in a partition. PostgreSQL's query planner can use these constraints to eliminate scanning some partitions. This feature is called constraint exclusion (check constraint on a table/partition tells the PostgreSQL planner that specific values will not be there in the table/partition. So, the planner can avoid scanning that table).

Compared to the indexes on the big single table, indexes on the partitions will be smaller, increasing the chances that they fit into memory.

We can also use partitioning to implement a tiered storage. Data that is less frequently accessed can be in partitions in a tablespace that is on a slow disk, whereas data that is frequently accessed go to partitions in a tablespace that is on a fast disk, and so on.

Another benefit of partitioning is ease of maintenance. Let's consider a data warehouse scenario where we have data for many years and as time goes on, the data for the oldest year can be removed. Without partitioning, this involves deleting a significant number of records in one go with a DELETE statement (which is resource-intensive) and the resultant empty space, subsequent heavy vacuuming, and so on. If the data is properly partitioned, a TRUNCATE statement is all it takes to get rid of the old data.

The steps to create partitioned tables are as follows:

1. Create a master table. This is the template for the child tables. This table will not really hold any data.
2. Create the child tables. These are the table which will store data. Any SQL against the master table will be diverted to one or more of the child tables available.
3. Create a trigger to achieve the redirection of SQL statements.

Now, let's try to see this with an example:

1. We will create a two-column transaction table with an ID and transaction date:

   ```
   CREATE TABLE tran(id integer PRIMARY KEY, trandate date);
   CREATE TABLE
   ```

2. We will create two child tables to store the transactions for the years 2013 and 2014:

   ```
   CREATE TABLE tran_y2013 (
   CHECK ( trandate >= DATE '2013-01-01' AND
   trandate < DATE '2014-01-01' )
   ) INHERITS (tran);
   CREATE TABLE
   CREATE TABLE tran_y2014 (
   CHECK ( trandate >= DATE '2014-01-01' AND
   trandate < DATE '2015-01-01' )
   ) INHERITS (tran);
   ```

Server Tuning

It's better to avoid functions, or at least avoid complex functions in the constraints, to make it easy for the planner.

> Note the `INHERITS` keyword we used while creating the child tables. Table inheritance is a very useful feature of PostgreSQL. Go through the details at http://www.postgresql.org/docs/current/static/ddl-inherit.html.

3. We have also added check constraints. Now, we will create the trigger function:

```
CREATE OR REPLACE FUNCTION trans_insert_trigger()
RETURNS TRIGGER AS $$
BEGIN
    IF ( NEW.trandate >= DATE '2014-01-01' AND
         NEW.trandate < DATE '2015-01-01' ) THEN
        INSERT INTO tran_y2014 VALUES (NEW.*);
    ELSIF ( NEW.trandate >= DATE '2013-01-01' AND
         NEW.trandate < DATE '2014-01-01' ) THEN
        INSERT INTO tran_y2013 VALUES (NEW.*);
    ELSE
        RAISE EXCEPTION 'Date out of range.  Fix the tran_insert_trigger() function!';
    END IF;
    RETURN NULL;
END;
$$
LANGUAGE plpgsql;
```

> For better performance, list triggers conditions in the order of probability of happening. A condition that has a high probability of returning TRUE should come before one with a low probability.

4. Attach the trigger to the master table:

```
CREATE TRIGGER insert_trans_trigger
    BEFORE INSERT ON tran
    FOR EACH ROW EXECUTE PROCEDURE trans_insert_trigger();
```

Now, we will insert a couple of records into the parent table to test our trigger:

```
INSERT INTO tran VALUES (1,'2014-01-01' );
INSERT 0 0
INSERT INTO tran VALUES (2,'2013-01-01' );
INSERT 0 0
SELECT * FROM tran;
```

```
 id | trandate
----+------------
  2 | 2013-01-01
  1 | 2014-01-01
(2 rows)

SELECT * FROM tran_y2013;
 id | trandate
----+------------
  2 | 2013-01-01
(1 row)

SELECT * FROM tran_y2014;
 id | trandate
----+------------
  1 | 2014-01-01
(1 row)
```

Let's see how queries are executed when we apply a filter on the `trandate` column:

```
EXPLAIN ANALYZE SELECT * FROM tran WHERE trandate=
'2013-01-01';
                       QUERY PLAN
-----------------------------------------------------------------
-----------------------------------------
 Append  (cost=0.00..36.75 rows=12 width=8) (actual
time=0.000..0.000 rows=1 loops=1)
   ->  Seq Scan on tran  (cost=0.00..0.00 rows=1 width=8) (actual
time=0.000..0.000 rows=0 loops=1)
         Filter: (trandate = '2013-01-01'::date)
   ->  Seq Scan on tran_y2013  (cost=0.00..36.75 rows=11 width=8)
(actual time=0.000..0.000 rows=1 loops=1)
         Filter: (trandate = '2013-01-01'::date)
 Total runtime: 0.000 ms
(6 rows)

EXPLAIN ANALYZE SELECT * FROM tran WHERE trandate=
'2014-01-01';
                       QUERY PLAN
-----------------------------------------------------------------
-------------------------------------
 Append  (cost=0.00..36.75 rows=12 width=8) (actual
time=0.000..0.000 rows=1 loops=1)
   ->  Seq Scan on tran  (cost=0.00..0.00 rows=1 width=8) (actual
time=0.000..0.000 rows=0 loops=1)
```

Server Tuning

```
            Filter: (trandate = '2014-01-01'::date)
   ->  Seq Scan on tran_y2014  (cost=0.00..36.75 rows=11 width=8)
(actual time=0.000..0.000 rows=1 loops=1)
            Filter: (trandate = '2014-01-01'::date)
 Total runtime: 0.000 ms
(6 rows)
```

The query went against the child tables. Usually, we index on the `trandate` column in the child tables to further improve performance.

Performance gains from such an approach can be expected only in cases where the query uses filters on the column(s) that drive the partitioning logic. In other cases, we will end up scanning all the child tables as follows:

```
EXPLAIN ANALYZE SELECT * FROM tran WHERE id = 1;
                        QUERY PLAN
---------------------------------------------------------
Append  (cost=0.00..73.50 rows=23 width=8) (actual time=0.274..0.289 rows=1 loops=1)
   ->  Seq Scan on tran  (cost=0.00..0.00 rows=1 width=8) (actual time=0.007..0.007 rows=0 loops=1)
            Filter: (id = 1)
   ->  Seq Scan on tran_y2013  (cost=0.00..36.75 rows=11 width=8)
(actual time=0.017..0.017 rows=0 loops=1)
            Filter: (id = 1)
            Rows Removed by Filter: 1
   ->  Seq Scan on tran_y2014  (cost=0.00..36.75 rows=11 width=8)
(actual time=0.015..0.020 rows=1 loops=1)
            Filter: (id = 1)
```

It is worth noting that there is a difference between the estimated and actual number for rows in the preceding plans.

Instead of deleting the data for a year, we can just drop the table:

```
DROP TABLE tran_y2013;
DROP TABLE
```

However, if someone attempts to insert data that should have gone to that child table, we get an error:

```
INSERT INTO tran values (1,'2013-01-01' );
ERROR:  relation "tran_y2013" does not exist
LINE 1: INSERT INTO tran_y2013 VALUES (NEW.*)
                    ^
QUERY:  INSERT INTO tran_y2013 VALUES (NEW.*)
CONTEXT:  PL/pgSQL function trans_insert_trigger() line 5 at SQL statement
```

> If we use ALTER TABLE tran_y2013 NO INHERIT tran instead of dropping the table, we will still have the data, but the partition table is delinked from the table tran.

Using triggers slows down inserts. Another way is to use the PostgreSQL rule system (http://www.postgresql.org/docs/current/static/sql-createrule.html). The overhead caused by rules is usually more than that caused by triggers. However, a rule is evaluated once per query, whereas the trigger is fired for each row. For tables with more bulk inserts, implementing partitioning using rules might be efficient.

Summary

In this chapter, we looked at a number of parameters that influence the execution plan and thus have an impact on execution times. We also covered two special data structures that can be used to improve performance.

In the next chapter, you will learn about a couple of PostgreSQL utilities.

9
Tools to Move Data in and out of PostgreSQL

In the previous two chapters, we covered optimizations at the query level, at the server level, and a bit at the data structure level. Once initial optimization and checks are carried out in the development or test environment, the next step is to prepare the production environment. Installation of database software and configuration of parameters can be done in a manner similar to how it was done in the development environment with the possibility that the production server has a higher configuration; we may be able to provide a bit more memory to the database.

Another important step in preparing the production environment is the creation of databases, users and roles, and population of master data. There are various ways of doing it. We will cover a couple of utilities that can be used to carry out these activities.

> Backup, recovery and scalability solutions are covered in *Chapter 10, Scaling, Replication, Backup, and Recovery.*

Setting up the production database – considerations

We typically create users and databases in the production environment, then create other objects (such as tables and views) and also populate some data before going live. The kind of cleaned and verified master data to be populated in the production environment depends on the system. Country and city master data, currencies and exchange rate master data, geoip data, domain-specific master data (such as product lists, warehouse lists, airports, and so on) all may need to be populated with scope for changes to the data in future.

The volume of data to be moved will also vary. It's possible that the new system, running on PostgreSQL, will replace a system that uses Oracle or MySQL. In such scenarios, data from the existing system should be migrated to the new system. These situations have a few added complexities:

- **Data volume**: The existing system has been live for a few years and most of the data needs to be migrated.
- **Database code rewrite**: The code written for Oracle or MySQL is unlikely to work with PostgreSQL. Code migration, testing, rewrite, and more testing will be involved.
- **Data transformation**: There will be a need to transform/manipulate the data before moving it to the new system. This will be true in most cases because the new data structures are usually not exact replicas of the data structures of the system that is being retired.

While the data volume issue can be handled by using the right options with PostgreSQL's built-in tools, the code rewrite and data transformation will require other tools. For moving data from Oracle to PostgreSQL, ora2pg (http://ora2pg.darold.net/), a Perl utility, offers different options (such as moving only specific tables or all tables, triggers, procedures and packages, selective migration of data with WHERE clauses, and so on). While the code does get converted to some extent, use of another utility, orafce (https://github.com/orafce/orafce), may be necessary to mimic the functionality of Oracle packages such as DBMS_OUTPUT.

> There are similar utilities available for other databases too. A comprehensive list is available at https://wiki.postgresql.org/wiki/Converting_from_other_Databases_to_PostgreSQL. When extensive data transformation/manipulation is necessary, a tool such as Pentaho (http://community.pentaho.com/projects/data-integration/) or Talend (http://www.talend.com/products/data-integration) can be used.

COPY

Now, let's look at the easiest way of moving data from PostgreSQL tables to files or the other way around: the COPY command. We will see the table to file options first:

```
postgres=# \c test
You are now connected to database "test" as user "postgres".
test=# CREATE TABLE myt (id int, nm varchar(20));
CREATE TABLE
test=# INSERT INTO myt VALUES(1,'First record');
INSERT 0 1
```

```
test=# INSERT INTO myt VALUES(2,'Second record');
INSERT 0 1
test=# COPY myt TO '/tmp/file.csv';
COPY 2
test=# \! cat /tmp/file.csv
1 First record
2 Second record
```

The simplest use of the command is COPY TABLE TO FILE. Instead of using the table name, we can use a SELECT command:

```
test=# \! rm /tmp/file.csv
test=# COPY ( select * from myt ) to '/tmp/file.csv';
COPY 2
test=# \! head /tmp/file.csv
1   First record
2   Second record
```

We named the file with the .csv extension, but the file generated is not really separated by comma. It used text as the default format with tab as the column separator. For the .csv output, we have to add the WITH CSV option:

```
test=# COPY ( SELECT * FROM myt ) TO '/tmp/file.csv' WITH CSV;
COPY 2
test=# \! head /tmp/file.csv
1,First record
2,Second record
```

If we want the column names to also be displayed, add the HEADER option. This may be necessary when we want to move the data to a spreadsheet, review and edit, and then move back to the table:

```
test=# COPY ( select * from myt ) to '/tmp/file.csv' WITH  CSV HEADER;
COPY 2
test=# \! head /tmp/file.csv
id,nm
1,First record
2,Second record
```

We can also write specific records as follows:

```
test=# COPY ( SELECT * FROM myt WHERE id =1 ) TO '/tmp/file.csv' WITH CSV;
COPY 1
test=# \! head /tmp/file.csv
1,First record
```

In a similar fashion, it's possible to SELECT specific columns. We can also join tables in the SELECT. It's not even necessary to SELECT from a table. We can also choose our delimiter (as long as it's a single one-byte character):

```
test=# \COPY (SELECT generate_series (1,2), 'AA') TO '/tmp/a.csv'
DELIMITER '?';
test=# \! cat /tmp/a.csv
1?AA
2?AA
```

When we copy data from a table to a file, the data in the file gets overwritten if it already exists. When we copy data from a file to a table, the data is appended to the data that exists in the table. The files are either read from the server or written to the server. Hence, the files must either reside on the server or be accessible from the server. If we connect to a remote PostgreSQL server from psql on our desktop, the output file created by the COPY command will be on the server. A minor change to the way the command is invoked from psql will write it to the local machine. Note this in the following sequence. We are connecting to a PostgreSQL server running on a remote machine, as shown in the following command:

```
postgres=# \c test
You are now connected to database "test" as user "postgres".
test=# COPY ( select * from myt ) to '/tmp/file.csv';
COPY 2
test=# \! cat  '/tmp/file.csv'
cat: /tmp/file.csv: No such file or directory
test=# \COPY ( select * from myt ) to '/tmp/file.csv'
test=# \! cat  '/tmp/file.csv'
1    First record
1    First record
```

Prefixing \ to copy created the file on the local machine rather than on the server. For more information on the differences between COPY and \copy, and details of options available with COPY, refer to http://www.postgresql.org/docs/current/static/sql-copy.html.

PostgreSQL 9.3 added the PROGRAM option to copy. So, we can now execute the COPY command, have programs such as awk or sed to massage/manipulate the data before the output goes into a file, use zip to compress the data, and so on.

```
test=# COPY myt  TO PROGRAM  'grep "First" > /tmp/file.csv  ';
COPY 2
test=# \! cat /tmp/file.csv
1    First record
```

Moving data from a file to a table is also pretty straightforward. This is done as follows:

```
test=# truncate myt;
TRUNCATE TABLE
test=# copy myt from '/tmp/file.csv';
COPY 1
test=# select * from myt;
 id  |      nm
----+--------------
  1 | First record
(1 row)
```

There are a few things to remember about COPY. It stops on the first error, and the rows that were inserted before the error occurred will not be visible or accessible. If we are copying from a file with hundreds of thousands of records and the error occurs in one of the last few records, this could be an issue. The table will end up occupying space on the disk and the data won't be accessible. Hence, it's better to ensure that the data is clean and properly formatted (if the data volume is significant), as shown here:

```
test=# \! cat '/tmp/file.csv';
1     First record
Bad     Second record
test=# TRUNCATE TABle myt;
TRUNCATE TABLE
test=# COPY myt FROM '/tmp/file.csv';
ERROR:  invalid input syntax for integer: "bad     Second record"
CONTEXT:  COPY myt, line 2, column id: "bad     Second record"
test=# SELECT * FROM myt;
 id | nm
----+----
(0 rows)
```

If we want to continue with the load process despite errors, we can use pg_bulkload.

Fast loading with pg_bulkload

The pg_bulkload utility is the one that provides a lot more flexibility than the COPY utility. The biggest advantage of pg_bulkload is speed. This utility lets us skip the shared buffers and WAL logging. This also implies a separate recovery process if something goes wrong. This is facilitated by postgresql, a script that comes with the pg_bulkload installation.

We will start with the installation of the utility. To do this, follow these steps:

1. Download the source with the following command:
   ```
   wget \
   http://pgfoundry.org/frs/download.php/3653/pg_bulkload-\
   3.1.6.tar.gz
   ```

2. Extract the contents as follows:
   ```
   tar xvf ./pg_bulkload-3.1.6.tar.gz
   ```

3. Change the directory with the following command:
   ```
   cd pg_bulkload-3.1.6
   ```

4. Make and install the binaries:
   ```
   make USE_PGXS=1
   ```

5. Then, use `su` with the following command:
   ```
   make USE_PGXS=1 install
   ```

6. Install the extension. Log in to the database where we will be using the utility and at the psql prompt:
   ```
   CREATE EXTENSION  pg_bulkload;
   CREATE EXTENSION
   ```

We will see what happens when we load the file we tried to load in the previous example.

We will create a control file with details of the source and target entities and a few other options. The contents of the control file are displayed using the `more` command:

```
more /tmp/file.ctl
TYPE = CSV
INPUT = /tmp/file.csv
DELIMITER = "    "
TABLE = myt
LOGFILE = /tmp/blk.log
PARSE_BADFILE = /tmp/parse.csv
```

We have a file with tab as the separator; we have mentioned this explicitly using the `DELIMITER` option. `PARSE_BADFILE` is the file to which all records that failed to load are written. Other parameters are self-explanatory. The database name is being passed when we invoke the following utility. The utility uses default settings for the server, database user, port, and so on. Now, we will invoke the utility from the shell prompt:

```
pg_bulkload /tmp/file.ctl -d test
```

Once the execution is over, we can see that the record with bad data has been written to `/tmp/parse.csv`:

```
more /tmp/parse.csv
bad      Second record
```

The log file has all the information pertaining to the execution (including execution time, number of rows skipped, number of rows successfully loaded, and so on). The record without any data issue has been inserted.

For other options and documentation, refer to `http://pgbulkload.projects.pgfoundry.org/pg_bulkload.html`.

Executing `pg_bulkload -help` at the shell prompt lists the available options.

> The `pg_bulkload` utility is similar to Oracle's SQL*Loader.

The tools covered so far meet our needs when we want to move a couple of tables from one system to another, or when we want to move master data from a `.csv` file to a master table. However, when we want to move all or quite a few data structures from a database with or without data or all the data without the data structures, `pg_dump` is the command we should use.

pg_dump

The `pg_dump` utility dumps the contents of the database in a file. Used without any options, it will use the default settings and dump the default database. In the following example, we will use the `-C` option. This option will generate the output with the command CREATE DATABASE so that we know which database was dumped:

```
# pg_dump -C > /tmp/a.sql
# grep "CREATE DATABASE" /tmp/a.sql | cut -f1-3 -d" "
CREATE DATABASE postgres
```

We will do the same for another database; use the `-d` option to specify the database and inspect the output. We can see that the database dumped was test:

```
pg_dump -C -d  test > /tmp/b.sql
```

Tools to Move Data in and out of PostgreSQL

The output file contains a command to set different values (such as `statement_timeout` and `lock_timeout`) followed by the `CREATE DATABASE` command because we used the `-C` option followed by SQL to create various database objects and then `COPY` commands to populate the tables with data. The file also contains commands to reset the sequences so that we don't have to worry about this when we use the file to populate a new database. For example, it will have SQL statements as follows:

```
SELECT pg_catalog.setval('batch_process_audit_process_id_seq', 9, true);
```

It's possible to redirect the output to another database in the same cluster or a database in a cluster on a remote machine, as shown in the following command:

```
test=# CREATE DATABASE test1;
CREATE DATABASE
test=# \c test1
You are now connected to database "test1" as user "postgres".
test1=# \d
No relations found.
test1=# \q
pg_dump -d test | psql -d test1
```

Now log in to psql on `test1`:

```
test1=# \d
                List of relations
 Schema |     Name     | Type  |  Owner
--------+--------------+-------+----------
 public | batch_error  | table | postgres
```

We dumped the database test and directed the output to the database `test1` via psql. We were able to do this because the default output from `pg_dump` consists of SQL commands. Other output formats, which may be more useful for large systems, are discussed later.

A couple points to note about `pg_dump` are as follows:

- It's non-blocking. Users can continue using the database even when a dump is being taken.
- The `pg_dump` utility provides a consistent dump. The database we restore it to will meet all constraints.

We will look at a few more useful options. We can use the `-c` option to generate commands to drop the objects. This way, we can ensure that the existing objects are dropped and recreated in the target database.

> The -j option (available from version 9.3) will start parallel jobs to generate the dump.

This is useful if we have a large database and enough CPU capacity to run a number of jobs in parallel. If we specify three as the number of jobs, four connections will be opened, one for the master processes and three for the worker processes. To use the -j option, we have to use -d, which stands for directory format. This is the only way multiple processes can write data in parallel. The dumps get written to a directory. For example, with `pg_dump -Fd test -j2 -f /tmp/dmp`, we are saying that there should be two workers, the output should be a custom dump (the -F option) in the directory format (d immediately after F) and the directory is /tmp/dmp. Note that we did not provide -d to specify the database. The first non-option argument is taken as the database name. The output format is compressed by default.

Let's inspect the directory and the files created:

```
ls -a /tmp/dmp/*
/tmp/dmp/2816.dat.gz    /tmp/dmp/2818.dat.gz    /tmp/dmp/2819.dat.gz
/tmp/dmp/2820.dat.gz    /tmp/dmp/toc.dat
```

There is a `toc` file (table of contents) and four numbered gzipped files. If we look at the contents of the files, we can see that each file contains data from one table. The `toc` file contains dependency information, COPY commands for the tables, scripts for functions, and so on. The best way to read the contents of `toc.dat` is to use `pg_restore`, which we will cover shortly. As we saw, the custom format (-F) creates zipped dump files. If we are not planning to run parallel workers, we can use the -Fc option and get the dump in a single file.

Filtering options

The `pg_dump` utility provides quite a few filtering options. We can use `--data-only` to generate files that contain only data, without CREATE statements, `--schema=` to generate the dump for a specific schema. If we need to retrieve only the object definition, which is often the case when we move from development to production environments, we can use the `--schema-only` option. To move specific tables, the `--table=` option can be used. Schema filters and table filters accept pattern matching. To generate only object definitions of tables whose names start with myt, we can execute the following command:

```
pg_dump test --table='myt*' --schema-only
```

Tools to Move Data in and out of PostgreSQL

In a similar fashion, it's possible to exclude schemas or tables using the `-exclude-schema` option or the `-exclude-table` option.

One version of `pg_dump` may not work seamlessly with other versions of PostgreSQL. For example, `pg_dump` cannot dump from PostgreSQL servers newer than its own version. For more information about version compatibility as well as details of options available with `pg_dump`, refer to http://www.postgresql.org/docs/current/static/app-pgdump.html.

The `pg_dump` utility does not dump database users because users are not linked to any specific database. We can use `pg_dumpall` to take care of this.

pg_dumpall

This `pg_dumpall` utility, as the name indicates, can be used to dump all the databases. It internally invokes `pg_dump`. As all databases get dumped, it doesn't matter which database we connect to. It does not support custom formats either; the output will always be in plain SQL format. The dump file will have SQL to create database users and groups, tablespaces, and other objects. The output generated can be fed to the psql client in another cluster to replicate the database cluster there.

> The script should be executed as a user with superuser privileges, as the addition of users, groups, and creation of databases will be involved.

This `pg_dumpall` utility has limited options compared to `pg_dump`. A few interesting options are `-data-only` (will provide a data dump without the object definitions), `--globals-only` (will dump roles and tablespaces), and `-roles-only` (will dump only roles). This `pg_dumpall` utility with the `--roles-only` option along with `pg_dump` for the databases, which are necessary, can be used to move users and databases from a development environment to a production environment.

pg_restore

This `pg_restore` utility can be used to restore two types of dumps: one created using the directory format (`-Fd` option) and those created using the custom format (`-Fc` option). Many of the options that are used while creating the dumps are applicable to `pg_restore` also, namely, `-data-only`, `--clean`, and `--create`.

Starting multiple workers to reduce load time is possible for both directory and custom format dumps using `-j n`, where n is the number of workers to be started. The `--no-tablespace` option is important. In the production system, we may not have a directory structure that is an exact replica of the directory structure in the development environment. In such situations, the restore process may error out because of missing directories (tablespaces). If we use the `-no-tablespace` option, the objects will be restored to the default tablespace. Two other very useful options are `--list` (lists the contents) and `-use-list` (lets us choose the objects to be restored). We will see an example for these three options. We will create a database and two tables in it: one in a new tablespace and the other in the default tablespace as follows:

```
postgres=# CREATE DATABASE tblspctst;
CREATE DATABASE
postgres=# \c tblspctst
You are now connected to database "tblspctst" as user "postgres".
tblspctst=# DROP TABLESPACE IF EXISTS mytablespace1;
```

Make postgres the owner of /pgdata from another shell session:

```
chown postgres /pgdata
Now login to psql
tblspctst=# \! mkdir /pgdata/mytblspc
tblspctst=# CREATE TABLESPACE mytablespace1 LOCATION
'/pgdata/mytblspc';
tblspctst=# CREATE TABLE myt (id integer) TABLESPACE
mytablespace;
CREATE TABLE
tblspctst=# CREATE TABLE myt1 (id integer);
CREATE TABLE
```

Now, we will create a custom dump as follows:

pg_dump -Fc tblspctst > tblspctst.dmp

Let's list the contents:

pg_restore --list tblspctst.dmp > tblspctst.lst

If we look at the contents, we can see that it has a header section with data about when it was created, what type of format it is, number of entries in the file, and so on. After this we have the items listed. The ; character marks a comment. Most of the contents are comments. The numbers at the beginning of the lines are the internal archive IDs assigned to the items. For example, we have:

```
2798; 0 257867 TABLE DATA public myt postgres
2799; 0 257870 TABLE DATA public myt1 postgres
```

We will use `pg_restore` with the list file. Instead of restoring to a database, we will direct the output to a file so that we can study the contents, as shown here:

```
pg_restore  -Fc -L tblspctst.lst tblspctst.dmp > a.sql
```

In `a.sql`, we will see the following entry before the SQL to create `myt`:

```
SET default_tablespace = mytablespace1;
```

We will edit the list file to remove all entries (except the one for `myt`) and use the `--no-tablespaces` option:

```
pg_restore --no-tablespaces -Fc -L tblspctst.lst tblspctst.dmp >\
b.sql
```

Now, the output file (`b.sql`) does not set the default tablespace and it does not have entries for other objects that are present in the dump.

Two other important and related options for `pg_restore` are `-single-transaction` and `-exit-on-error`. When we use the `-single-transaction` option, we are telling the restore to be rolled back if there is an error. The entire restore process is one transaction (all or nothing). The `-single-transaction` option can't be used with parallel workers.

> The `pg_restore` utility can't restore from plain SQL dumps, and psql can't be used to restore from custom dumps.

Summary

In this chapter, we covered a few utilities that can be used to move data and data structures from a development environment to a production environment. In the next chapter, we will cover more topics related to production deployment, namely, scaling and failover options.

10
Scaling, Replication, and Backup and Recovery

In the previous chapter, we saw how to move data from one PostgreSQL cluster to another or from one database in a cluster to another in the same cluster. We also covered various options that can be used while creating the files that are used to move data. How can we restore the data from a file to a database cluster and what are the options available while restoring the data were also covered.

In this chapter, we will cover a few concepts about scalability and failover. Then, we will see a couple of ways of achieving scalability and failover-ability with tools available in the PostgreSQL ecosystem.

Scalability and ability to recover from failures are critical for databases. These are two different concepts, although the same tool or approach can take care of both. We will first look at scalability and then at the ability to recover from failures.

Scalability

Performance issues can be identified during the performance testing phase before we go live with our system. There are a number of tools and websites available to conduct performance tests as well as to identify bottlenecks. JMeter (http://jmeter.apache.org/) is a free and very capable performance testing tool. Monitoring tools such as New Relic (http://newrelic.com/) help us identify bottlenecks when we are conducting performance tests. These are just pointers. We will not cover how to conduct performance tests.

Even in cases where performance tests were conducted and response times met our expectations, the number of users might go up beyond our expectations over time. From a business perspective, it's definitely a good thing to happen. However, this might lead to increased application response times. Tracking the requests and responses from the browser all the way to the database might tell us that it's the database that is the bottleneck. This means that we have run into a scalability issue at the database layer. Here, the average load went up slowly over time, resulting in an increase in response times.

Another possible scenario is one where the number of requests went up by a magnitude, far higher than what we ever expected, although for a short period of time. For example, there was a promotional offer - "First 100 passengers get LAX-JFK air tickets for $1". As soon as customers heard about the offer, they immediately hit the website, resulting in a huge spike in the number of requests to the application server and database server. This is a situation where the peak load exceeded our estimates and the system failed to respond.

In many such scenarios, scalability issues can be traced to:

- Poorly written queries (missed a WHERE clause?)
- Keeping default database parameters
- Not creating enough/right indexes
- Not fully exploiting available object types (materialized views and partitions)
- Not using the right data types (used VARCHAR to store dates?)
- Code issues resulting in transactions locking each other
- Not using proper normalization techniques while designing tables

As we go from the first to the last of the preceding listed items, fixing the issues probably takes more and more effort. Rewriting a query is usually very easily done while redesigning a couple of tables warrant changes to the application code in many places.

Once we realize that there is a scalability issue at the database layer, the next thing to do would be to ask "How can we scale?" Once we have tried the action items previously listed, we conclude that our hardware is just not sufficient to handle the load. We must explore the possibility of increasing the processing power and/or memory available to handle the system. There could be issues at the storage level too (for example, use of inappropriate RAID level). However, we will not cover this. Here are a few links with discussions on RAID levels:

- `https://wiki.postgresql.org/wiki/Community_Disk_Tuning_Guide#Hardware_related`

- `http://serverfault.com/questions/235049/choosing-the-right-raid-level-for-postgresql-database`
- `http://serverfault.com/questions/453767/postgresql-raid-configuration`

We have two possible approaches to scaling at hardware level and then different possibilities under them.

Vertical scaling

In this approach, we move from a small machine to a bigger one. For example, we move from a 16 GB two quad-core CPU machine to a 32 GB four quad-core CPU machine. If we use virtualized machines, it might involve just allocating more cores/RAM from the host machine. Either way, we should review and change the `postgresql.conf` parameters after the upgrade. All the parameters that are related to memory (for example, `shared_buffers`) and CPU (mainly planner related) should be reviewed after the upgrade.

The advantage of vertical scaling is that no code change is necessary. The disadvantage is that we may again run into scalability issues as databases do not scale linearly to infinite number of cores. Different blogs and studies available on the Web reveal that PostgreSQL stops scaling linearly after a specific number of cores. The number of cores beyond which PostgreSQL stops scaling linearly depends on the version of PostgreSQL and Linux.

> PostgreSQL cannot use more than one core to process a query. So, if we have a really heavy query that is taking time, adding cores to the server will not help. We will have to use more powerful cores.

Another disadvantage with vertical scaling is that we have to estimate with reasonable accuracy the kind of load the system will have to support in the next couple of years. If we overestimate, we will end up with underutilized servers. If we underestimate, we have to go the procurement route to buy a beefier server. With virtualization technologies, which make it possible to allocate cores/RAM as per need, and VPS providers who make it possible to upgrade with half an hour to may be a couple of hours of downtime, this disadvantage (procurement and migration) is alleviated to some extent. One more disadvantage is that the prices of servers also go up significantly as we move up from a small to medium-sized server to one with many CPUs/cores and more than, say, 64 GB of memory.

Horizontal scaling

When we scale horizontally, we do not add more cores or memory to one machine. We add more machines to the environment to spread the load over more machines. This implies more PostgreSQL clusters. This approach has many variations; we will look at some of them later. The obvious advantage is that we will be able to scale much more than with the vertical approach. Now, we are no longer stuck at 32 (or 64) cores. Another advantage is that we can add servers gradually as per requirements. We could add one more node and see whether it's sufficient to handle the load. If not, add one more. If adding one node was able to handle the load and bring down the response time to acceptable levels, we are done for the time being. We can add more nodes when we notice that the existing nodes are fully utilized and response times have started deteriorating.

Horizontal scaling has a few disadvantages:

- We have more clusters to monitor
- We have to ensure that backup and recovery mechanisms are in place for these clusters
- We have more possible points of failure
- Changes to application setup and configuration will be necessary

Let's look at the possible variations of horizontal scaling. We will start with the easiest one: master-slave replication with read/write separation.

Master-slave(s) with read/write separation

One server (master) accepting all writes and one or more servers (slaves) responding to most of the reads is the easiest way to scale. This is the low-hanging fruit of horizontal scaling approaches. This does not require significant code change. This approach offers the ability to scale to a large number of nodes as far as reads are concerned.

Ability to scale, as far as writes is concerned, is limited to one node. This is one disadvantage of this approach. If the application has a high write to read ratio, this approach takes a toll on the infrastructure, as the writes have to be replicated to all the slaves.

We will first cover concepts related to implementing this approach. In this approach, the replication of data from master to slaves can be done using PostgreSQL's built-in replication capability or using a middleware solution (pgpool-II). We will use PostgreSQL's built-in method and cover different replication possibilities offered by PostgreSQL.

All replication possibilities offered by PostgreSQL involve the use of **Write Ahead Logs (WAL)**. These logs, we saw earlier, record all the changes that have been made to the data. Once a file is filled, the server moves on and starts writing to the next file. Once the changes that have been committed are flushed to the corresponding data files, the data in the WAL files is no longer useful and can be overwritten. We can archive the logs before they are overwritten using the `archive_command` parameter in `postgresql.conf`.

We have:

- WAL files that are being written to
- WAL files that have been filled and are waiting to be archived
- WAL files that have been archived

When we move WAL files (which have been filled) to another server or use them on another cluster in the same server, it's called log shipping. Log shipping is asynchronous. There can be a delay before data that is committed on the master server appears on the slave. The slaves are eventually consistent with the master, not always consistent with the master. This also means that there is a chance of data loss when the primary server crashes, as there may be transactions which have not been shipped yet. If we keep a low `archive_timeout` value, files switching will happen frequently and the lag on the secondary server will go down. However, this also increases the volume of data transferred across the network.

In earlier versions of PostgreSQL (8.*), the archived WAL logs were used to keep a cluster ready for failover. The cluster would run in recovery mode and it was not possible to connect to the server until recovery was complete, that is, the primary failed over.

Hot standby was introduced in PostgreSQL 9.0. This was a major change because now we could connect to the standby server and execute queries. So, scalability for reads was possible. Still, the standby could lag behind the primary as the WAL logs had to be shipped. This lag was reduced by adding streaming replication.

Streaming replication

It's possible to get the WAL records as soon as they are generated without waiting for the log files to be filled. This reduces the lag. In streaming replication, the slave/standby connects to the master/primary and gets the WAL records. An entry for `primary_conninfo` in a file named `recovery.conf` is what it takes to move replication from log shipping to streaming replication. Here is how log shipping is different from streaming replication:

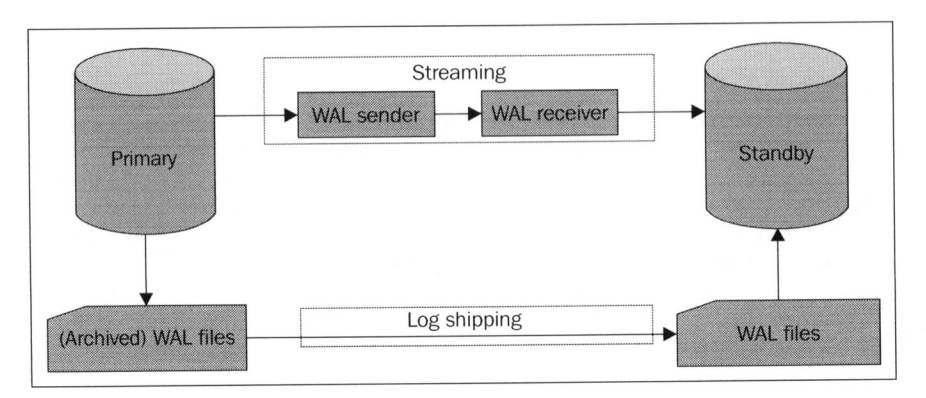

We will now see how to set up streaming replication because this approach lets us scale horizontally with read-write separation with minimum lag. It also lets the standby be promoted as primary in case of a failure. After this, we will see **Point-in-time recovery (PITR)**.

Configuring primary

We have to make a few changes to the primary before we can start streaming the logs. This involves making changes to the configuration settings in `postgresql.conf` and `pg_hba.conf` and setting up archiving. To do this, follow these steps:

1. First we will make a few changes in `postgresql.conf`:

   ```
   wal_level = hot_standby
   ```

   As we move from minimal to archive to the `hot_standby` values for `wal_level`, the amount of information recorded in WAL files go up:

   ```
   archive_mode = on
   archive_command = 'rsync -av %p /pgdata/archive/'
   ```

   The preceding parameters decide what should be done with the archived WAL files:

   ```
   archive_timeout = 10
   ```

Chapter 10

A WAL switch will be forced after this many seconds have elapsed since the last switch, and there has been any database activity, including a single checkpoint. In streaming replication, we are streaming WAL records as they are generated and are used to keep the standby in sync. We are not dependent on the archived WAL files to keep the standby in sync:

`max_wal_senders = 2`

This is the maximum number of concurrent connections from standby servers that can connect to the master for streaming:

`wal_keep_segments = 10`

This defines the number of past log files to be kept in `pg_xlog`. As each segment is of 16 MB (default), we will have about 160 MB of files with this setting. If space is not an issue, this number can be increased to ensure that the standby gets the changes before primary archives the WAL files. In fact, it's a good idea to increase this number to much more than the value of 10.

2. Next is an entry in `pg_hba.conf`:

   `host    replication       postgres 127.0.0.1/32    trust`

   > We are setting up the master and standby on the same machine. In production, these must be on different machines. Think about what would happen if we have non-default tablespaces and we try to have both master and standby on the same server. Having master and standby on different servers does imply a few changes to the steps outlined here, such as enabling password-less `ssh`/`scp` between the servers.

3. Create the archive directory with the following command:

   `mkdir /pgdata/archive`

4. Restart the server as follows:

   `pg_ctl restart`

Now, the primary is up and running with all the necessary configuration changes.

> It's a good idea to have these settings in the secondary also. As and when a failover happens, we will be able to configure a new secondary server to connect to the new primary server.

Scaling, Replication, and Backup and Recovery

Configuring secondary

This involves initializing the cluster and making configuration changes. To do this, follow these steps:

1. We will initialize a cluster on `/pgdata/standby`:

    ```
    initdb --pgdata=/pgdata/standby
    ```

2. Go to `/pgdata/standby`, edit `postgresql.conf` and set it:

    ```
    listen_addresses = '127.0.0.1'
    hot_standby = on
    ```

    The `hot_standby` parameter takes effect only when the server is in the archive recovery or standby mode. When this is set to on, queries can be executed during recovery.

3. In the same directory, create a file named `recovery.conf` with the following entries:

    ```
    standby_mode = 'on'
    primary_conninfo = 'host=127.0.0.1 port=2345 user=postgres'
    restore_command = 'cp /pgdata/archive/%f "%p"'
    trigger_file = '/pgdata/standby/down.trg'
    ```

> The master is running on port (2345). Change the port entry in `postgresql.conf` for master and restart master, in case it is not. If it's at the default port (5432), this should be used in `primary_conninfo` here and the standby server should be running on a different port

We will use the `postgres` user to connect to the primary server using the trust authentication. It's better to create a user with `REPLICATION` and `LOGIN` privileges along with a password and an md5 authentication mode. If we create a user called `myreplicationuser` for replication purposes, the entry made in `pg_hba.conf` in the primary node will look like the following command:

```
host    replication     myreplicationuser 127.0.0.1/32    md5
```

The entry in `recovery.conf` on secondary will be:

```
primary_conninfo = 'host=127.0.0.1 port=2345 user= myreplicationuser password=thepassword'
```

The `recovery.conf` file is read on cluster startup. Normally, PostgreSQL will scan the file, complete recovery, and rename the file to `recovery.done`. As we have enabled `standby_mode`, it will continue running in standby mode, connecting to the server mentioned in the `primary_conninfo`, and keep streaming the XLOG records.

Making the standby in synch with primary

Now, we will make sure that the database folders are in sync. Note that we have just initialized the secondary cluster and not started the server. It's better to drop any big tables/databases created for testing purpose to reduce the synching time. Make sure you drop non-default tablespaces because we will create the secondary on the same server. If we don't drop non-default tablespaces, both the primary and the secondary will end up pointing to the same directory and cause issues.

In a production setup, the secondary cluster must be on a different machine. Some changes to the configuration files and scripts will be necessary to make this work when the clusters are on separate machines (for example, the failover script).

1. In a psql session on the primary node, execute the following command:

    ```
    SELECT pg_start_backup('mybackup');
    ```

    The `pg_start_backup` command forces a checkpoint in the cluster and writes a file with information about the activity. Once the function is executed, we can have a look in the data directory and we will see a file called `backup_label`. It has information about the start WAL location, the checkpoint location, time, and a few other pieces of information. We can inspect the contents of the file using `more` commands:

    ```
    more /pgdata/9.3/backup_label
    START WAL LOCATION: 3/FA000028 (file 0000000100000003000000FA)
    CHECKPOINT LOCATION: 3/FA000060
    BACKUP METHOD: pg_start_backup
    BACKUP FROM: master
    START TIME: 2014-07-01 08:25:25 IST
    LABEL: mybackup
    ```

2. Open an `ssh` session as postgres, go to `/pgdata/9.3`, and rsync like this:

    ```
    rsync -avz --exclude postmaster.pid --exclude pg_hba.conf \
    --exclude postgresql.conf --exclude postmaster.opts \
    --exclude pg_xlog /pgdata/9.3/ /pgdata/standby
    ```

    Note that we have excluded a few files and rsynced everything else. The files excluded were the postmaster `pid` file with the process ID, the postmaster options file, which tells us the options used while starting the server, and the two configuration files. The WAL directory was also excluded.

3. In the psql session, execute the following command:

   ```
   SELECT pg_stop_backup();
   ```

   This function causes a WAL segment switch; WAL segments are archived. In the archive directory, we can see a file with extension `backup`:

   ```
   000000010000000300000FA.00000028.backup
   ```

   It has all the information we had in `backup_label` plus two pieces of information when the process stopped and the WAL location at which it stopped:

   ```
   STOP WAL LOCATION: 3/FB000050 (file 0000000100000003000000FB)
   STOP TIME: 2014-07-01 08:28:34 IST
   ```

4. Ensure that the PGDATA directory is set to the secondary server's directory and start the cluster:

   ```
   pg_ctl start
   server starting...
   LOG:  entering standby mode
   .....
   LOG:  database system is ready to accept read only connections
   ...
   LOG:  started streaming WAL from primary
   ```

We can see the words streaming and read only. We are good to go. If you did not change the port for the primary to `2345`, you will get an error.

There are multiple ways to ensure that the standby is in read-only mode. On the standby, at psql, try executing the SQL statement:

```
CREATE TABLE a(id int);
ERROR:  cannot execute CREATE TABLE in a read-only transaction
STATEMENT:  CREATE TABLE a(id int);
ERROR:  cannot execute CREATE TABLE in a read-only transaction
```

Also, you can execute the following SQL statement:

```
SHOW transaction_read_only;
 transaction_read_only
-----------------------
 On
```

This is the correct way of testing if a node is in read-only mode. We can try the same on the primary node:

```
SHOW transaction_read_only;
transaction_read_only
----------------------
Off
```

So far, we have set up streaming replication. When we make any change to the data or data structures in the primary, it will be reflected in the secondary cluster.

> A good comparison of various replication options to achieve availability and scalability is available at http://www.postgresql.org/docs/current/static/different-replication-solutions.html.

Connection pooling, load balancing, and failover with pgpool-II

There are quite a few solutions available for replication, connection pooling, load balancing, and failover. We will use pgpool-II for the following reasons:

- It provides load balancing. The pgpool-II middleware can distribute SELECTs over a number of servers, which are configured in pgpool.conf, depending on the weight assigned to the servers. It does not send the same query to more than one server when we use it in the manner described in the following sections. We have to be careful with functions that change data and get executed via SELECT. Look up the black_function_list feature of pgpool-II to deal with this issue.

- It provides connection pooling. Acquiring a connection always has a minor overhead attached to it. Reusing connections is crucial to performance. The pgpool-II middleware provides connection pooling with parameters to fix the number of pools as well as the number of connections in a pool. It reuses a connection when a request for a new connection comes in and has the same properties (user, database, and protocol).

- It provides failover capability for cluster. This is achieved via a script that we have to write. In the event of pgpool-II detecting failure of the primary node, it can execute the script. In the script, we can trigger a standby promotion.

- It provides HA for pgpool-II: This is done so that pgpool-II does not become a single point of failure.

Scaling, Replication, and Backup and Recovery

One disadvantage of using PostgreSQL's streaming capability with pgpool-II is that we end up replicating all the databases and tables in the cluster. It's not possible to selectively replicate specific databases or tables. A replication solution such as Slony (http://slony.info/) can be used if we want to replicate only part of the changes from the master node. If we are looking for a solution that provides connection pooling and nothing more, we need to look at pgbouncer.

Now, let's cover pgpool-II, which provides quite a few useful features:

Configuring pgpool-II

We will use pgpool-II (version 3.3.3). We will download the source and untar it:

```
wget -O pgpool-II-3.3.3.tar.gz    \
http://www.pgpool.net/download.php?f=pgpool-II-3.3.3.tar.gz &&    \
tar -xzvf pgpool-II-3.3.3.tar.gz
```

Next, use cd to go to the directory, configure, and install:

```
cd pgpool-II-3.3.3 && ./configure && make && sudo make install
```

Next, use cd to go to the sql/pgpool-recovery directory, execute make, and make install. These steps will create an extension (a sql file) under /usr/local/pgsql/share/extension/. Then, we need to connect to the template1 database (psql) on the master node and execute the following command:

```
CREATE EXTENSION pgpool_recovery;
```

Now, we will set up configuration. We can find a few sample configuration files in /usr/local/etc:

```
pgpool.conf.sample    pgpool.conf.sample-master-slave
pgpool.conf.sample-replication    pgpool.conf.sample-stream
pool_hba.conf.sample
```

We will use pgpool.conf.sample-stream as we have set up streaming replication. We will also create a user to be used for health and streaming replication checks. In the psql session on the primary node, create the following user, which will be used for online recovery:

```
CREATE USER pgpooluser WITH PASSWORD 'pgpool';
```

Editing the pgpool config files and starting pgpool can be done as the root user. Now, let's see the changes we have to make to pgpool.conf:

```
cd /usr/local/etc
cp pgpool.conf.sample-stream pgpool.conf
cp pool_hba.conf.sample pool_hba.conf
```

The changes to be made to `pgpool.conf` are provided here with descriptions:

`listen_addresses = '127.0.0.1'`

This is similar to the `postgresql.conf` configuration. We are telling pgpool-II which interfaces to listen on 1:

`backend_hostname0 = '127.0.0.1'`
`backend_port0 = 2345`

The backend with number 0 is treated as master. As we are using streaming replication, this is not relevant. We can have only one master. The node data we will see later in log files will refer to this number:

`backend_weight0 = 0`

We can decide the load balancing ratio by setting this. The value here is set to 0 and the value for the secondary is set to 1 to ensure that SELECT queries always go to standby. The weights should be adjusted after taking into consideration the number of nodes, write/read ratio and similar factors. If we have 3 nodes and we set the weight to 0, 1, and 2 for node 0, node 1, and node 2 respectively, 0 SELECT statements will go to node 0, about one-third of the SELECT statements will go to node 1 and two-thirds of the SELECT statements will go to node 2:

`backend_data_directory0 = '/pgdata/9.3'`
`backend_hostname1 = '127.0.0.1'`
`backend_port1 = 5432`
`backend_weight1 = 1`
`backend_data_directory1 = '/pgdata/standby'`
`backend_flag1 = 'DISALLOW_TO_FAILOVER'`

If the standby fails, we do not want to try and failover to another node:

`num_init_children = 8`

This is the number of pools. This multiplied by `max_pool` the (number of connections per pool) should be less than the maximum number of connections set in the PostgreSQL node minus `superuser_reserved_connections`, if all connections are going to one PostgreSQL node:

`log_statement = on`
`log_per_node_statement = on`

Scaling, Replication, and Backup and Recovery

These should be turned off in production. We are setting these on to see load balancing and read/write separation:

```
sr_check_user = 'pgpooluser'
sr_check_password = 'pgpool'
health_check_period = 10
```

Check for health every 10 seconds:

```
health_check_user = 'pgpooluser'
health_check_password = 'pgpool'
failover_command = '/usr/local/pgsql/failover.sh %d /pgdata/standby/down.trg'
```

The `failover` command can be any script. Our script is just a few lines. Create a script named `failover.sh` in `/usr/local/pgsql`:

```
#! /bin/sh
# Arguments: $1: failed node id. $2: trigger file
failed_node=$1
trigger_file=$2
# Do nothing if standby goes down.
if [ $failed_node = 1 ];
then exit 0;
fi
# Create the trigger file.
/bin/touch $trigger_file
exit 0;
```

Provide execute permission on the file:

```
chmod +x /usr/local/pgsql/failover.sh
```

The script checks whether it is the secondary node that failed. If so, do nothing. If it's not, create the trigger file using the `touch` command. When the trigger file is spotted by the secondary node, it will cause streaming replication to end and the standby will open in read/write mode. Note that `/pgdata/standby/down.trg` is the value we set for `trigger_file` in `recovery.conf` for the secondary node:

```
mkdir -p /var/run/pgpool
```

Now start `pgpool`:

```
pgpool   -n > /tmp/pgpool.log 2>&1 &
```

Let's create a database to test `pgpool`. On the primary node, connect to psql. Ensure that we are connecting via `pgpool` by specifying the correct port (`9999`):

```
psql -p 9999
postgres=#CREATE DATABASE pgp;
postgres=#   SHOW pool_nodes;
 node_id | hostname  | port | status | lb_weight | role
---------+-----------+------+--------+-----------+---------
 0       | 127.0.0.1 | 2345 | 2      | 0.000000  | primary
 1       | 127.0.0.1 | 5432 | 2      | 1.000000  | standby
postgres=# SHOW pool_processes;
pool_pid |     start_time       | database | username |
create_time     | pool_counter
---------+----------------------+----------+----------+--------------
--------+--------------
 13722   | 2014-07-01 15:52:47  |          |          |
|
 13723   | 2014-07-01 15:52:47  | pgp| postgres  | 2014-07-01 15:52:51
| 1
 13724   | 2014-07-01 15:52:47  |          |          |
|
```

Test read/write separation

We will open a psql session, insert a record, delete a record, execute a couple of `SELECT`s, and see how pgpool-II is handling all this:

```
psql -p 9999
postgres=# \c pgp
You are now connected to database "pgp" as user "postgres"
pgp=# CREATE TABLE tbl(id INT);
pgp=# SELECT * FROM tbl;
id
----
(0 rows)

pgp=# INSERT INTO tbl VALUES(1);
INSERT 0 1
pgp=# SELECT * FROM tbl;
id
----
  1
(1 row)
```

```
pgp=# DELETE FROM tbl;
DELETE 1
pgp=# SELECT * FROM tbl;
 id
----
(0 rows)
```

In an `ssh` session, let's open the log file:

```
more /tmp/pgpool.log
```

It starts with the following lines:

```
find_primary_node: primary node id is 0
```

```
2014-07-01 16:57:25 LOG:    pid 15361: DB node id: 1 backend pid: 15388 statement: SELECT * FROM tbl;
2014-07-01 16:57:37 LOG:    pid 15361: statement: INSERT INTO tbl VALUES(1);
2014-07-01 16:57:37 LOG:    pid 15361: DB node id: 0 backend pid: 15387 statement: INSERT INTO tbl VALUES(1);
2014-07-01 16:57:40 LOG:    pid 15361: statement: SELECT * FROM tbl;
2014-07-01 16:57:40 LOG:    pid 15361: DB node id: 1 backend pid: 15388 statement: SELECT * FROM tbl;
2014-07-01 16:57:45 LOG:    pid 15361: statement: DELETE FROM tbl;
2014-07-01 16:57:45 LOG:    pid 15361: DB node id: 0 backend pid: 15387 statement: DELETE FROM tbl;
2014-07-01 16:57:50 LOG:    pid 15361: statement: SELECT * FROM tbl;
2014-07-01 16:57:50 LOG:    pid 15361: DB node id: 1 backend pid: 15388 statement: SELECT * FROM tbl;
```

We can see that the `INSERT`/`DELETE` statements are all going to node 0, and `SELECT` statements are going to node 1.

Test failover

Now, let's test failover. Stop the primary server:

```
pg_ctl stop
psql -p 9999
postgres=# \c pgp
You are now connected to database "pgp" as user "postgres".
pgp=# SHOW port;
 port
```

```
------
  5432
(1 row)
pgp=# INSERT INTO tbl values(100);
INSERT 0 1
pgp=# SHOW transaction_read_only;
transaction_read_only
----------------------
off
(1 row)
```

From the port value, it's clear that we are connected to the secondary server. It's now in read/write mode. We can see a file named recovery.done in the data directory of the secondary node:

pwd

/pgdata/standby

[postgres@MyCentOS standby]$ ls rec*

recovery.done

In pgpool.log in /tmp, we can see the following entries:

```
ERROR: pid 16229: health check failed. 0 th host 127.0.0.1 at port
2345 is down
LOG:    pid 16229: set 0 th backend down status
LOG:    pid 16229: starting degeneration. shutdown host
127.0.0.1(2345)
LOG:    pid 16229: Restart all children
LOG:    pid 16229: execute command: /usr/local/pgsql/failover.sh 0
/pgdata/standby/down.trg
LOG:    pid 16229: find_primary_node_repeatedly: waiting for
finding a primary node
LOG:    pid 16229: find_primary_node: primary node id is 1
LOG:    pid 16229: failover: set new primary node: 1
LOG:    pid 16229: failover done. shutdown host 127.0.0.1(2345)
...
LOG:    pid 16270: statement: SHOW transaction_read_only;
```

The sequence of events is as follows:

1. The pgpool-II middleware realizes that the master is down.
2. It executes the failover script.
3. The failover script creates the trigger file in the slave's data directory.

4. The slave, who keeps polling for the trigger file, notices it.
5. The slave reboots in read/write mode (earlier it was in read-only mode) and completes recovery.
6. The slave renames `recovery.conf` to `recovery.done`.

In most failover scenarios, there is one issue that is to be tackled. Assume that the primary server (node 0) is unavailable for some time because of a network issue; we fail over to the secondary server (node 1). After some time, network issues are resolved and node 0 is available again. The application must not start connecting to node 0 now. It has missed all the writes that went to the secondary node in the interim and will not be up-to-date. The node 1 is now in read/write mode and won't be able to accept transactions from the primary.

> The process of restoring operations to the original primary server is called failback.

The pgpool-II middleware handles this situation as well. For pgpool-II, node 1 is now the primary node. Once we recover node 0 (or if it came up automatically), we must restart pgpool-II with the `-D` option (D for discard) so that it again treats node 0 as primary. If we restart without the `-D` option, it will continue to work with node 1 as primary. In effect, pgpool-II ensures that the primary (which is marked as down) does not get written to without anybody noticing it. It does this by recording the status in a `pgpool_status` file under `/tmp/`. To ensure that this approach works okay, we have to ensure that all PostgreSQL connections do go through pgpool-II.

> Using `pg_terminate_backend()` to stop a PostgreSQL process will trigger a failover with pgpool-II. Do not use `pg_terminate_backend()` to terminate a backend if you are using pgpool-II.

There are quite a few things that have been left out in the preceding sections. For example, we used TRUST authentication, which is not recommended in production systems. Typically, we use md5. Using md5 in `postgresql.conf` will in turn necessitate md5 in the `hba` configuration file for pgpool-II also. We will need to create a password file for pgpool-II if we use md5 to stream replication. Refer to http://www.pgpool.net/docs/latest/pgpool-en.html#md5 for details.

We can configure one more pgpool-II instance and set up a watchdog process so that pgpool-II itself is not a single point of failure. Details are available at http://www.pgpool.net/pgpool-web/contrib_docs/watchdog_master_slave/en.html.

The pgpool-II middleware has an admin interface (pgpoolAdmin) which provides a good UI to monitor and control pgpool-II. Online recovery (revering a failed node without stopping pgpool-II and PostgreSQL) is possible using pgpool-II. Parameters like backend_data_directory need to be set only if we are using this. It's also possible to list whitelist/blacklist functions so that pgpool-II knows which functions will not write to the database and which will. The pgpool-II middleware can also cache result sets to further reduce the response time.

> The pgpool's cache mechanism can cache SELECT statements and results. The result can be returned from the cache (if the same SELECT statement is executed again and the data in the tables did not change). If data in the tables changes, all caches related to the tables need to be deleted. If this happens frequently, there may be a drop in performance when compared to an environment where the cache is not enabled. A decision on whether to enable the cache should be made after considering how frequently the tables get updated.
>
> A quick tutorial on how to set this up is available at http://www.pgpool.net/pgpool-web/contrib_docs/memqcache/en.html.

In short, pgpool-II is a great tool (capable of a number of settings) and we can tweak these setting to achieve a lot.

Now, we will move on to some more theory and concepts that deal with horizontal scaling.

One reason we decided to go with horizontal scaling is that we can keep adding nodes if we are choking on reads. Recollecting our discussion from an earlier chapter on tuning, most applications have a high read to write ratio. If we are able to scale for reads, by adding more nodes as and when necessary, it is quite an achievement. How should we add more nodes? There are several choices. The following diagram shows sample configurations:

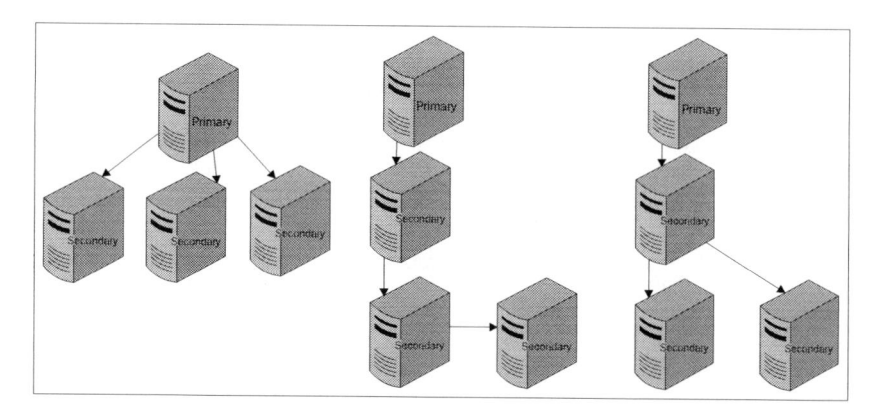

In the first one, three standby servers are fed from a primary server. The primary server will usually be under quite a bit of load because all writes are going against it. Hence, it's not recommended to add the overhead of feeding too many secondary servers. Which secondary server should take over in the case of primary failure is another item to be figured out. In addition to this issue, other secondary servers will stop getting updates once the primary server goes down.

In the second option, the load will be more or less evenly balanced with each server feeding at most one secondary server. However, one issue with this approach is that there can be significant delay for the last server in the chain to catch up. The third option where a secondary server feeds more than one server avoids this issue. In the second and third options, it's clear which secondary server should take over in the event of a primary failure. In the second and third cases, if the secondary server that is fed from primary goes down, we will have a system where the writes are working, reads are successful, but the reads will not be fetching current data (as replication from primary is no longer working).

It's better not to failover automatically from a secondary server. If there are consecutive failures happening at primary and then secondary (now acting as primary) servers, surely manual intervention and root cause analysis is necessary.

Scheduling backups from a secondary server can avoid load spikes on the primary server during backups.

When we use a secondary node to feed another one, it's referred to as cascading replication. When we use cascading replication, chances of significant lag between the primary and the secondary node at the farthest end are high. So, a write can go to the master; the user who initiated the transaction gets a message communicating successful commit. When the user tries to retrieve the data, it might go to a node that has not yet received the changes. One way of avoiding this is to use synchronous replication. With synchronous replication, the primary node waits for confirmation from standby before committing the change. Configuration-wise, two changes are necessary:

First, specify an application name in the `primary_conninfo` in `recovery.conf`. So, `primary_conninfo = 'host=127.0.0.1 port=2345 user=postgres'` becomes `primary_conninfo = 'host=127.0.0.1 port=2345 user=postgres application_name=myapp'`.

Also, we must make an entry for this in `postgreql.conf` of the primary:

```
synchronous_standby_names = 'myapp'
synchronous_commit = on
```

Now, we can check the status on primary with the following command:

```
postgres=# SELECT  application_name,sync_state FROM pg_stat_replication;
 application_name | sync_state
------------------+------------
 myapp            | sync
(1 row)
```

Note that synchronous replication is bound to have an impact on response times for write transactions on the master server.

Sharding

Sharding usually means splitting data horizontally; we have 1000 records. We consider splitting them into 10 shards of 100 records and hosting the shards on 10 different servers. When we normalize tables, data gets split vertically. In sharding, data gets split into horizontal blocks. It does sound like partitioning, but here, the partitions/shards are on different servers. Although we said 1000 records, typically the number will be far higher that 1000 (many millions). In sharding, all the database servers will be in read/write mode. There will be some logic that processes each record, figure out which shard it should go to, and send it there. For reads too, similar logic works. Postgres-XC with the CREATE TABLE syntax that can use the DISTRIBUTE BY HASH option is a good example (http://postgres-xc.sourceforge.net/docs/1_0/ddl-basics.html).

> Postgres-XC is a write-scalable PostgreSQL solution. This is different from PostgreSQL project. It has a few components to be taken care of (global transaction manager, coordinator, and data node). Unless write scalability is really a major issue, it's recommended to go with vanilla PostgreSQL.

A system that is expected to handle millions of users can be split across servers with users whose names start with A-C hosted on one server, D-G on another, and so on. It's important to study the data, figure out the number of users whose names start with each letter, then decide the distribution. If we don't do this, some servers might end up hosting many users and some others very few users. Ensuring uniform distribution of data based on users' names is not an easy task and hence sharding by name is not recommended. Splitting can be done based on the location of the user, or age or any other appropriate parameter.

A set of master data (country, currency), which needs to be accessed frequently from each server, can be replicated on all the servers. Such data should require minimum updates. Sharding should be done so that there is minimal or no need to fetch data from more than one server. Inter-database-server communication should also be kept to a minimum. Instagram's case study of how they sharded with PostgreSQL is definitely worth a read (`http://instagram-engineering.tumblr.com/post/10853187575/sharding-ids-at-instagram`).

How data should be sharded really depends on the application and the problem we are trying to solve.

Splitting an application module-wise (application sharding) and hosting them on different machines is also sometimes referred to as sharding. Let's look at a solution which takes care of all booking and travel-related aspects of an airline. This can easily be split into the following modules:

- Availability and booking
- Check-in
- Frequent flyer and loyalty rewards
- Crew management
- Cargo management
- Aircraft movement tracking

Availability module is one which will need to scale quickly depending on demand for the airline's flights. It's tricky to predict the maximum number of concurrent hits during a promotion, as we discussed earlier. What about the availability expectations of this module? Well, it will have an impact on revenue if the availability module goes down for half an hour or so.

However, this is nothing compared to the situation if the check-in module goes down. There will be long queues at the counters, possible disruption in flight schedules and havoc. In short, the situation will be far more serious than the one where the availability module was not responding. What about the scalability requirements of the check-in module? Given that the number of counters is a known factor, we can predict with far more accuracy the maximum number of transactions per second (tps) the check-in module will need to handle. In short, different modules in the same application can have different scalability and availability requirements. It makes sense to shard/split an application into modules based on the scalability and availability requirements.

With sharding, we need to ensure that a lot of attention and care is paid to how the application is sharded, or how data in tables is distributed across servers at the design and coding stages. Change to the architecture at later stages will be quite difficult to implement. We might end up moving data from one server to another because of a change in the data distribution logic; we might have to make configuration changes so that the queries go to the server where the data has been relocated. In short, a lot of effort will be spent when we decide to change the sharding strategy. This is the key disadvantage of these approaches.

Multi-master full replication

In this approach, all data will be replicated to all database clusters. If we have a setup with four PostgreSQL clusters, each write transaction will be written four times. Reads can go to any server because the assumption is that the servers are in sync. Writes can go against any server and will need to be replicated to other database servers from the application/web tier/a database replication tool. PostgreSQL's built-in replication can't be used in this approach because only one server (master) can be started in write mode. Other clusters (slaves) will be in read-only mode.

Multi-master replication for entire datasets is not often recommended because of many reasons. It's possible that the same data point might get modified in two different servers at the same time. Then, we have to identify which is the change that must be accepted by all servers.

Transactions must successfully be committed on all the servers before the user is notified of a successful write. This can result in a significant drag on performance. If we don't ensure that transactions are successfully committed on all servers, it can lead to unpredictable results. Let's assume that a user fills a form and clicks on submit. It's successfully committed in three of the four servers. If the user's next read goes to the server where data was not successfully committed, the user will end up wondering what happened to the form he submitted. He might try submitting the form again. This issue can be mitigated by a sticky connection (requests from a client will always go to the same node). Another solution is to ensure that writes to specific datasets always go to specific nodes.

The approaches covered so far are not by any means the only ones available, but are the most frequently used ones.

Let's take a look at the approaches we covered so far before we move to the next topic:

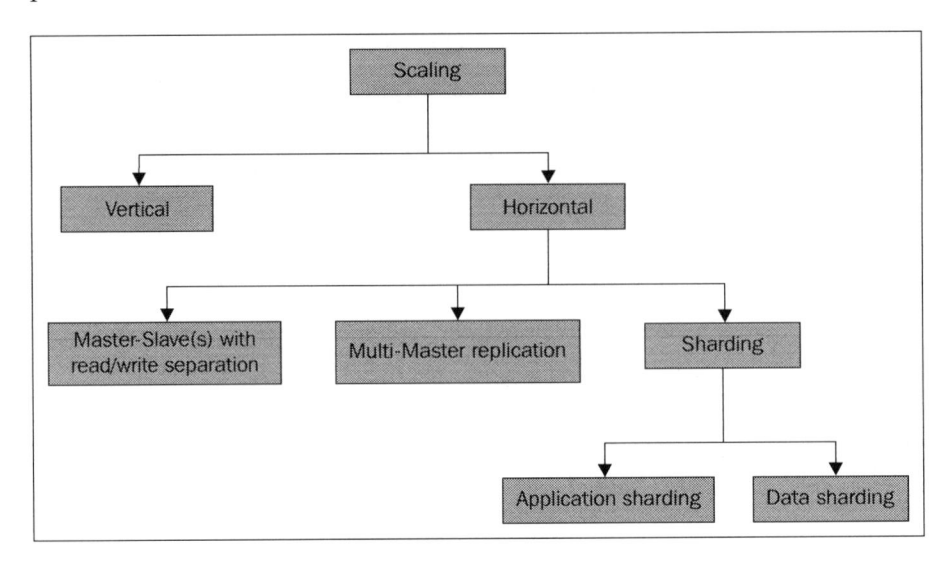

```
                          Scaling
                         /       \
                   Vertical     Horizontal
                               /    |    \
            Master-Slave(s) with  Multi-Master  Sharding
            read/write separation  replication  /      \
                                      Application    Data
                                        sharding    sharding
```

Point-in-time recovery

We covered scalability and one way to scale horizontally and failover. We failed over to a node, which contains all transactions, which were committed till the primary went down.

Sometimes, we want to go back in time, retrieve the database cluster at a specific point in time, and then start afresh. For example, we made a release in production last evening. Sanity testing told us things looked fine and we made the system open to users. Sometime this morning, customer support tells us that there is some issue with the system and many orders entered after the release did not look right. Once we are sure that there is a critical bug, the first thing we want to do is to roll back the changes.

On the application side, it's relatively easy. Get the previous release from version control system and deploy it. What about the database? If it's a small cluster (a few GBs), it's always possible to take a full backup before each release and restore from that. In case of big databases, that is not a practical solution. We cannot take a full backup of a database with hundreds of GB frequently. We have to resort to a backup taken some time ago and replay the transactions until a point in time (point-in-time recovery, so to speak). The time to replay will depend on how much catch up has to be done.

Once the replay to a point in time is over, we can open the database for exclusive access to admin and the customer support team. This can be opened in another server/port. Then, go through all the transactions made after the release, make these entries in the recovered cluster, and open the system for business. This is easier said than done.

PostgreSQL allows you to restore the database to a specific point in time by using one of the three options:

- `recovery_target_name`: This option is to be used with named restore points. The `pg_create_restore_point` can be used to create named restore points. The occasions to create restore points are typically before major production releases/upgrades of the application. Recovering a target name is probably the easiest of the three options available.

- `recovery_target_time`: This option can be used when we know we made a mistake and realize it sometime later, and we remember the approximate time that we dropped a table or deleted some records in the morning. Although we are specifying a timestamp value, recovery will stop only after the transaction running at that point in time are committed. So, if we have long running transactions, we would want to provide a value that is a bit earlier than the exact time at which we made a mistake. This can be used with the `pause_at_recovery_target` option. We keep the earliest possible timestamp, start recovering, look at the data in the server. Once we are sure that we have reached the correct point, we use `pg_xlog_replay_resume` to stop recovery and open the database for normal use.

- `recovery_target_xid`: This option can be used if we know the `transactionid` after which the database was corrupted; we can use that to recover until that transaction.

For demonstration, we will use the target name option along with `pause_at_recovery_target` options. Let's use the same setup we used earlier. We can go to `/pgdata/standby` and execute `rm -rf *` to clean the directory. This time, we will not use `rsync`. We will use `pg_basebackup`, which creates a binary copy of the database cluster. The cluster will be put in and out of backup mode automatically:

```
pg_basebackup -D /pgdata/standby --format=plain \
--write-recovery-conf --xlog-method=fetch   --verbose -h 127.0.0.1
```

The `-D` option is used to specify the target directory. We are using the plain format. It's possible to use the tar format. We used the recovery `conf` option to generate a sample recovery file. We will edit that later. The output from the command is as follows:

```
transaction log start point: 4/8D000028 on timeline 1
transaction log end point: 4/8E000050
pg_basebackup: base backup complete
```

Scaling, Replication, and Backup and Recovery

As happened when we took a backup last time, there is a backup file in the cluster directory:

`more 000000010000000400000008D.00000028.backup`

```
START WAL LOCATION: 4/8D000028 (file 000000010000000400000008D)
STOP WAL LOCATION: 4/8E000050 (file 000000010000000400000008E)
CHECKPOINT LOCATION: 4/8D000060
BACKUP METHOD: streamed
BACKUP FROM: master
START TIME: 2014-07-02 11:47:33 IST
LABEL: pg_basebackup base backup
STOP TIME: 2014-07-02 11:49:33 IST
```

As our plan is to bring up the standby even while the primary is running, we will change the port to `5432`. Also, we want to read from the new cluster. So, enable `hot_standby`. Archive should go to `/pgdata/standby_archive`. We need to edit this too.

So, changes made to the `postgresql.conf` file for the secondary node will be as follows:

```
port = 5432
hot_standby = on
archive_command = 'rsync -av %p /pgdata/standby_archive/%f '
```

Create the directory using the following command:

`mkdir /pgdata/standby_archive`

Now, let's edit `recovery.conf`. We will add the following two lines:

```
pause_at_recovery_target = true
recovery_target_name = patch_of_2014_07_02
```

On the primary, we will create a table, insert some data, create a restore point, and insert some more data. We will restore to the point before the last batch was inserted:

```
psql -d pgp
pgp=# CREATE TABLE myt(id integer);
CREATE TABLE
pgp=# INSERT INTO myt SELECT generate_series(1,100);
INSERT 0 100
pgp=# SELECT pg_create_restore_point('patch_of_2014_07_02');
 pg_create_restore_point
-------------------------
 4/93000090
```

[204]

```
(1 row)
pgp=# INSERT INTO myt SELECT generate_series(1000,1100);
INSERT 0 101
pgp=# SELECT count(*), min(id), max(id) FROM myt;
 count | min | max
-------+-----+------
   201 |   1 | 1100
(1 row)
```

Now let's start the secondary database:

```
pg_ctl start
```

If we check the log file, these are the important sections:

```
entering standby mode..
recovery stopping at restore point "patch_of_2014_07_02", time
2014-07-02 12:08:57.507946+05:30
recovery has paused
Execute pg_xlog_replay_resume() to continue
```

Connect to psql on the secondary node:

```
postgres=# \c pgp
You are now connected to database "pgp" as user "postgres".
pgp=# SELECT min(id), max(id), count(*) FROM myt;
 min | max | count
-----+-----+-------
   1 | 100 |   100
(1 row)
pgp=# CREATE TABLE a(id integer);
ERROR:  cannot execute CREATE TABLE in a read-only transaction
The database is still in read-only mode.
pgp=# SELECT pg_xlog_replay_resume();
 pg_xlog_replay_resume
-----------------------

(1 row)
pgp=# CREATE TABLE a(id integer);
CREATE TABLE
pgp=# SELECT min(id), max(id), count(*) FROM myt;
 min | max | count
-----+-----+-------
   1 | 100 |   100
(1 row)
```

We are done. The new cluster is open in read/write mode and the transaction which we wanted to omit has been omitted.

We will see a few useful functions that deal with replication/failover:

This returns `True` for standby node and `False` for primary:

```
SELECT pg_last_xlog_receive_location();
```

This retrieves the last transaction location that was streamed by the secondary. Executing the function on the primary retrieves no data:

```
SELECT pg_last_xlog_replay_location();
```

This retrieves the last transaction replayed during recovery:

```
select pg_last_xact_replay_timestamp();
```

This retrieves the latest timestamp when a transaction was replayed on the secondary.

Refer to the following links for details of recovery settings and system administration functions:

- http://www.postgresql.org/docs/current/static/recovery-target-settings.html
- http://www.postgresql.org/docs/current/static/functions-admin.html

Summary

In this chapter, we covered very important concepts of scaling, failover, backup, and recovery. We also covered scalability options at the database layer. We shortlisted one of the options (horizontal scaling with primary/secondary setup and read/write separation) and covered the most basic setup possible with pgpool-II. We also briefly touched upon backup and recovery scenarios and covered what is a mandatory step before making a major release in production: baselining the database state. We saw how to recover this baseline.

In the next chapter, we will look at troubleshooting PostgreSQL issues. Connection issues, queries not responding and similar problems will be covered.

11
PostgreSQL – Troubleshooting

In the previous chapter, we covered a few scalability, backup, and recovery concepts. We also saw how pgpool-II can be used with PostgreSQL's streaming replication to achieve horizontal scalability with read/write separation. We had a look at point-in-time recovery with PostgreSQL's inbuilt tools.

From installation to designing databases, optimization, and scaling, we covered a lot. Unfortunately, there will be hiccups when we try something new. In this chapter, we will cover common problems we are likely to run into when we work with PostgreSQL and how to troubleshoot them. The errors/issues range from connection issues to a query that is not responding. We will start with connection issues.

Connection issues

So, we installed PostgreSQL and are trying to connect via psql from a remote host. However, we get the following error:

```
psql: could not connect to server: Connection refused
        Is the server running on host "192.168.56.101" and accepting
        TCP/IP connections on port 5432?
```

The first thing we need to do is log in to the machine where PostgreSQL is supposed to be running and check whether the server process is there. We can use the `ps` command to find this out:

    ps aux | grep postgres

If we don't see the processes: the writer process, wal writer process, and so on, we know that the server has not started. We can start the service and try again. If we get the same error again, the next step is to confirm that it's indeed listening at the port we are trying to connect to. To do this, use the following command:

    ss -anp | grep postgres

We should see entries for port `5432`. We can also log in to the database server, connect to psql, and try the following commands:

```
postgres=# SHOW port;
 port
------
 5432
postgres=# SHOW listen_addresses;
 listen_addresses
------------------
 localhost
```

Correcting the entry for `listen_addresses` and port in `postgresql.conf` and restarting the server (or using the correct options in psql) should take us one step closer. The `listen_addresses` in `postgresql.conf` tells PostgreSQL on which interfaces it should listen for requests, while the address entries in `pg_hba.conf` tells PostgreSQL from which addresses it should let users through. On the other hand, if we are getting the following error, there are a few steps that you need to take:

```
psql: could not connect to server: No route to host
        Is the server running on host "192.168.56.101" and accepting
        TCP/IP connections on port 5432?
```

We need to check `iptables` (on CentOS/similar OS) or any other firewall-blocking software on the database server. Note the difference in errors (this one said `No route to host`, whereas the first error said `Connection refused`).

Once we resolve the firewall issue, we should be able to connect. These cover the process/listen address/port/firewall checks. In short, we need to:

- Check whether the server is running
- Verify that there are no firewalls blocking the port
- Check whether it's listening at the expected interfaces
- Check whether we got the port right

Authentication and permission issues

Once we are past the initial stage, the next set of errors is a result of incorrect or missing entries in `pg_hba.conf:`, the host-based authentication file found under the data directory. The location/name of the file can be set using the `hba_file` parameter in `postgresql.conf`.

The most likely error we will see will be similar to the following:

```
psql: FATAL:  no pg_hba.conf entry for host "192.168.56.1", user
"postgres", database "postgres"
```

The message mentions a host, a user, and a database. These are precisely the entries we should provide in `pg_hba.conf`. It has entries similar to the following screenshot:

```
# "local" is for Unix domain socket connections only
local   all             all                                     trust
# IPv4 local connections:
host    all             all             127.0.0.1/32            trust
# IPv6 local connections:
host    all             all             ::1/128                 trust
# Allow replication connections from localhost, by a user with the
# replication privilege.                  Database  User  Host
#local   replication     postgres                                trust
#host    replication     postgres        127.0.0.1/32            trust
#host    replication     postgres        ::1/128                 trust
```

The entry marked host can be a hostname, an IP address range or a special keyword.

> Note that most of the lines in the screenshot are commented as they begin with #.

We must reload the configuration for the changes to take effect with the following command:

```
pg_ctl reload
```

Now, we will be able to connect.

It's possible to use very specific entries in `pg_hba.conf`, such as the one we used, by specifying the host, user, and database. In a live deployment scenario, we could make a couple of entries for the IP addresses of the web servers (live and failover) while specifying the application user and application database and not allow anything/anyone else through. For administrative tasks, we can allow PostgreSQL to connect from localhost and from one or two other machines (the machines used by DBA). When specifying the host IP address range, we can specify /32,/24,/16,/0 as CIDR masks for IPv4 addresses and thus allow connections from more machines in the network. This mask indicates the number of higher-order bits of the client IP address that must match. If we use 32 as the mask for an IPv4 address, PostgreSQL will accept connections only from this specific IP. If we use 0, PostgreSQL will accept requests from all IPv4 addresses. For a discussion on Classless Inter-Domain Routing, refer to http://en.wikipedia.org/wiki/Classless_Inter-Domain_Routing.

Once the connection errors are resolved, an error that newcomers usually run into is as follows:

```
ERROR:  relation "mytb" does not exist
```

This usually happens when we use upper or a mix of upper and lowercase letters while creating the table and used quotes. For example:

```
postgres=> CREATE TABLE  "Mytb" ( id INTEGER);
CREATE TABLE
postgres=> SELECT  * FROM Mytb;
ERROR:  relation "mytb" does not exist
LINE 1: SELECT  * FROM Mytb;
                       ^
postgres=> SELECT  * FROM "Mytb";
 id
----
(0 rows)
```

The other usual suspect is that the object is in another schema and `search_path` is not set properly.

There might be instances where you will get the following error:

```
ERROR:  permission denied for relation mytb
```

It will be a matter of, well, not having permission. We can give permissions and check it with the following command:

```
postgres=> \dp+ mytb
                                Access privileges
 Schema | Name  | Type  |     Access privileges       | Column access privileges
--------+-------+-------+-----------------------------+--------------------------
 public | mytb  | table | postgres=arwdDxt/postgres+ |
        |       |       |        | myuser=r/postgres
 |
```

Parameter changes not effective

When we change a parameter, but can't see the effect, there are quite a few possible reasons. Some parameters need a server restart. These are marked in the configuration file as follows:

```
# (change requires restart)
```

Then, there are parameters that can be set by a reload of the configuration file after making changes in the file. Reloading the parameters can be done using the following command:

```
pg_ctl reload
```

The same can be achieved by executing at psql:

```
SELECT pg_reload_conf();
```

We can know whether a server restart is required for a parameter change to take effect by querying `pg_settings`:

```
postgres=# SELECT DISTINCT  context FROM pg_settings;
  context
------------
 backend
 user
 internal
 postmaster
 superuser
 sighup
```

If the context says `postmaster`, then a restart of the cluster is required. However, if the context says `sighup`, `pg_ctl` a reload will do. For example:

```
SELECT  name, context FROM  pg_settings WHERE  name IN ( 'archive_command','port');
      name       |  context
-----------------+------------
 archive_command | sighup
 port            | postmaster
```

Another thing to check is did we make the change in the right file? We can find the file used by the server as follows:

```
postgres=# SHOW config_file;
         config_file
-----------------------------
 /pgdata/9.3/postgresql.conf
```

[211]

PostgreSQL – Troubleshooting

In some cases, when we have an invalid parameter value, PostgreSQL will just ignore the value and continue with the default one. Refer to the entries in the log file in the following screenshot:

```
user=,db= LOG:   received SIGHUP, reloading configuration files
user=,db= LOG:   parameter "default_text_search_config" changed to "pg_catalog.english_ouch"
user=[unknown],db=[unknown] LOG:  connection received: host=[local]
user=postgres,db=postgres LOG:  connection authorized: user=postgres database=postgres
user=postgres,db=postgres LOG:  duration: 1.000 ms  statement: show default_text_search_config;
user=postgres,db=postgres LOG:  disconnection: session time: 0:00:08.159 user=postgres database=postgres host=[local]
user=,db= LOG:   received smart shutdown request
user=,db= LOG:   autovacuum launcher shutting down
user=,db= LOG:   shutting down
user=,db= LOG:   database system is shut down
user=,db= LOG:   database system was shut down at 2014-12-01 12:04:32 IST
user=,db= LOG:   database system is ready to accept connections
user=,db= LOG:   autovacuum launcher started
user=,db= LOG:   received SIGHUP, reloading configuration files
user=,db= LOG:   invalid value for parameter "lc_monetary": "en_US.UTF-8_ouch"
user=,db= LOG:   configuration file "/pgdata/9.3/postgresql.conf" contains errors; unaffected changes were applied
```

> PostgreSQL does not come with a validator. We must check and ensure that the new values have taken effect.

Query not responding

Sometimes, we execute a query and we wait and wait. Nothing happens! We do not want to kill the query. What if it has just completed processing and is about to fetch us the results? And yes, it may be an update or some other SQL that will make changes to the data and we have to execute it anyway. The best thing to do in such situations is to find out what exactly is happening in the database. There are a couple of views that are very useful when we want to see what is happening in the database.

The `pg_stat_activity` view keeps track of all the activities in the database. Note that this view does not have transactions that have been completed. Only live queries can be retrieved from this view. We will cover the important columns in this view:

Columns	Content
`datid` and `datname`	These columns have the OID of the database and name of the database the user is connected to.
`pid`	This is the ID of the backend process created for a connection. When we connect to PostgreSQL using psql, there are two processes associated (we can get from a process listing). One is `pid` of the psql command. The other one is the backend process created for the session by PostgreSQL. It's the ID of the backend process that is tracked in the `pid` column.

Columns	Content
application_name	When we connect using psql, this will read psql. We can set this using SET application_name at psql or pass it as a parameter when we connect using JDBC (jdbc:postgresql://host:5435/db?ApplicationName=TheApp). When there are many connections to a cluster from different applications, setting this value will make it easier to find out which application is executing which query.
client_addr, client_hostname, and client_port	These are all attributes of the client that established the connection.
state	This tells us whether the backend is active or idle.
waiting	If the value is true, it means it's waiting for a lock.
query	This tells us about the query being executed.

Let's see the values in the most important columns when there is a lock. Take three psql sessions to connect to the same database. Set the application name in two of them, start transactions that wait, and see the data in pg_stat_activity in the third one:

- Session 1:

    ```
    pgp=# SET application_name = 'lockingclient';
    SET
    pgp=#  BEGIN;
    BEGIN
    pgp=# SELECT * FROM myt FOR UPDATE;
     id
    ----
      2
    ```

- Session 2:

    ```
    pgp=#  SET application_name = 'waitingclient';
    SET
    pgp=# SELECT * FROM myt FOR UPDATE;
    ```

- Session 3: Refer to the following screenshot:

```
pgp=# SELECT  pid ,waiting, query ,state ,application_name FROM pg_stat_activity;
 pid  | waiting |                           query                                   |       state         | application_name
------+---------+-------------------------------------------------------------------+---------------------+------------------
 2362 | f       | SELECT * FROM myt FOR UPDATE;                                     | idle in transaction | lockingclient
 1955 | f       | SELECT  pid ,waiting, query ,state ,application_name FROM pg_stat_activity; | active    | psql
 2383 | t       | SELECT * FROM myt FOR UPDATE;                                     | active              | waitingclient
(3 rows)
```

PostgreSQL – Troubleshooting

The next important view to be used when our queries are not responding is `pg_locks`. The important columns are shown in the following table:

Columns	Content
locktype	This is the lock on the entire table, page, or tuple
database	This is the OID of the database
relation	This is the OID of the table
pid	This is the process ID of the backend process
mode	This is the lock mode held or requested for

Now, let's see how we can write a query to fetch the most relevant information for transactions in process with the following command:

```
SELECT  pl.locktype, pl.mode, pc.relname,pl.pid , psa.state,
psa.query
FROM pg_locks pl JOIN pg_class pc ON pl.relation=pc.oid
JOIN pg_stat_activity psa ON pl.pid=psa.pid
WHERE relname='myt';
```

The following screenshot illustrates the preceding command:

```
locktype |        mode        | relname | pid  |       state        |           query
---------+--------------------+---------+------+--------------------+-------------------------------
relation | RowShareLock       | myt     | 2383 | active             | SELECT * FROM myt FOR UPDATE;
relation | RowShareLock       | myt     | 2362 | idle in transaction| SELECT * FROM myt FOR UPDATE;
tuple    | AccessExclusiveLock| myt     | 2383 | active             | SELECT * FROM myt FOR UPDATE;
```

However, this gives only data about all locks in the system. It does not tell us who is blocking whom. To get this information, we need to use a query like this:

```
SELECT waiting1.pid                AS waiting_pid,
       waiting2.usename            AS waiting_user,
       waiting2.query              AS waiting_statement,
        blocking1.pid              AS blocking_pid,
        blocking2.usename          AS blocking_user,
        blocking2.query            AS blocking_statement
    FROM  pg_locks waiting1
    JOIN pg_stat_activity waiting2  ON
            waiting1.pid = waiting2.pid
    JOIN pg_locks blocking1 ON
            waiting1.transactionid = blocking1.transactionid
         AND waiting1.pid != blocking1.pid
    JOIN pg_stat_activity blocking2 ON
            blocking1.pid = blocking2.pid
    WHERE NOT waiting1.granted;
```

Chapter 11

The following screenshot illustrates the preceding command:

```
 waiting_pid | waiting_user |         waiting_statement       | blocking_pid | blocking_user |       blocking_statement
-------------+--------------+---------------------------------+--------------+---------------+---------------------------------
        2383 | postgres     | SELECT * FROM myt FOR UPDATE;   |         2362 | postgres      | SELECT * FROM myt FOR UPDATE;
```

These views cover information we can get from the database about what is happening, who is locking whom, and so on. The data available in PostgreSQL views is rather basic when it comes to tracking what exactly a query is doing. Very often, we will need to go to the next level, that is, the operating system level to find out what is happening and see why an operation (reading/writing) is taking time.

We will look at a few Linux utilities that are useful to look at the activities from the OS level.

The first one is strace. It traces system calls and signals. If we have a query that is not seemingly doing anything, we can get its process ID and do a strace. If we strace the process that started a transaction, acquired the locks, and then used COMMIT, it will look like strace -p 2362, as shown in the following screenshot:

```
recvfrom(10, "Q\0\0\0\vBEGIN;\0", 8192, 0, NULL, NULL) = 12
gettimeofday({1417433268, 958239}, NULL) = 0
gettimeofday({1417433268, 959239}, NULL) = 0
gettimeofday({1417433268, 960240}, NULL) = 0
gettimeofday({1417433268, 961240}, NULL) = 0
write(2, "\0\0h\0\342\16\0\0t2014-12-01 16:57:48 IST"..., 113) = 113
gettimeofday({1417433268, 963241}, NULL) = 0
sendto(10, "C\0\0\0\nBEGIN\0Z\0\0\0\5T", 17, 0, NULL, 0) = 17
recvfrom(10, "Q\0\0\0*UPDATE myt SET name='a' WHE"..., 8192, 0, NULL, NULL) = 43
gettimeofday({1417433277, 132074}, NULL) = 0
gettimeofday({1417433277, 132074}, NULL) = 0
kill(2623, SIGUSR1)                     = 0
read(31, "\0\0\0\0\0\0\0\0\4\0\264\0\260\30\0 \4 \0\0\0\0\320\237\\\0\240\237\\\0"..., 8192) = 8192
lseek(44, 0, SEEK_END)                  = 450560
lseek(44, 0, SEEK_END)                  = 450560
open("base/331880/578005_fsm", O_RDWR)  = 45
lseek(45, 0, SEEK_END)                  = 24576
lseek(45, 0, SEEK_SET)                  = 0
read(45, "\0\0\0\0\0\0\0\0\0\0\0\30\0\0 \0 \4 \0\0\0\0\0\0\0\0\0\0\0\0\0\0"..., 8192) = 8192
lseek(44, 0, SEEK_END)                  = 450560
gettimeofday({1417433277, 161084}, NULL) = 0
gettimeofday({1417433277, 162085}, NULL) = 0
write(2, "\0\0\210\0\342\16\0\0t2014-12-01 16:57:57 IST"..., 145) = 145
gettimeofday({1417433277, 163085}, NULL) = 0
sendto(10, "C\0\0\0rUPDATE 1\0Z\0\0\0\5T", 20, 0, NULL, 0) = 20
recvfrom(10, "Q\0\0\0\fCOMMIT;\0", 8192, 0, NULL, NULL) = 13
gettimeofday({1417433281, 284515}, NULL) = 0
gettimeofday({1417433281, 284515}, NULL) = 0
gettimeofday({1417433281, 284515}, NULL) = 0
write(41, "u\320\5\0\1\0\0\0\0\0\210\274\25\0\0\0-\n\0\0\0\0\0\0\0\246\310\0\0\0\0\0"..., 8192) = 8192
fdatasync(41)                           = 0
gettimeofday({1417433281, 287516}, NULL) = 0
gettimeofday({1417433281, 288516}, NULL) = 0
write(2, "\0\0j\0\342\16\0\0t2014-12-01 16:58:01 IST"..., 115) = 115
sendto(9, "\2\0\0\0\320\3\0\0h\20\5\0\t\0\0\0\1\0\0\0\1\0\0\0\0\0\0\0\0\0\0\0"..., 976, 0, NULL, 0) = 976
sendto(9, "\2\0\0\0\0000\2\0\0h\20\5\0\5\0\0\0\0\0\0\0\0\0\0\0\0\0\0\0\0\0\0"..., 560, 0, NULL, 0) = 560
gettimeofday({1417433281, 290517}, NULL) = 0
sendto(10, "C\0\0\0\vCOMMIT\0Z\0\0\0\5I", 18, 0, NULL, 0) = 18
recvfrom(10, "X\0\0\0\4", 8192, 0, NULL, NULL) = 5
gettimeofday({1417433301, 167412}, NULL) = 0
gettimeofday({1417433301, 167412}, NULL) = 0
write(2, "\0\0\225\0\342\16\0\0t2014-12-01 16:58:21 IST"..., 158) = 158
exit_group(0)                           = ?
Process 3810 detached
```

In the output, we can see that there are open, seek, and write activities. Such output gives us a better idea about what the server is doing in response to our read/write requests.

Strace is really useful when we are using a middleware (such as pgpool-II) and are unable to connect. Setting the number of children to 1 in pgpool-II and then running a strace on this process will tell us a lot about where it's failing. For more interesting ways of using strace, refer to http://www.thegeekstuff.com/2011/11/strace-examples/.

Once we find out what the database is doing, we might want to find out whether the issue/bottleneck is at the processor level or at the I/O level. The utilities to see what is happening in the Linux-based system include:

- `top` and `htop`: This top command as well as its more user-friendly version: `htop` are great at telling us about the processes running on the system, their memory and CPU utilization, and how long they have been running.
- `vmstat`: This command provides us virtual memory information. How much memory is available, how much is cached, how much is used, and so on. It does provide information about CPU utilization, the number of processes waiting for CPU time, and so on.
- `vmstat 2`: This command will keep printing the information every 2 seconds.
- `iostat`: This utility provides a wealth of information about disk read/writes. If we suspect that we are facing an I/O bottleneck, this is the command to use. It displays the statistics every 2 seconds if we use `iostat 2`.
- `mpstat`: This command is similar to `vmstat` and `iostat` (with more information available on the individual CPU or core).

There is a lot of overlap when it comes to the data provided by the commands listed previously. However, each command provides more detailed information on one of the three possible issues: memory issues, I/O wait, or CPU bottleneck. Examples and options for these commands are available at http://www.thegeekstuff.com/2011/07/iostat-vmstat-mpstat-examples/.

Summary

In this chapter, we covered how to troubleshoot a few issues that are commonly raised in the PostgreSQL forums. While this is by no means an exhaustive list, these are the issues that someone who is a novice in PostgreSQL is likely to run into.

The next chapter will cover quite a few assorted topics: a few special data types, a tool to analyze the PostgreSQL log, and the interesting features in PostgreSQL 9.4.

12
PostgreSQL – Extras

In the previous chapter, we saw how to troubleshoot the initial hiccups faced by people who are new to PostgreSQL. We also covered a couple of PostgreSQL views and Linux utilities that help us see what is exactly happening when we are in a no-response situation.

In this chapter, we will cover a variety of topics. We will look at a few useful, but not commonly used data types. We will also cover pgbadger, a nifty third-party tool that can run through a PostgreSQL log. This tool can tell us a lot about what is happening in the cluster. Also, we will look at a few key features that are part of the PostgreSQL 9.4 release. We will cover a couple of useful extensions.

Interesting data types

We will start with the data types. PostgreSQL does have all the common data types we see in databases. These include:

- The number data types (`smallint`, `integer`, `bigint`, `decimal`, `numeric`, `real`, and `double`)
- The character data types (`varchar`, `char`, and `text`)
- The binary data types
- The date/time data types (including `date`, `timestamp without timezone`, and `timestamp with timezone`)
- `BOOLEAN` data types

However, this is all standard fare. Let's start off by looking at the `RANGE` data type.

[217]

RANGE

This is a data type that can be used to capture values that fall in a specific range. Let's look at a few example use cases.

Cars can be categorized as compact, convertible, MPV, SUV, and so on. Each of these categories will have a price range. For example, the price range of a category of cars can start from $15,000 at the lower end and the price range at the upper end can start from $40,000.

We can have meeting rooms booked for different time slots. Each room is booked during different time slots and is available accordingly.

Then, there are use cases that involve shift timings for employees. Each shift begins at a specific time, ends at a specific time, and involves a specific number of hours on duty. We would also need to capture the swipe-in and swipe-out time for employees.

These are some use cases where we can consider range types. Range is a high-level data type; we can use `int4range` as the appropriate subtype for the car price range scenario. For the meeting rooms and shift use cases, we can consider `tsrange` or `tstzrange` (if we want to capture time zone as well).

There are a number of very useful functions and operators available with range data types at http://www.postgresql.org/docs/current/interactive/functions-range.html#RANGE-OPERATORS-TABLE. Hence, it makes sense to explore the possibility of using range data types in most scenarios, which involve:

- From and to timestamps/dates for room reservations
- Lower and upper limit for price/discount ranges
- Scheduling jobs
- Timesheets

Let's now look at an example. We have three meeting rooms. The rooms can be booked and the entries for reservations made go into another table (basic normalization principles). How can we find rooms that are not booked for a specific time period, say, `10:45` to `11:15`? We will look at this with and without the range data type:

```
CREATE TABLE rooms(id serial, descr varchar(50));

INSERT INTO rooms(descr)
SELECT concat('Room ', generate_series(1,3));
```

```
CREATE TABLE  room_book (id serial , room_id integer, from_time
timestamp, to_time timestamp , res tsrange);

INSERT INTO room_book (room_id,from_time,to_time,res)
values(1,'2014-7-30 10:00:00', '2014-7-30 11:00:00', '(2014-7-30
10:00:00,2014-7-30 11:00:00)');

INSERT INTO room_book (room_id,from_time,to_time,res)
values(2,'2014-7-30 10:00:00', '2014-7-30 10:40:00', '(2014-7-30
10:00,2014-7-30 10:40:00)');

INSERT INTO room_book (room_id,from_time,to_time,res)
values(2,'2014-7-30 11:20:00', '2014-7-30 12:00:00', '(2014-7-30
11:20:00,2014-7-30 12:00:00)');

INSERT INTO room_book (room_id,from_time,to_time,res)
values(3,'2014-7-30 11:00:00', '2014-7-30 11:30:00', '(2014-7-30
11:00:00,2014-7-30 11:30:00)');
```

PostgreSQL has the OVERLAPS operator. This can be used to get all the reservations that overlap with the period for which we wanted to book a room:

```
SELECT room_id FROM room_book WHERE (from_time,to_time) OVERLAPS
('2014-07-30 10:45:00','2014-07-30 11:15:00');
```

If we eliminate these room IDs from the master list, we have the list of rooms available. So, we prefix the following command to the preceding SQL:

```
SELECT id FROM rooms
EXCEPT
```

We get a room ID that is not booked from 10:45 to 11:15. This is the old way of doing it. With the range data type, we can write the following SQL statement:

```
SELECT id FROM rooms
EXCEPT
SELECT room_id FROM room_book WHERE res   && '(2014-07-30
10:45:00,2014-07-30 11:15:00)';
```

> Do look up GIST indexes to improve the performance of queries that use range operators.

PostgreSQL – Extras

Another way of achieving the same is to use the following command:

```
SELECT id FROM rooms
EXCEPT
SELECT room_id FROM room_book WHERE
'2014-07-30 10:45:00' < to_time AND '2014-07-30 11:15:00' >
from_time;
```

Now, let's look at the finer points of how a range is represented. The range values can be opened using [or (and closed with] or). [means include the lower value and (means exclude the lower value. The closing (] or)) has a similar effect on the upper values.

When we do not specify anything, [) is assumed, implying include the lower value, but exclude the upper value. Note that the lower bound is 3 and upper bound is 6 when we mention 3,5, as shown here:

```
SELECT   int4range(3,5,'[)') lowerincl ,int4range(3,5,'[]')
bothincl,
int4range(3,5,'()') bothexcl , int4range(3,5,'[)') upperexcl;
 lowerincl | bothincl | bothexcl | upperexcl
-----------+----------+----------+-----------
 [3,5)     | [3,6)    | [4,5)    | [3,5)
```

Using network address types

The network address types are cidr, inet, and macaddr. These are used to capture IPv4, IPv6, and Mac addresses. Let's look at a few use cases.

When we have a website that is open to the public, a number of users from different parts of the world access it. We may want to analyze the access patterns. Very often, websites can be used by users without registering or providing address information. In such cases, it becomes even more important that we get some insight into the users based on the country/city and similar location information. When anonymous users access our website, an IP is usually all we get to link the user to a country or city. Often, this becomes our not-so-accurate unique identifier (along with cookies) to keep track of repeat visits, to analyze website-usage patterns, and so on.

The network address types can also be useful when we develop applications that monitor a number of systems in different networks to check whether they are up and running, to monitor resource consumption of the systems in the network, and so on.

While data types (such as VARCHAR or BIGINT) can be used to store IP addresses, it's recommended to use one of the built-in types PostgreSQL provides to store network addresses. There are three data types to store network addresses. They are as follows:

- inet: This data type can be used to store an IPV4 or IPV6 address along with its subnet. The format in which data is to be inserted is Address/y, where y is the number of bits in the netmask.
- cidr: This data type can also be used to store networks and network addresses. Once we specify the subnet mask for a cidr data type, PostgreSQL will throw an error if we set bits beyond the mask, as shown in the following example:

```
CREATE TABLE  nettb (id serial, intclmn inet, cidrclmn cidr);
CREATE TABLE
INSERT INTO  nettb (intclmn , cidrclmn) VALUES ('192.168.64.2/32', '192.168.64.2/32');
INSERT 0 1
INSERT INTO  nettb (intclmn , cidrclmn) VALUES ('192.168.64.2/24', '192.168.64.2/24');
ERROR:   invalid cidr value: "192.168.64.2/24"
LINE 1: ...b (intclmn , cidrclmn) VALUES ('192.168.64.2/24', '192.168.6...

DETAIL:  Value has bits set to right of mask.
INSERT INTO  nettb (intclmn , cidrclmn) VALUES ('192.168.64.2/24', '192.168.64.0/24');
INSERT 0 1
SELECT * FROM nettb;
 id |     intclmn      |    cidrclmn
----+------------------+------------------
  1 | 192.168.64.2     | 192.168.64.2/32
  2 | 192.168.64.2/24  | 192.168.64.0/24
```

Let's also look at a couple of useful operators available within network address types. Does an IP fall in a subnet? This can be figured out using <<=, as shown here:

```
SELECT id,intclmn FROM nettb ;
 id |   intclmn
----+--------------
  1 | 192.168.64.2
  3 | 192.168.12.2
  4 | 192.168.13.2
  5 | 192.168.12.4
```

PostgreSQL – Extras

```
SELECT id,intclmn FROM nettb where intclmn <<=
inet'192.168.12.2/24';
 id |    intclmn
  3 | 192.168.12.2
  5 | 192.168.12.4

SELECT id,intclmn FROM nettb where intclmn <<=
inet'192.168.12.2/32';
 id |    intclmn
  3 | 192.168.12.2
```

The operator used in the preceding command checks whether the column value is contained within or equal to the value we provided. Similarly, we have the equality operator, greater than or equal to, bitwise AND, bitwise OR, and other standard operators.

The `macaddr` data type can be used to store Mac addresses in different formats.

The complete list of operators and functions available with network data types is available at http://www.postgresql.org/docs/current/static/functions-net.html#CIDR-INET-OPERATORS-TABLE.

> For better indexing support and performance optimization, check out the ip4r project at http://ip4r.projects.pgfoundry.org/.

hstore for key-value pairs

A key-value store available in PostgreSQL is `hstore`. Many applications have requirements that make developers look for a schema-less data store. They end up turning to one of the NoSQL databases (Cassandra) or the simple and more prevalent stores such as Redis (http://redis.io/) or Riak (http://basho.com/riak/). While it makes sense to opt for one of these if the objective is to achieve horizontal scalability, it does make the system a bit complex because we now have more moving parts. After all, most applications do need a relational database to take care of all the important transactions along with the ability to write SQL to fetch data with different projections. If a part of the application needs to have a key-value store (and horizontal scalability is not the prime objective), the `hstore` data type in PostgreSQL should serve the purpose. It may not be necessary to make the system more complex by using different technologies that will also add to the maintenance overhead.

Sometimes, what we want is not an entirely schema-less database, but some flexibility where we are certain about most of our entities and their attributes but are unsure about a few. For example, a person is sure to have a few key attributes such as first name, date of birth, and a couple of other attributes (irrespective of his nationality). However, there could be other attributes that undergo change. A U.S. citizen is likely to have a **Social Security Number** (**SSN**); someone from Canada has a **Social Insurance Number** (**SIN**). Some countries may provide more than one identifier. There can be more attributes with a similar pattern.

How do we store these attributes (which vary in number and name) if we are using the same data structure? Attempting to design such tables usually leads one to the **Entity-attribute-value** (**EAV**) model at (http://en.wikipedia.org/wiki/Entity-attribute-value_model), where we list the entity IDs, attribute IDs, and values in a table. There is usually a master attribute table (which links the IDs to attribute names) and a master table for the entities. Writing queries against tables designed on an EAV approach can get tricky. Using hstore may be an easier way of accomplishing the same. Let's see how we can do this using hstore with a simple example.

The hstore key-value store is an extension and has to be installed using CREATE EXTENSION hstore. We will model a customer table with first_name and an hstore column to hold all the dynamic attributes:

```
CREATE TABLE customer(id serial, first_name varchar(50),
dynamic_attributes hstore);
INSERT INTO customer  (first_name ,dynamic_attributes) VALUES
   ('Michael','ssn=>"123-465-798" '),
   ('Smith','ssn=>"129-465-798" '),
   ('James','ssn=>"No data" '),
   ('Ram','uuid=>"1234567891" , npr=>"XYZ5678",
ratnum=>"Somanyidentifiers" ');
```

Now, let's try retrieving all customers with their SSN, as shown here:

```
SELECT first_name,  dynamic_attributes FROM   customer
       WHERE dynamic_attributes ? 'ssn';
 first_name |  dynamic_attributes
  Michael   | "ssn"=>"123-465-798"
   Smith    | "ssn"=>"129-465-798"
   James    | "ssn"=>"No data"
```

PostgreSQL – Extras

Also, those with a specific SSN:

```
SELECT first_name,dynamic_attributes FROM  customer
      WHERE dynamic_attributes -> 'ssn'= '123-465-798';
first_name |  dynamic_attributes
Michael    | "ssn"=>"123-465-798"
```

If we want to get records that do not contain a specific SSN, just use the following command:

```
WHERE NOT dynamic_attributes -> 'ssn'= '123-465-798'
```

Also, replacing it with `WHERE NOT dynamic_attributes ? 'ssn';` gives us:

```
first_name |                         dynamic_attributes
-----------+------------------------------------------------------
  Ram      | "npr"=>"XYZ5678", "uuid"=>"1234567891",
"ratnum"=>"Somanyidentifiers"
```

As is the case with all data types in PostgreSQL, there are a number of functions and operators available to fetch data selectively, update data, and so on. Refer to http://www.postgresql.org/docs/current/static/hstore.html for an exhaustive list.

We must always use the appropriate data types. This is not just for the sake of doing it right, but because of the number of operators and functions available with a focus on each data type; `hstore` stores only text. We can use it to store numeric values, but these values will be stored as text. We can index the `hstore` columns to improve performance. The type of index to be used depends on the operators we will be using frequently.

json/jsonb

JavaScript Object Notation (JSON) is an open standard format used to transmit data in a human-readable format. It's a language-independent data format and is considered an alternative to XML. It's really lightweight compared to XML and has been steadily gaining popularity in the last few years.

PostgreSQL added the JSON data type in Version 9.2 with a limited set of functions and operators. Quite a few new functions and operators were added in Version 9.3. Version 9.4 adds one more data type: `jsonb`. which is very similar to `json`.

The `jsonb` data type stores data in binary format. It also removes white spaces (which are insignificant) and avoids duplicate object keys. As a result of these differences, `jsonb` has an overhead when data goes in, while `json` has extra processing overhead when data is retrieved (consider how often each data point will be written and read). The number of operators available with each of these data types is also slightly different. As it's possible to cast one data type to the other, which one should we use depends on the use case. If the data will be stored as it is and retrieved without any operations, `json` should suffice. However, if we plan to use operators extensively and want indexing support, `jsonb` is a better choice. Also, if we want to preserve whitespace, key ordering, and duplicate keys, `json` is the right choice.

Now, let's look at an example. Assume that we are doing a proof of concept project for a library management system. There are a number of categories of items (ranging from books to DVDs). We wouldn't have information about all the categories of items and their attributes at the piloting stage. For the pilot stage, we could use a table design with the `json` data type to hold various items and their attributes:

```
CREATE TABLE items (
    item_id serial,
    details json
);
```

Now, we will add records. All DVDs go into one record, books go into another, and so on:

```
INSERT INTO items (details) VALUES
('{
                "DVDs" :[
                        {"Name":"The Making of Thunderstorms",
"Types":"Educational",
                        "Age-group":"5-10","Produced By":"National
Geographic"
                        },
                        {"Name":"My nightmares", "Types":"Movies",
"Categories":"Horror",
                        "Certificate":"A",
"Director":"Dracula","Actors":
                                [{"Name":"Meena"},{"Name":"Lucy"},{"Nam
e":"Van Helsing"}]
                        },
                        {"Name":"My Cousin Vinny", "Types":"Movies",
"Categories":"Suspense",
                        "Certificate":"A", "Director": "Jonathan
Lynn","Actors":
                                [{"Name":"Joe "},{"Name":"Marissa"}] }]
    }'
    );
```

PostgreSQL – Extras

A better approach would be to have one record for each item. Now, let's take a look at a few JSON functions:

```
SELECT    details->>'DVDs' dvds, pg_typeof(details->>'DVDs') datatype
    FROM items;
SELECT    details->'DVDs' dvds  ,pg_typeof(details->'DVDs') datatype
    FROM items;
```

Note the difference between `->>` and `->` in the following screenshot. We are using the `pg_typeof` function to clearly see the data type returned by the functions. Both return the JSON object field. The first function returns text and the second function returns JSON:

```
test=# SELECT    details->>'DVDs' dvds, pg_typeof(details->>'DVDs') datatype
test-#     FROM items;
                                    dvds                                    | datatype
----------------------------------------------------------------------------+----------
 [ {"Name":"The Making of Thunderstorms" , "Types":"Educational",          +| text
           "Age-group":"5-10" ,"Produced By":"National Geographic"          +|
          },                                                                +|
         {"Name":"My nightmares", "Types":"Movies", "Categories":"Horror", +|
          "Certificate":"A", "Director": "Dracula","Actors":                +|
              [{"Name":"Meena"},{"Name":"Lucy"},{"Name":"Van Helsing"}]     +|
          },                                                                +|
         {"Name":"My Cousin Vinny", "Types":"Movies", "Categories":"Suspense",+|
          "Certificate":"A", "Director": "Jonathan Lynn","Actors":          +|
              [{"Name":"Joe "},{"Name":"Marissa"}]                          +|
          }                                                                 +|
         ]                                                                  |
(2 rows)

test=# SELECT    details->'DVDs' dvds  ,pg_typeof(details->'DVDs') datatype
test-#     FROM items;
                                    dvds                                    | datatype
----------------------------------------------------------------------------+----------
 [ {"Name":"The Making of Thunderstorms" , "Types":"Educational",          +| json
           "Age-group":"5-10" ,"Produced By":"National Geographic"          +|
          },                                                                +|
         {"Name":"My nightmares", "Types":"Movies", "Categories":"Horror", +|
          "Certificate":"A", "Director": "Dracula","Actors":                +|
              [{"Name":"Meena"},{"Name":"Lucy"},{"Name":"Van Helsing"}]     +|
          },                                                                +|
         {"Name":"My Cousin Vinny", "Types":"Movies", "Categories":"Suspense",+|
          "Certificate":"A", "Director": "Jonathan Lynn","Actors":          +|
              [{"Name":"Joe "},{"Name":"Marissa"}]                          +|
          }                                                                 +|
         ]                                                                  |
(2 rows)
```

Now, let's try something a bit more complex: retrieve all movies in DVDs in which Meena acted with the following SQL statement:

```
WITH tmp (dvds) AS
(SELECT json_array_elements(details->'DVDs') det  FROM items)
SELECT * FROM tmp , json_array_elements(tmp.dvds#>'{Actors}') as a
WHERE
    a->>'Name'='Meena';
```

We get the record as shown here:

```
                            dvds                                   |       value
-------------------------------------------------------------------+-----------------
{"Name":"My nightmares", "Types":"Movies", "Categories":"Horror", +| {"Name":"Meena"}
                "Certificate":"A", "Director": "Dracula","Actors": +|
                     [{"Name":"Meena"},{"Name":"Lucy"},{"Name":"Van Helsing"}] +|
                }                                                  |
```

We used one more function and a couple of operators. The `json_array_elements` expands a JSON array to a set of JSON elements. So, we first extracted the array for DVDs. We also created a temporary table, which ceases to exist as soon as the query is over, using the `WITH` clause. In the next part, we extracted the elements of the array actors from DVDs. Then, we checked whether the Name element is equal to Meena.

The complete list of operators and functions available for JSON data type is available at http://www.postgresql.org/docs/current/static/functions-json.html.

> Also look up PL/V8 at http://pgxn.org/dist/plv8/doc/plv8.html, which lets us write JavaScript functions that are callable from SQL.

XML

PostgreSQL added the xml data type in Version 8.3. **Extensible Markup Language (XML)** has a set of rules to encode documents in a format that is both human-readable and machine-readable. This data type is best used to store documents. XML became the standard way of data exchanging information across systems. XML can be used to represent complex data structures such as hierarchical data. However, XML is heavy and verbose; it takes more bytes per data point compared to the JSON format. As a result, JSON is referred to as fat-free XML. XML structure can be verified against XML **Schema Definition Documents (XSD)**. In short, XML is heavy and more sophisticated, whereas JSON is lightweight and faster to process.

> We need to configure PostgreSQL with `libxml` support (`./configure --with-libxml`) and then restart the cluster for XML features to work. There is no need to reinitialize the database cluster.

Inserting and verifying XML data

Now, let's take a look at what we can do with the xml data type in PostgreSQL:

```
CREATE TABLE tbl_xml(id serial, docmnt xml);
INSERT INTO tbl_xml(docmnt ) VALUES ('Not xml');
INSERT INTO tbl_xml (docmnt)
      SELECT  query_to_xml( 'SELECT now()',true,false,'') ;
SELECT xml_is_well_formed_document(docmnt::text), docmnt
      FROM tbl_xml;
```

Then, take a look at the following screenshot:

```
 xml_is_well_formed_document |                          docmnt
-----------------------------+------------------------------------------------------------
 f                           | Not xml
 t                           | <table xmlns:xsi="http://www.w3.org/2001/XMLSchema-instance">+
                             |                                                             +
                             | <row>                                                       +
```

First, we created a table with a column to store the XML data. Then, we inserted a record, which is not in the XML format, into the table. Next, we used the `query_to_xml` function to get the output of a query in the XML format. We inserted this into the table. Then, we used a function to check whether the data in the table is well-formed XML.

Generating XML files for table definitions and data

We can use the `table_to_xml` function if we want to dump the data from a table in the XML format. Append `and_xmlschema` so that the function becomes `table_to_xml_and_xmlschema`, which will also generate the schema definition before dumping the content.

If we want to generate just the definitions, we can use `table_to_xmlschema`.

PostgreSQL also provides the `xpath` function to extract data as follows:

```
SELECT xpath('/table/row/now/text()',docmnt) FROM tbl_xml
     WHERE id = 2;
              xpath
-----------------------------------
{2014-07-29T16:55:00.781533+05:30}
```

An exhaustive list of the XML functions available in PostgreSQL is available at http://www.postgresql.org/docs/current/static/functions-xml.html.

> Using properly designed tables with separate columns to capture each attribute is always the best approach from a performance standpoint and update/write-options perspective. Data types such as `json/xml` are best used to temporarily store data when we need to provide feeds/extracts/views to other systems or when we get data from external systems. They can also be used to store documents. The maximum size for a field is 1 GB. We must consider this when we use the database to store text/document data.

Geometry and geography

PostgreSQL provides a good set of data types to capture geometric data. They include point, line, circle, path, and a few others. A set of geometric functions and operators are also available. If anything more sophisticated is necessary, PostGIS (http://postgis.net/) is recommended. PostGIS, probably, has the most comprehensive set of data types and functions one might need to manage **Geographic Information Systems (GIS)**. PostGIS is an open source spatial database extender for PostgreSQL. It's available under GNU General Public License.

Foreign Data Wrappers

From PostGIS, which can be installed as an extension and caters to a specific set of users whose work involve a lot of geometry/geography data, we will move on to an extension that pretty much everyone working with PostgreSQL will find useful: **Foreign Data Wrappers (FDW)**. FDW provides a means to access data outside a PostgreSQL cluster. The data may be on a filesystem, on a MySQL server, or another PostgreSQL cluster. We will take a look at two examples: one accessing a file and another accessing a PostgreSQL. The steps usually involve:

1. Installing the extension.
2. Creating a server object. This provides details of the server (such as IP and port or path).

3. Creating user mapping. This involves providing the authentication information to connect to other databases. This step may or may not be necessary depending on the type of server object.
4. Creating the foreign table. This creates a table that maps to another table or file on the server object.

FDW for files

We will walk through an example:

1. Install the extension as follows:
   ```
   CREATE EXTENSION file_fdw;
   ```

2. Create the server object with the following command:
   ```
   CREATE SERVER file_server FOREIGN DATA WRAPPER file_fdw;
   ```

3. Create the foreign table. The syntax is very similar to the standard CREATE TABLE syntax. We have the keyword FOREIGN and need to mention the server object it points to:
   ```
   CREATE FOREIGN TABLE file_to_tbl(
       id integer, name varchar(40)
   )
   SERVER file_server
   OPTIONS (
       delimiter ',',
       filename '/home/postgres/names.csv',
       format 'csv'
   );
   ```

We are done. If we do a SELECT statement from the table now, it will fail as there is no file. So, let's create a file named names.csv in /home/postgres with data that looks like this:

```
1,Jayadevan
2,Steve
3,Jones
4,Anne
5,Julie
```

Now, we can fetch data from the table as follows:

```
SELECT * FROM file_to_tbl;
 id |   name
----+-----------
  1 | Jayadevan
  2 | Steve
  3 | Jones
  4 | Anne
  5 | Julie

SELECT * FROM file_to_tbl where id = 4;
 id | name
----+------
  4 | Anne
```

A good use case for this would be to create similar tables for web logs and other log files. Analyzing data is always easy using SQL. We can search for errors, get a count of the errors, and so on. We can split the log file into different columns and do a sort based on the session ID or username to find out the sequence of actions a user carried out, compare the total number of GETs Vs POSTs, and so on.

PostgreSQL FDW

While we can get a lot of data from log files, a major chunk of the data we need for analysis can be in a database. This could include more information about the users. We can get the session IDs and action sequences from log files, but what about data pertaining to users who created these sessions? If we are performing all the analysis in a data warehouse environment, we will need to pull this information from the transactional system. This usually means a foreign data wrapper for the database. The extra information to be provided to set up this wrapper will be the user authentication information.

1. Let's create a new user for this:

    ```
    CREATE USER myuser1 PASSWORD 'myuser';
    ALTER USER myuser1 WITH CREATEDB;
    ```

2. Connect to pgp (an existing database) as postgres and create the table that will be accessed using FDW:

    ```
    CREATE TABLE prod_table (id serial, name varchar(50));
    INSERT INTO prod_table (name) VALUES ('Scott'), ('Thomson');
    GRANT SELECT on prod_table to myuser1;
    ```

3. Log in as `myuser1` to PostgreSQL and create the database where the FDW will be created with the following command:

   `CREATE DATABASE reports;`

4. Log in as `postgres` to the new database (reports) and install the extension:

   `CREATE EXTENSION postgres_fdw ;`

5. Create the server object:

   ```
   CREATE SERVER f_prod FOREIGN DATA WRAPPER postgres_fdw
   OPTIONS (
       dbname 'pgp',
       host '192.168.56.101',
       port '5432'
   );
   ALTER SERVER f_prod OWNER TO myuser1;
   ```

6. Then, create the user mapping:

   ```
   CREATE USER MAPPING FOR myuser1 SERVER f_prod OPTIONS (
           user 'myuser1',
   password 'myuser'
   );
   ```

7. Next, log in as `myuser1` to reports and create the foreign table:

   ```
   CREATE FOREIGN TABLE prod_table (
       id integer ,
       name varchar(100)
   )
   SERVER f_prod;

   SELECT * FROM prod_table;
   ```

Data wrappers – other aspects

The performance of queries executed via a data wrapper will vary a lot, depending on the remote server we are connecting to. Whether we can write to the foreign table depends on the data wrapper. PostgreSQL wrapper allows you to write, assuming the user connecting to the remote server has the appropriate privileges. Data wrappers are available for a large number of SQL and NoSQL databases. The following link provides the extensions: http://pgxn.org/tag/fdw/.

The link https://wiki.postgresql.org/wiki/Foreign_data_wrappers also provides an overview of most of the wrappers available.

pgbadger

Now, we will look at a must-have tool if we have just started with PostgreSQL and want to analyze the events taking place in the database.

> For those coming from an Oracle background, this tool provides reports similar to AWR reports, although the information is more query-centric. It does not include data regarding host configuration, wait statistics, and so on.

Analyzing the activities in a live cluster provides a lot of insight. It tells us about load, bottlenecks, which queries get executed frequently (we can focus more on them for optimization). It even tells us if the parameters are set right, although a bit indirectly. For example, if we see that there are many temp files getting created while a specific query is getting executed, we know that we either have a buffer issue or have not written the query right.

For pgbadger to effectively scan the log file and produce useful reports, we should get our logging configuration right as follows:

```
log_destination = 'stderr'
logging_collector = on
log_directory = 'pg_log'
log_filename = 'postgresql-%Y-%m-%d.log'
log_min_duration_statement = 0
log_connections = on
log_disconnections = on
log_duration = on
log_line_prefix = '%t [%p]: [%l-1] user=%u,db=%d '
log_lock_waits = on
track_activity_query_size = 2048
```

It might be necessary to restart the cluster for some of these changes to take effect.

We will also ensure that there is some load on the database using pgbench. It's a utility that ships with PostgreSQL and can be used to benchmark PostgreSQL on our servers. We can initialize the tables required for pgbench by executing the following command at the shell prompt:

pgbench -i pgp

PostgreSQL – Extras

This creates a few tables on the `pgp` database. We can log in to psql (database `pgp`) and check:

```
\dt
          List of relations
 Schema |       Name        | Type  |  Owner
--------+-------------------+-------+----------
 public | pgbench_accounts  | table | postgres
 public | pgbench_branches  | table | postgres
 public | pgbench_history   | table | postgres
 public | pgbench_tellers   | table | postgres
```

Now, we can run `pgbench` to generate load on the database with the following command:

pgbench -c 5 -T10 pgp

The `T` option passes the duration for which `pgbench` should continue execution in seconds, `c` passes the number of clients, and `pgp` is the database.

> For more details on how to use pgbench, refer to http://www.postgresql.org/docs/current/static/pgbench.html.

Now, to use pgbadger, you can download it from https://github.com/dalibo/pgbadger.

At the shell prompt, execute:

wget https://github.com/dalibo/pgbadger/archive/master.zip

Once the file is downloaded, unzip the file using the following command:

unzip master.zip

Use `cd` to move to the directory `pgbadger-master` as follows:

cd pgbadger-master

Execute the following command:

```
./pgbadger /pgdata/9.3/pg_log/postgresql-2014-07-31.log -o myoutput.html
```

Replace the log file name in the command with the actual name. It will generate a `myoutput.html` file.

Chapter 12

The HTML file generated will have a wealth of information about what happened in the cluster with great charts/tables. In fact, it takes quite a bit of time to go through the report. Here is a sample chart that provides the distribution of queries based on execution time:

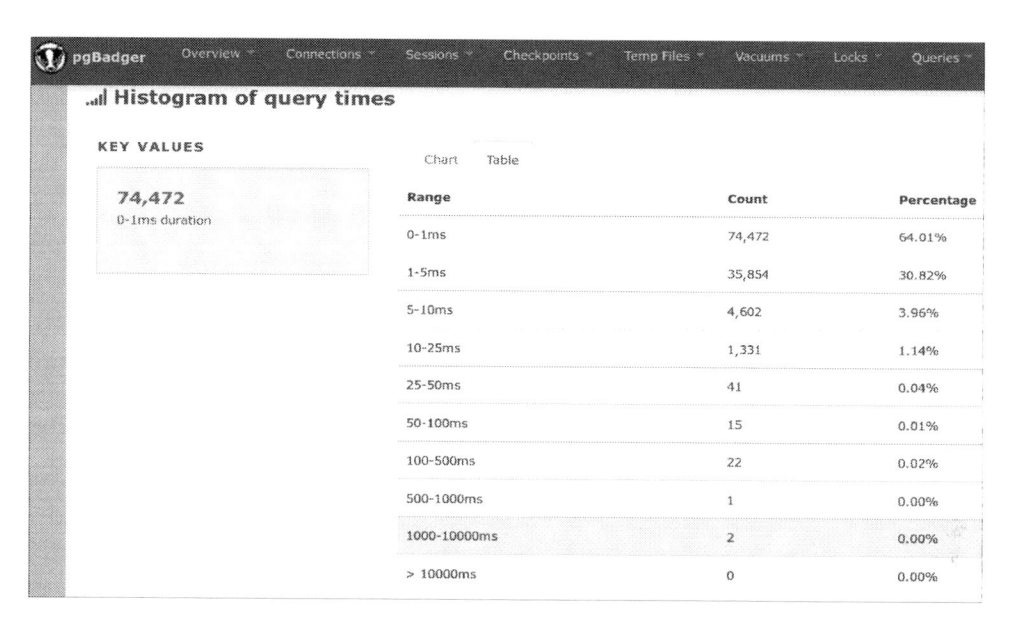

Histogram of query times

KEY VALUES

74,472
0-1ms duration

Range	Count	Percentage
0-1ms	74,472	64.01%
1-5ms	35,854	30.82%
5-10ms	4,602	3.96%
10-25ms	1,331	1.14%
25-50ms	41	0.04%
50-100ms	15	0.01%
100-500ms	22	0.02%
500-1000ms	1	0.00%
1000-10000ms	2	0.00%
> 10000ms	0	0.00%

The following screenshot gives an idea about the number of performance metrics provided by the report:

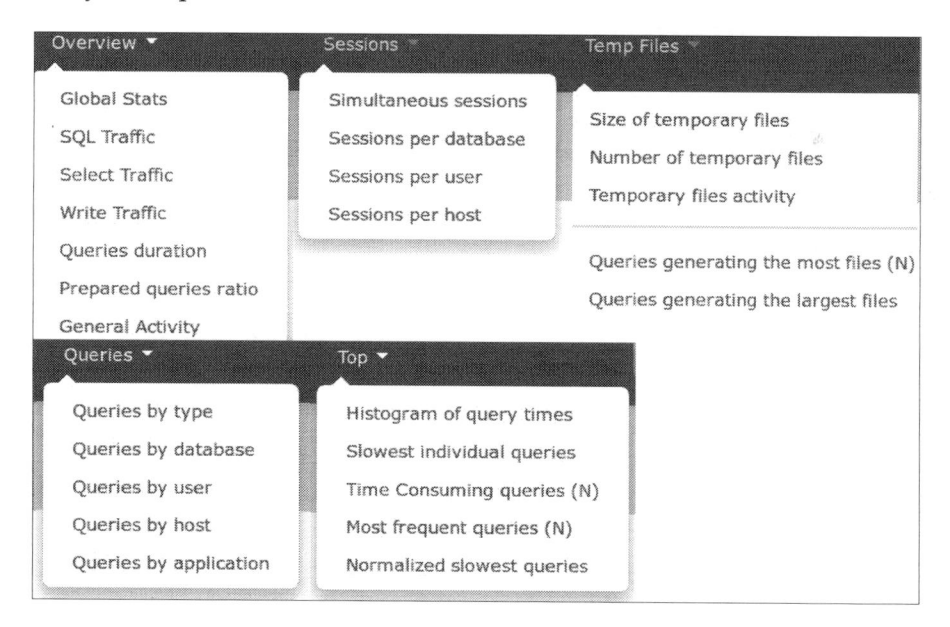

Overview
- Global Stats
- SQL Traffic
- Select Traffic
- Write Traffic
- Queries duration
- Prepared queries ratio
- General Activity

Sessions
- Simultaneous sessions
- Sessions per database
- Sessions per user
- Sessions per host

Temp Files
- Size of temporary files
- Number of temporary files
- Temporary files activity
- Queries generating the most files (N)
- Queries generating the largest files

Queries
- Queries by type
- Queries by database
- Queries by user
- Queries by host
- Queries by application

Top
- Histogram of query times
- Slowest individual queries
- Time Consuming queries (N)
- Most frequent queries (N)
- Normalized slowest queries

[235]

PostgreSQL – Extras

If our objective is to troubleshoot performance bottlenecks, the slowest individual queries and most frequent queries under the top drop-down list is the right place to start. Once the queries are identified, locks, temporary file generation, and so on can be studied to identify the root cause. Of course, **EXPLAIN** is the best option when we want to refine individual queries.

If the objective is to understand how busy the cluster is, the **Overview** section and **Sessions** are the right places to explore.

> The logging configuration used may create huge log files in systems with a lot of activity. Tweak the parameters appropriately to ensure that this does not happen.

With this, we covered most of the interesting data types, an interesting extension, and a must-use tool from PostgreSQL ecosystem. Now, let's cover a few interesting features in PostgreSQL Version 9.4.

Features over time

An excellent snapshot of how PostgreSQL has changed over versions features-wise is available at http://www.postgresql.org/about/featurematrix/. Applying filters in Versions 8.0, 9.0, and 9.4 gives us a good idea about how quickly features are getting added to the database.

Interesting features in 9.4

Each version of PostgreSQL adds many features grouped into different categories (such as performance, backend, data types, and so on). We will look at a few features that are more likely to be of interest (because they help us improve performance or they make maintenance and configuration easy).

Keeping the buffer ready

As we saw earlier, reads from disk have a significant overhead compared to those from memory. There are quite a few occasions when disk reads are unavoidable. Let's see a few examples.

In a data warehouse, the **Extract, Transform, Load** (ETL) process, which may happen once a day usually, involves a lot of raw data getting processed in memory before being loaded into the final tables. This data is mostly transactional data. The master data, which does not get processed on a regular basis, may be evicted from memory as a result of this churn.

Reports typically depend a lot on master data. When users refresh their reports after ETL, it's highly likely that the master data will be read from disk, resulting in a drop in the response time. If we could ensure that the master data as well as the recently processed data is in the buffer, it can really improve the user experience.

In a transactional system like an airline reservation system, a change to the fare rule may result in most of the fares being recalculated. This is a situation similar to the one described previously, ensuring that the fares and availability data for the most frequently searched routes in the buffer can provide a better user experience. This also applies to an e-commerce site selling products. If the product/price/inventory data is always available in memory, it can be retrieved very fast.

So, how can we ensure that the data is available in the buffer? A pg_prewarm module has been added as an extension to provide this functionality. The basic syntax is very simple: SELECT pg_prewarm('tablename');. This command will populate the buffers with data from the table. It's also possible to mention the blocks that should be loaded into the buffer from the table.

> You must use PostgreSQL 9.4 for trying out the code in the following sections.

We will install the extension in a database, create a table, and populate some data. Then, we will stop the server, drop buffers (OS), and restart the server. We will see how much time a SELECT count(*) takes. We will repeat the exercise, but we will use pg_prewarm before executing SELECT count(*) at psql:

```
CREATE EXTENSION pg_prewarm;
CREATE TABLE myt(id SERIAL, name VARCHAR(40));
INSERT INTO myt(name) SELECT concat(generate_series(1,10000),'name');
```

Now, stop the server using pg_ctl at the shell prompt:

```
pg_ctl stop -m immediate
```

Clean OS buffers using the following command at the shell prompt (will need to use sudo to do this):

```
echo 1 > /proc/sys/vm/drop_caches
```

The command may vary depending on the OS. Restart the cluster using pg_ctl start.

Then, execute the following command:

```
SELECT COUNT(*) FROM myt;
Time: 333.115 ms
```

PostgreSQL – Extras

We should repeat the steps of shutting down the server, dropping the cache, and starting PostgreSQL. Then, execute `SELECT pg_prewarm('myt');` before `SELECT count(*)`.

The response time goes down significantly. Executing `pg_prewarm` does take some time, which is close to the time taken to execute the `SELECT count(*)` against a cold cache. However, the objective is to ensure that the user does not experience a delay.

```
SELECT COUNT(*) FROM myt;
 count
-------
 10000
(1 row)
Time: 7.002 ms
```

Better recoverability

A new parameter called `recovery_min_apply_delay` has been added in 9.4. This will go to the `recovery.conf` file of the slave server. With this, we can control the replay of transactions on the slave server. We can set this to approximately 5 minutes and then the standby will replay the transaction from the master when the standby system time is 5 minutes past the time of commit at the master. This provides a bit more flexibility when it comes to recovering from mistakes. When we keep the value at 1 hour, the changes at the master will be replayed at the slave after one hour. If we realize that something went wrong on the master server, we have about 1 hour to stop the transaction replay so that the action that caused the issue (for example, accidental dropping of a table) doesn't get replayed at the slave.

Easy-to-change parameters

An `ALTER SYSTEM` command has been introduced so that we don't have to edit `postgresql.conf` to change parameters. The entry will go to a file named `postgresql.auto.conf`. We can execute `ALTER SYSTEM SET  work_mem='12MB';` and then check the file at psql:

```
\! more postgresql.auto.conf
# Do not edit this file manually!
# It will be overwritten by ALTER SYSTEM command.
work_mem = '12MB'
```

We must execute `SELECT pg_reload_conf();` to ensure that the changes are propagated.

Logical decoding and consumption of changes

Version 9.4 introduces physical and logical replication slots. We will look at logical slots as they let us track changes and filter specific transactions. This lets us pick and choose from the transactions that have been committed. We can grab some of the changes, decode, and possibly replay on a remote server. We do not have to have an all-or-nothing replication. As of now, we will have to do a lot of work to decode/move the changes.

Two parameter changes are necessary to set this up. These are as follows:

The `max_replication_slots` parameter (set to at least 1) and `wal_level` (set to logical). Then, we can connect to a database and create a slot as follows:

```
SELECT * FROM
pg_create_logical_replication_slot('myslot','test_decoding');
```

The first parameter is the name we give to our slot and the second parameter is the plugin to be used. `test_decoding` is the sample plugin available, which converts WAL entries into text representations as follows:

```
INSERT INTO myt(id) values (4);
INSERT INTO myt(name) values ('abc');
```

Now, we will try retrieving the entries:

```
SELECT * FROM pg_logical_slot_peek_changes('myslot',NULL,NULL);
```

Then, check the following screenshot:

```
 location  | xid  |                                data
-----------+------+------------------------------------------------------------------
 0/17F9178 | 1820 | BEGIN 1820
 0/17F9178 | 1820 | table public.myt: INSERT: id[integer]:4 name[character varying]:null
 0/17F91F8 | 1820 | COMMIT 1820
 0/17F92F0 | 1821 | BEGIN 1821
 0/17F92F0 | 1821 | table public.myt: INSERT: id[integer]:10003 name[character varying]:'abc'
 0/17F9378 | 1821 | COMMIT 1821
```

This function lets us take a look at the changes without consuming them so that the changes can be accessed again:

```
SELECT * FROM pg_logical_slot_get_changes('myslot',NULL,NULL);
```

This is shown in the following screenshot:

```
STATEMENT:  SELECT * FROM pg_logical_slot_get_changes('myslot',NULL,NULL);
 location  | xid  |                               data
-----------+------+-------------------------------------------------------------
 0/17F9178 | 1820 | BEGIN 1820
 0/17F9178 | 1820 | table public.myt: INSERT: id[integer]:4 name[character varying]:null
 0/17F91F8 | 1820 | COMMIT 1820
 0/17F92F0 | 1821 | BEGIN 1821
 0/17F92F0 | 1821 | table public.myt: INSERT: id[integer]:10003 name[character varying]:'abc'
 0/17F9378 | 1821 | COMMIT 1821
(6 rows)

Time: 25.009 ms
warm=# SELECT * FROM pg_logical_slot_get_changes('myslot',NULL,NULL);
LOG:  starting logical decoding for slot myslot
DETAIL:  streaming transactions committing after 0/17F9450, reading WAL from 0/17F91F8
STATEMENT:  SELECT * FROM pg_logical_slot_get_changes('myslot',NULL,NULL);
LOG:  logical decoding found consistent point at 0/17F91F8
DETAIL:  running xacts with xcnt == 0
STATEMENT:  SELECT * FROM pg_logical_slot_get_changes('myslot',NULL,NULL);
 location | xid | data
----------+-----+------
(0 rows)
```

This function is similar to the peek function, but the changes are no longer available to be fetched again as they get consumed.

Summary

In this chapter, we covered a few data types that data architects will find interesting. We also covered what is probably the best utility available to parse the PostgreSQL log file to produce excellent reports. We also looked at some of the interesting features in PostgreSQL version 9.4, which will be of interest to data architects.

Index

A

access methods 126
ACID properties, transactions
  about 76
  atomicity 76
  consistency 76
  durability 85
  isolation 76, 77
Advanced Packaging Tool (APT) 1
approaches, performance optimization
  indexing 125
  normalization 125
  partitioning 125
autonomous subtransaction
  URLs 43
autovacuum 37-41

B

background writer 36
base directory 15
buffer cache
  inspecting 25-28

C

cardinality 141
checkpoint
  about 29-32
  URL 31
checkpoint_segments parameter 149
cidr data type 221
cluster, initializing
  about 11-13
  directories 14
  files created 17
  processes spawned 17
command-line tools 105
Commit Log (CLOG) buffer 54
Common Table Expression (CTE)
  about 140
  URL 140
config directory 4
contrib directory 4
COPY command
  about 168
  URL 170
CPU-related cost settings 155-157
CREATE TABLE command
  URL 59
current_schema function 63

D

daemon process
  starting with 21-23
database design tool 93
databases
  about 61
  facts 123, 124
database tools
  about 91
  uses 92
Data Definition Language (DDL) 91
data modeling 91
data types
  about 217
  Foreign Data Wrappers 229
  geography data 229
  geometry data 229

[241]

pgbadger 233, 234
range data type 218-220
XML 227
default_statistics_target parameter 151
doc directory 4

E

effective_cache_size 53, 148, 149
Enterprise Resource Planning (ERP) 67
executables, PostgreSQL
  building 8
executor 125
EXPLAIN
  URL 130
Extensible Markup Language. *See* XML
Extract, Transform, and Load (ETL)
      process 150, 236

F

features, PostgreSQL 9.4
  better recoverability 238
  buffer, keeping ready 236, 237
  consumption of changes 239, 240
  easy-to-change parameters 238
  logical decoding 239
Foreign Data Wrappers (FDW)
  about 229, 230
  aspects 232
  example 230
  for files 230, 231
  PostgreSQL FDW 231, 232
  URL 232
fsync 36
functions
  optimizing 143
  URL 143

G

Geographic Information Systems (GIS) 229
global directory 16
GNU Compiler Collection (GCC) 4
GUI tools 105

H

horizontal scaling
  about 182
  connection pooling 189
  disadvantages 182
  failover capability 189
  master-slave(s), with read/write
      separation 182, 183
  multi-master full replication 201
  pgpool-II, using 189
  sharding 199
  streaming replication 184
hot_standby level 36
hstore, key-value pairs
  about 222-224
  URL 224

I

IMMUTABLE functions 143
index-only scans
  URL 132
inet data type 221
initdb
  about 55
  URL 13
isolation, ACID properties
  SQL standard isolation levels 77
isolation levels, PostgreSQL
  read committed 80, 81
  repeatable read 82
  serializable level 83-85

J

JavaScript Object Notation (JSON) 224
JMeter
  URL 179
join strategies 127
json_array_elements 227
jsonb data type 225
json data type
  about 225
  example 225-227
  URL 227

L

Liquibase
 about 92
 URL 92
logging process 41-45

M

macaddr data type 222
maintenance, with
 maintenance_work_mem 51-53
main window, pgAdmin
 about 108
 Object Browser pane 108
 Server Groups 108
 Servers 108
 Statistics tab 108
 Tools menu 110, 111
makefile, PostgreSQL
 configuring 5-7
 creating 5-7
materialized views 157-160
memory
 sorting, work_mem used 49-51
meta-commands, psql 117-119
multi-master full replication 201
Multiversion Concurrency Control (MVCC)
 about 38, 77
 URL 90
 using 86-89

N

network address types
 about 220
 cidr 221
 inet 221
 macaddr 222
 URL 222
 using 220-222
New Relic
 URL 179
numeric data types
 URL 28

O

ora2pg
 about 168
 URL 168
orafce
 URL 168

P

parameters, impacting query plan and performance 151, 152
parser 125
partitioned tables
 about 160
 creating 161
 example 161-165
performance optimization strategies
 about 130
 DISTINCT, using 134
 foreign keys, indexing 130-132
 function executions, reducing 138-140
 functions, optimizing 143-145
 functions, using in FILTER clause 134-136
 ORDER BY, using 133
 partial indexes 142
 SELECT *, using 132
 SQL statements, reducing 137, 138
 UNION ALL, using 134
pgAdmin
 about 105
 for Linux-based systems 105
 for Windows 105
 main window 108
 Query tool 111-113
 server, adding 106, 107
 URL 105
pgbadger
 about 233-236
 download link 234
pgbench
 URL 234
pg_bulkload utility
 about 171
 installing 172, 173
 URL 173

pg_clog directory 16
pg_ctl utility 14
PGDATABASE variable 120
pg_dumpall utility 176
pg_dump utility
  about 173-175
  URL 176
PGHOST variable 120
pg_locks view
  about 214
  columns 214
pg_multixact directory 16
pgpool-II
  about 197
  configuring 190-192
  connection pooling 189
  failover capability 189
  failover, testing 194, 195
  HA 189
  load balancing 189
  read/write separation, testing 193, 194
  using 189
PGPORT variable 120
pg_restore utility 176-178
pg_serial directory 16
pg_service.conf file
  URL 107
pg_snapshots directory 16
pg_stat_activity view
  about 212
  columns 212
pg_statistic
  URL 151
pg_stat_tmp directory 16
pg_subtrans directory 16
pg_tblspc directory 16
pg_twophase directory 16
PGUSER variable 120
pg_xlog directory 16
planner 126
PL/V8
  URL 227
point-in-time recovery 202-206
PostGIS
  about 229
  URL 229

PostgreSQL
  about 1
  cluster 55, 56
  dependencies, for compiling source 4, 5
  MVCC, using 86-89
  point-in-time recovery 202-206
  troubleshooting 207
  URL 44
  URL, for documentation 71
  URL, for rule system 165
PostgreSQL 9.4
  features 236
  URL 236
PostgreSQL installation
  about 1
  changes, inspecting 10
  cluster, initializing 11-13
  contents, inspecting 3, 4
  executables, building 8
  extensions, working with 18
  files, moving to correct directories 9
  makefile, configuring 5-7
  makefile, creating 5-7
  options 1, 2
  source, downloading 2
  source, extracting 3
Postgres-XC 199
privileges 67-71
production database
  considerations 167, 168
  COPY command 168-171
  database code rewrite 168
  data transformation 168
  data volume 168
  fast loading, with pg_bulkload 171-173
  filtering options 175
  pg_dump utility 173-175
  setting up 167, 168
profiling 102
psql
  \d command 115-117
  \h command 117
  \s command 121
  about 105, 114
  connection options 114, 115

environment, setting up 120, 121
meta-commands 117-119
psql --help command 114

Q

query execution components
about 125
access methods 126
executor 125
join strategies 127
parser 125
planner 125
rewriter 125
Query tool, pgAdmin 111-113

R

RAID levels
URLs 180
range data type
about 218-220
hstore, key-value pairs 222-224
jsonb data type 225
json data type 224
network address types, using 220-222
URL 218
readline 5
Real Application Clusters (RAC) 55
recovery_target_name option 203
recovery_target_time option 203
recovery_target_xid option 203
Red Hat Package Manager 1
reverse engineering 100
rewriter 125
roles 67-71
RPM Package Manager (rpm) commands 1

S

scalability
about 179
horizontal scaling 182
issues 180
vertical scaling 181
schemas
about 62
use cases 67

search_path 63-66
selectivity 141
seq_page_cost 153
sequences
URL 28
serializable isolation level
URL 85
serializable snapshot isolation level
URL 85
server tuning
about 147
connections, managing 149, 150
CPU costs 155
maintenance, managing 149, 150
materialized views 157
parameters, impacting query plan and performance 151-154
partitioned tables 160
writes, managing 149, 150
server-wide memory settings
about 147
effective_cache_size 148, 149
shared_buffers 147, 148
severity levels
ERROR 42
FATAL 42
INFO 42
LOG 42
NOTICE 42
PANIC 42
WARNING 42
sharding 199-201
shared buffer 23, 24
shared_buffers parameter 147, 148
Slony
URL 190
Social Insurance Number (SIN) 223
Social Security Number (SSN) 223
Solid State Disks (SSDs) 153
source, PostgreSQL
downloading 2
extracting 3
URL 2
SQL, generating
about 97-99
data model, exporting 101

[245]

profiling 102
reverse engineering 100
SQL Power Architect
  about 91
  download link 93
  installing 93, 94
  tables, creating 95, 96
SQL standard isolation levels, transactions
  read committed 78
  read uncommitted 78
  repeatable reads 78, 79
  serializable 79
SQL tuning
  about 123
  common approaches, for optimization 125
  execution plan, finding 128, 129
  performance optimization strategies 130
  query execution components 125
src directory 3
STABLE functions 143
stats collector process 46-49
strace
  URL 216
streaming replication
  about 184
  database folders, synchronizing 187-189
  primary, configuring 184, 185
  secondary, configuring 186
  setting up 184

T

tablespaces
  about 56 58
  temporary objects, managing with temporary tablespaces 59, 60
  views 61
table_to_xml function 228
TOra
  URL 92
track_functions 138
transactions
  about 73
  ACID properties 76, 77
  working with 73-76
troubleshooting
  authentication issues 208, 209

connection issues 207, 208
parameter changes not effective 210-212
permission issues 208, 209
PostgreSQL 207
query not responding 212-216

U

utilities, Linux-based system
  htop 216
  iostat 216
  mpstat 216
  top 216
  vmstat 216
  vmstat 2 216
utilities, Windows systems
  URL 1

V

vertical scaling 181
views, tablespaces
  about 61
  URL 61
Virtual Private Server (VPS) 153
VOLATILE functions 143

W

WAL(Write Ahead Log)
  about 32-34
  incremental backup 34
  point-in-time recovery 34
  receiver 49
  recovery 34
  replication 34-36
  sender 49
  writer process 32-34
wal_buffers memory 36
wal_sync_method
  URL 36
web2py
  about 74
  URL 74
work_mem
  used, for sorting memory 49-51

X

xmax column 87
xmin column 87
XML
  about 227
  data, inserting 228
  data, verifying 228
  files, generating for table definitions and data 228
xml data type 227

XML functions
  URL 229
XML Schema Definition Documents (XSD) 227

Y

Yellow dog Updater Modified (yum) 1

Z

zlib 5

Thank you for buying
PostgreSQL for Data Architects

About Packt Publishing

Packt, pronounced 'packed', published its first book, *Mastering phpMyAdmin for Effective MySQL Management*, in April 2004, and subsequently continued to specialize in publishing highly focused books on specific technologies and solutions.

Our books and publications share the experiences of your fellow IT professionals in adapting and customizing today's systems, applications, and frameworks. Our solution-based books give you the knowledge and power to customize the software and technologies you're using to get the job done. Packt books are more specific and less general than the IT books you have seen in the past. Our unique business model allows us to bring you more focused information, giving you more of what you need to know, and less of what you don't.

Packt is a modern yet unique publishing company that focuses on producing quality, cutting-edge books for communities of developers, administrators, and newbies alike. For more information, please visit our website at www.packtpub.com.

About Packt Open Source

In 2010, Packt launched two new brands, Packt Open Source and Packt Enterprise, in order to continue its focus on specialization. This book is part of the Packt Open Source brand, home to books published on software built around open source licenses, and offering information to anybody from advanced developers to budding web designers. The Open Source brand also runs Packt's Open Source Royalty Scheme, by which Packt gives a royalty to each open source project about whose software a book is sold.

Writing for Packt

We welcome all inquiries from people who are interested in authoring. Book proposals should be sent to author@packtpub.com. If your book idea is still at an early stage and you would like to discuss it first before writing a formal book proposal, then please contact us; one of our commissioning editors will get in touch with you.

We're not just looking for published authors; if you have strong technical skills but no writing experience, our experienced editors can help you develop a writing career, or simply get some additional reward for your expertise.

[PACKT] open source
community experience distilled
PUBLISHING

PostgreSQL Replication

ISBN: 978-1-84951-672-3   Paperback: 250 pages

Understand basic replication concepts and efficiently replicate PostgreSQL using high-end techniques to protect your data and run your server without interruptions

1. Explains the new replication features introduced in PostgreSQL 9.

2. Contains easy to understand explanations and lots of screenshots that simplify an advanced topic like replication.

3. Teaches PostgreSQL administrators how to maintain consistency between redundant resources and to improve reliability, fault-tolerance, and accessibility.

PostgreSQL Server Programming

ISBN: 978-1-84951-698-3   Paperback: 264 pages

Extend PostgreSQL and integrate the database layer into your development framework

1. Understand the extension framework of PostgreSQL, and leverage it in ways that you haven't even invented yet.

2. Write functions, create your own data types, all in your favourite programming language.

3. Step-by-step tutorial with plenty of tips and tricks to kick-start server programming.

Please check www.PacktPub.com for information on our titles

PostGIS Cookbook

ISBN: 978-1-84951-866-6   Paperback: 484 pages

Over 80 task-based recipes to store, organize, manipulate, and analyze spatial data in a PostGIS database

1. Integrate PostGIS with web frameworks and implement OGC standards such as WMS and WFS using MapServer and GeoServer.
2. Convert 2D and 3D vector data, raster data, and routing data into usable forms.
3. Visualize data from the PostGIS database using a desktop GIS program such as QGIS and OpenJUMP.

PostgreSQL 9 Admin Cookbook

ISBN: 978-1-84951-028-8   Paperback: 360 pages

Solve real-world PostgreSQL problems with over 100 simple yet incredibly effective recipes

1. Administer and maintain a healthy database.
2. Monitor your database ensuring that it performs as quickly as possible.
3. Tips for backup and recovery of your database.

Please check **www.PacktPub.com** for information on our titles